for Teresita
with love,
D '86

Farm Women

Institute for Research in Social Science Monograph Series

Published by the University of North Carolina Press in association with the Institute for Research in Social Science at the University of North Carolina at Chapel Hill

Farm Women

Work, Farm, and Family in the United States

by Rachel Ann Rosenfeld

The University of North Carolina Press
Chapel Hill and London

To my parents,
Ethel and Jerome Rosenfeld

Manufactured in the United States of America

Library of Congress Cataloging in Publication Data

Rosenfeld, Rachel.
Farm women.

Bibliography: p.
Includes index.
1. Women in agriculture—United States—Case studies.
2. Farmers' wives—Employment—United States—Case studies. 3. Rural women—United States—Case studies.
4. United States—Rural conditions. I. Title.
HD6073.A292U67 1985 331.4'83'0973 85-13945
ISBN 0-8078-1674-4

Design by Heidi Perov

Contents

List of Tables and Figures

Tables

Figures

Preface

Less than 3 percent of the U.S. population lives and works on farms. Social scientists and people in general tend to forget about this segment of the country or to think of it as marginal. Yet the state of U.S. agriculture influences the country's standard of living through the cost of food and affects its trade balance and foreign policy by providing agricultural surplus for export. There are women connected in some way with most U.S. farms, but the work of these women is even less noticed, since farming is thought to be done by men. This book focuses attention on some of the nation's farm women—those who operate their own farms or are wives of farm operators. It looks at the way the nature of their farms and their families shape the work they do, on and off the farm, with or without pay. While this is not the first book on the subject of farm women, it is the first to use data from a national sample. I hope that this book not only proves valuable for understanding farm women's lives but also stimulates others to look into the Farm Women Survey data set for further research and possible follow-up.

Although I lived on a farm for two years as a child and have parents who live in a rural area, I did not turn to farm women as a research topic until 1979, when as a Senior Study Director at the National Opinion Research Center, with an interest in women and work, I was asked if I would like to be principal investigator of a survey of farm women, funded by the U.S. Department of Agriculture. Farm women and their work sounded interesting, so I enthusiastically agreed. In the fall of 1979, NORC and USDA signed a cooperative research agreement (58-319T-9-0376) to carry out a national survey of farm women.

During the survey I worked with a number of people at NORC and USDA who deserve to be acknowledged here. Calvin Jones was the NORC Project Director. He kept the process going, participated in all stages of the survey—from initial conception to writing the report (Jones and Rosenfeld 1981)—and is largely responsible for the high quality of the data. Lorayn Olson provided able research assistance. Paul Sheatsley, a NORC Senior Survey Director, gave us advice on the questionnaire and survey design. At USDA, Carol Forbes had developed the idea for the survey, concerned about farm women's complaints that they did not have equal access to USDA resources. Peggy Ross (of the Economic Development Division of the Economic Research Service) was USDA Project Officer, acting both as participant in the survey development and as a tactful, effective liaison between NORC and USDA. She later was kind enough to send me a copy of her own work with these data. Frances Hill, then of the University of Texas, was our main consultant.

The report from the survey was soon sold out. Papers on farm women and families began to cite its results, but it was hard for people to get access to copies of the report. Further, the report gave only an initial description of the women's work and the determinants of it. At the 1982 Wingspread Seminar on the Role of Women in North American Agriculture, Christine Gladwin and Carolyn Sachs suggested the need for a book based on the Farm Women Survey data. Sachs, who was finishing her own book on farm women, later sent me a copy of her manuscript which helped considerably in my writing of the first chapter, and Gladwin sent copies of her papers on Florida farm families, which were important to the off-farm employment chapter.

In Chapel Hill, where I had begun teaching in the Department of Sociology, Mary Ellen Marsden, then at the Institute for Research in Social Science, proposed that a book on farm women be part of the IRSS series of the University of North Carolina Press. She, Iris Tillman Hill, Editor-in-Chief at UNC Press, and Angell Beza at IRSS all helped shepherd this book through the publication process. The Endowment Committee of the University of North Carolina College of Arts and Sciences for Scholarly Publications, Artistic Exhibitions, and Performances contributed a subsidy toward publication costs.

The Carolina Population Center, at the University of North Carolina, provided most of the resources that made the analysis and writing of the book possible. The Word Processing staff at CPC, especially Mandy Lyerly, Catheryn Brandon, David Claris, Jeff Slagle, Nancy Kuzil, and Bill Dolbee, produced version after version of the manuscript and the final floppy disks and tables that went to the UNC Press. Lynn Igoe, CPC editor, gave much help with the references and index.

A number of people made valuable comments on the manuscript, for which I am grateful. Shelley Pendleton, Lu Ann Jones, and Sherryl Kleinman (who *tried* to get me to take out excess words) made suggestions on the first chapter; John Scanzoni and Susan Olzak on chapter 4 (family decision making); J. Miller McPherson and David Knoke on chapter 6 (voluntary organizational involvement); Kathryn Ward on both chapter 1 and chapter 7 (women's role identification). Joan Huber (in amazing detail) and Eugene Wilkening (with useful references to his own work) made recommendations about the total manuscript. François Nielsen not only read parts of the manuscript, but also offered advice, support, and excellent meals. Although he did not comment directly on this book, Aage Sørensen's ongoing intellectual and methodological advice has made a contribution here.

Finally, I would like to thank all the farm women and farm women researchers who have shared with me their experiences and given reality to the numbers.

Farm Women

1
Women, Work, and Farming

As a majority of humankind, women clearly comprise the largest "group" in the world. Yet they also participate in nearly every other group within society. This simultaneous oneness and diversity has confounded almost everyone who has tried to come to grips with it.—William H. Chafe, Women and Equality: Changing Patterns in American Culture

One of the most dramatic changes in our country over this century has been the decline in the proportion of the population living and working on farms. At the turn of the century, almost half of the people in the United States lived on farms. In 1920, 30 percent did. By 1980, only about 3 percent of the population were farm residents (Smuts 1959; Banks and DeArc 1981). While fewer people now live on farms, the proportion of farmers and farm managers who are women has increased, from 3 percent in 1950 to 5 percent in 1970, and to almost 10 percent in 1979 (Kalbacher 1983). The proportion of farm land owned by women has increased as well (Geisler et al. 1985). Further, almost all farm families include both a husband and a wife, and in very many cases the wife as well as the husband provides farm labor (U.S. Department of Commerce 1983). Yet we know little about U.S. farm and ranch women. This book is about the work these women do and how they feel about it. It uses data from the 1980 Farm Women's Survey—the first national survey of U.S. women on agricultural operations.[1]

Cross-cultural accounts of women and their work show that women have been important providers of food for much of human history (Blumberg 1978; Friedl 1975; O'Kelly 1980). In hunting and gathering societies, women provided about 60 to 80 percent of the food, mostly through their gathering activities (Aronoff and Crano 1975). Many social scientists (e.g., Blumberg 1978) speculate that women, not men, discovered how to cultivate plants through the knowledge they accumulated while gathering. In horticultural societies, which cultivate plants with digging stick or hoe technology, women were often the primary farmers. In agrarian societies based on the use of the plow, fertilizer, irrigation, and draft animals, men took on the dominant roles in agriculture. Women's role in production was reduced, but definitely not eliminated.

Women also help produce food in industrialized societies, but their part often goes unnoticed. In fact, most people, including social scientists, pay little attention to farming in such societies. A major reason for this is that agricultural work occupies only a small part of the population in industrialized societies. But an additional reason for the neglect of farming and women's part in it is social scientists' characterization of the consequences of industrialization. Industrialization, they argue, separated work and family. The preindustrial family was the center of both production and consumption, and all members of the family contributed to its economic viability. For the family in industrialized societies, however, work, and especially work for pay, is believed to happen outside the home. The home is seen as a consumption and reproduction unit, not a productive one. Social scientists' acceptance of what Kanter (1977b) calls the myth of family and work as separate spheres means, among other things, that they did not study women's work, because they assumed that women's major adult roles were within the family. It also means that family farms—in which the workplace and the family are often indistinguishable both physically and psychologically—did not fit their conceptions of a workplace and were left out of studies of work and occupations.[2] In this book, however, I will look at women's work on and for farms in the United States.

This book's investigation of women and their work in what is considered an atypical workplace—the farm—can inform research on women's work in industrialized societies by pointing to interconnections of family and the workplace that we might not think to examine in a more "usual" group. In addition, the results of such a study will have implications for U.S. agricultural policy. If women are an important part of the farm economy, then policies about and contact with U.S. farms will need to take this into account. The results are important as well for policies related to agriculture in Third World countries. Recognition that even in a highly developed country such as the U.S. women are important, and feel themselves important, in agricultural production might increase the sensitivity of policymakers to the position of women in agriculture in developing countries.

In this chapter, I set up the conceptual framework and some specific hypotheses with which to study U.S. farm women. Before one can talk about farm women's work, one needs to have a definition of work and an understanding of how it applies to women. The next section develops this conceptualization. Farm women work and live in a particular workplace—the farm. To give a sense of the context in which farms operate, the subsequent section traces changes in agriculture over this century and outlines the structure of farming today. The chapter then turns to what we know about changes in farm women's work over time before developing hypotheses as to the nature and variation in these women's current work.

Women and Work

For most people, work means a job held outside the home for pay. In fact, this tends to be the only type of work people recognize as such. In this book, however, I define work much more broadly: work is effort resulting in some product or service. It can be done for pay (such as a wage or salary) but at times receives no remuneration. It can be done in the home or outside it. Figure 1.1 shows the four types of work to which this definition leads.

Most of the research on "work" has been on work for pay outside the home (cell 1). Until recently, men have been the major wage earners. Although there have always been some women who have earned a living outside the home, only a minority of U.S. women were employed early in the twentieth century (Smuts 1959). Since the 1950s, however, the proportion of women, and especially mothers of young children, who are employed or actively looking for employment has increased dramatically. In 1950, 33.9 percent of women sixteen and over were in the labor force. By 1980 this percentage had jumped to 51.2. In 1950 the labor force participation rate for women with children under six years of age was 11.9

Figure 1.1. *Types of Work*

	Direct pay	No direct pay
Outside home	1. Wage work	4. Volunteer work
In home	2. In-home business or employment ("cottage industry")	3. Housework, childcare

percent; in 1979 it was 43.2 percent (Hayghe and Johnson 1980).[3] The research on women's paid work outside the home has likewise increased in the past 15 years.[4]

Cottage industry (production within the home for pay, cell 2) evolved in the transition to an industrialized society (e.g., Gullickson 1981). At the turn of the century, even in urban areas, women earned money working in the home. They took in boarders, sewed, made cigars, and produced craft objects. The opportunities to earn money through these activities, however, decreased as declining migration reduced the demand for rooms in private homes, as laws forbade home work in the tobacco, garment, and food industries, and as factory-produced goods and commercial services competed with those provided by women at home (Smuts 1959).

Little is known about such work today. Perhaps as a response to the depressed economy of the early 1980s, however, newspaper articles and self-help books on how to start home businesses abound. Some speculate that computer terminals will make home the workplace for women and perhaps even for men. Work for pay in the home may become more common in the future (Langway 1984).

Unpaid work inside the home (cell 3) was and is primarily women's work. What women do for the home has not been seen as real work, with a few exceptions (e.g., Oakley 1974, and Schooler et al. 1984). Some time-budget studies of what is done in the home do exist. One notable finding from such research is that even when the woman is employed, she is the one who does most of the child care and housework. When a married woman is employed, her husband does not increase his household work very much, if at all, though on average the woman spends fewer hours a week on housework (Vanek 1974; Meissner et al. 1975; Stafford 1980; Pleck 1979). Also there has been only a little recognition that the work women do seemingly just for the home may be part of a husband's career progress, as when the wife takes on responsibility for entertaining her husband's business associates (e.g., Kanter 1977a). Work within the home, then, can be part of a two-person career, where only one person is recognized as working.

Cell 4—work without pay outside the home—includes volunteer work, work in voluntary organizations, and political activity. While earlier research found women to have fewer organizational memberships than men, recent evidence shows men and women to have about the same degree of involvement in voluntary organizations (McPherson and Smith-Lovin 1982; Duncan and Duncan 1978; Hanks and Eckland 1978; though see Knoke and Thomson 1977). Political participation, such as working for candidates or attending political meetings, is also now about the same for women and men (Lynn 1979:411; Carroll 1979; Duncan and Duncan 1978:118–19). Women seem to do more volunteer work than men, however. In 1981, 56 percent of all U.S. adult volunteers were women (Granthan 1982). According to a 1965 study, 21 percent of U.S. women 14 and over did some volunteer work, compared with 15 percent of the men. The women doing volunteer work contributed an average of 5.4 hours per week; the men, 5 hours (cited in Mueller 1975:331).

In general, then, women do more of the unpaid work in our society than men. If one does not consider types of work other than paid employment, then one misses important work contributions, especially of women. At the same time, one needs to keep in mind that not all kinds of work are equally valued in a given society. Often the work that is seen as most important is done largely by men, such as paid employment in our society. The extent to which women do the "important" work in a given society is therefore of special interest.

In the study of work, one needs not only a broad enough definition of the concept but also recognition of possible interconnections among the different sorts of work. For women, probably the most critical interrelationship is between their unpaid work in the home and other sorts of work. Blumberg (1978:25), among others, has argued that one crucial factor that affects the extent to which women participate in the main economic work of a society is the degree to which women can combine child care with economic activities. Women's responsibilities for rearing children, as well as for maintaining families in general, have been used to explain at least in part the historical exclusion of women from factory work, differences between men's and women's labor force participation rates generally, and sex differences in wages and occupational locations. Although more mothers of young children are employed today, they are still less likely to have jobs than other women (Cramer 1980; Waite 1981). Polachek (1981:68) reported that "differences in labor force commitment *alone* account for much of the difference in professional and menial employment [by sex]. If women were to have full commitment to the labor force, the number of women professionals would increase by 35 percent, the number of women in managerial professions would more than double, and women in menial occupations would decrease by more than 25 percent." Oppenheimer (1970) has described women's occupations as those with relatively little on-the-job training such that it is easy for a woman to move into and out of the job as her childrearing and family duties dictate. Wolf and Rosenfeld (1978) presented some evidence that predominantly female occupations are those easiest to reenter. Consistently over this half of the twentieth century, women employed full-time over the entire year have earned only about 60 percent of what men earn (Hayghe and Johnson 1980). This lower pay has been explained by their irregular labor force participation, which in turn results from their home responsibilities (e.g., Polachek 1975). Explanations for sex segregation and the wage gap based on the extent and nature of women's work in the home, however, do not always hold up empirically.[5] Nor do such explanations resolve the question of why women do most of the unpaid work, even when biological imperatives, such as that they nurse children, are no longer in force (e.g., Huber and Spitze 1983). But when accepted by women and employers, these explanations support the existing situation.

At the same time, what occurs in one domain reinforces the situation in others. Because women are employed less regularly than men and at lower wages, they are more dependent on the husband's wage. Thus it makes economic sense for them to provide services without pay within the home and in the community, since their time is worth less than a man's in the labor force. Since more of their work is not paid or is paid at a lower rate, and since work in a market society such as ours tends to be valued by how much it earns, women's work is valued (and recognized) less than men's. One comes full circle. What looks like a rational choice argument (e.g., Becker 1981) becomes tautological. Further, there is always the assumption in these explanations that women have husbands. When they do not, they suffer, whether because of the difficulties of combining household work with paid work, because of low-wage job opportunities, or both. One indicator of this is that in 1980, 34 percent of persons in female-headed households lived in poverty (as officially defined) compared with 8 percent of people in other types of families (U.S. Department of Commerce 1983: Table 781).

The second major factor (in addition to compatibility with child care) that according to Blumberg (1978) affects women's involvement in a society's principal economic activities is the availability of male labor: When the supply of male labor is less than the demand, then women step in. Women's labor potential has been useful to our society. When demand for labor or certain kinds of labor has increased, women have entered employment. When they are no longer needed, they retire. For example, during World Wars I and II, women did "men's" work to fill in for men in the armed forces. After the wars, men replaced them (Greenwold 1981; Anderson 1979). Over the last half century, the demand for clerical workers seems to have stimulated women's labor force participation (Oppenheimer 1970). Milkman (1976), however, shows that even during the Depression, men did not take over "women's" jobs.

Within the family, too, the woman may take up the slack, providing the extra income needed to keep the family out of poverty or at a higher standard of living (Oppenheimer 1977), even though she earns less than a man and continues to be responsible for child care and home maintenance. When men are laid off during hard times, women may be able to provide all of the family's income if fewer jobs usually assigned to women than to men are cut back.

This sort of reasoning helps explain why child care does not always take precedence over other sorts of work. As Friedl (1975) emphasizes, the nature of the economic work women do may affect the number and spacing of children they bear. In the United States Cramer (1980) showed that, although fertility affects employment in the short run, employment affects fertility in the long run. And when there are children, women do not always stay home to care for them. Accounts of nineteenth-century working-class families depicted cases where women neglected infants in order to go out and earn the wage necessary for the family's survival. In our times there is concern about "latch key" children and the quality of day care. Thus, to understand women's work, not only must one look at the interrelationships among different kinds of work the women do, but also one needs to consider the extent and nature of the work of men (and possibly other family members).

FARM WOMEN'S WORK

The research that exists on farm women is similar to the general research on women and work in that it "has been done in regard to women as helpers, mothers, and wives" (Joyce and Leadley, 1977: 34). In the late 1970s some scholars criticized this approach and produced research that went beyond it (e.g., Boulding 1980). A conceptualization of work such as that in Figure 1.1 helps point out that farm women do a wide range of work on and off the operation.

Many women on family farms do work that falls into all of the cells in the figure. As will be seen, they almost inevitably do housework. Sometimes this housework is above and beyond that of city and other rural women, as when they prepare meals not only for their immediate family but also for other farm workers. Colman and Elbert (1983:3), for example, report one of the women in their study "when asked to enumerate the hours spent in farm versus home tasks, opened the lid of her washing machine, revealing a common mixture of barn suits, children's jeans, and furniture slipcovers all tumbling around in the soapy water." Farm women often raise and process food for the family's use. Many do farm work without direct pay as "unpaid family labor." At least some farm women have other businesses in the home that bring in money. Many are employed off the farm, often to help the farm's cash flow. Finally, at least some farm women join agricultural and community organizations to improve the position of family farms and increase their ties with the community. Thus farm women do work outside the home for both family and farm. Even work done within the home may be seen as a contribution to the operation in terms of support services.

Given the range of sorts of work farm women do, it is necessary to look at the interrelationships among the different kinds of activities for an understanding of farm women's work lives. Further, because many farms are family businesses it is even more important to take into account the work of other family members. What especially a husband or adult son does on and off the farm can determine what is left for the woman to do. Also, because children may be part of the farm labor force, their work contributions, rather than simply their presence, must be considered in analyzing women's work. The atypicality of the farm as a workplace in industrial society thus highlights issues that are important in the study of work in general and of women's work in particular. The boundaries between "work" and "family" become artificial, and one is forced to analyze the links between the two.

The topic of women's work brings up the further topic of the sexual division of labor, that is, not just what women do but also how the work in general is divided between women and men. In this book I will be concentrating on farm *women's* work. At some points, though, I will also look directly at how women and men divide various types of work—whether it is usually assigned to one particular sex, whether women and men seem to substitute for each other when necessary, or whether women and men do the work together. Rural people have been described as rather conservative in their sex role attitudes (e.g., Flora and Johnson 1978; Dunne 1980; Kain and Divecha 1983). Yet, because home work and farm work occur in proximity to one another and even off-farm work may support the farm, some observers have suggested that the division of labor within farm couples may actually be less sex-typed than is work for the nonfarm population. (See the discussion in Fassinger and Schwarzweller 1982.) As I will discuss later in this chapter, various accounts show that crossing sex role boundaries usually goes only one way, as is true generally: women do "men's" work on the farm as necessary, but men do not ordinarily do "women's" work. Further, women are still unlikely to do certain critical kinds of "men's" work. Social scientists looking at what happens to women's work in developing countries have noticed that women are excluded from certain key tasks that link the individual's or family's work to the larger economy as countries increasingly enter a market (as compared with a subsistence) economy (e.g., Bourque and Warren 1981; Boserup 1970). There are hints that in the United States, too, women are less likely than men to do work that provides such contact with markets.

A further topic related to that of women's work is women's status (e.g., Chafetz 1984; Blumberg 1978). Status is a relative concept: One must be able to say women's status as compared with what. The comparison may be with men's, but it may also be with women in other places, classes, or times (e.g., Ward 1984). Status is a multidimensional concept as well, although the extent to which women do valued work in a society is one variable thought to affect status. With information primarily on work and primarily on women at only one time, I will not attempt to say much about women's overall status. The information in this book, however, may provide background information for those who are engaged in study of this topic.

In this book, then, I will be looking at farm women's work on and off the farm, done with or without pay. In examining any particular type of work, I will bring in the other types of work the woman does, especially child care. At the same time, I will look at how the work of other family members (especially the husband, if there is one) affects what the woman does. In some cases I will be able to see how wives and husbands divide labor. The topic of status (which includes women's power over resources) will have to wait for other authors. Before saying more about farm women's work, we turn to trends in farming generally.

The U.S. Family Farm

Does it still make sense to talk about the family farm? One view is that the traditional family farm—owned, run, and worked by family members—is disappearing, that it is a remnant of a former type of society and is being replaced by corporate agriculture. Some of the trends in present day agriculture seem consistent with the idea that the traditional family farm is disappearing. The number of farms has decreased dramatically, and their size has increased. In 1935 there were over 6.8 million farms in the United States. In 1960 there were just under 4 million, and in 1982 there were 2.4 million. The 1935 farm averaged 155 acres, while the 1982 farm averaged almost three times that size—433 acres (U.S. Department of Commerce 1983:652). At the same time farms are more productive than ever before. Sales are more concentrated. In 1964, for example, 1.28 million farms accounted for 90 percent of farm sales; in 1974, 825,000 farms did (U.S. Department of Agriculture 1979). Further, the percent of sales accounted for by farms organized as corporations has increased. In 1969 they accounted for 14 percent of farm product sales, and in 1974, 18 percent (U.S. Department of Agriculture 1979:7). There have been changes in the type of labor involved, too. While the absolute number of people in the farm work force has declined, the relative proportion of hired farm labor has increased, and the employment of hired farm workers has become more concentrated on a smaller number of large farms (Goss et al. 1980:110). Thus, farming in the United States has become more productive, concentrated, centralized, and dependent on hired rather than family labor, with corporate farms accounting for an increasing part of farm production.

On the other hand, there is evidence that the nature of agriculture places limits on the extent to which it can be organized like any other business and that the U.S. family farm is likely to continue—and that indeed it is continuing, although its form has changed. The family farm today is intimately tied in to the larger economy and is affected by changes in that economy. To understand the U.S. family farm as a workplace (and women's part in such a workplace), it is important to place it in modern industrialized capitalistic society rather than to see it as an extension of an earlier type of society.

Agriculture may be unattractive to many corporations for two reasons. One is that production time is longer than labor time. That is, the time it takes for crops to ripen and animals to grow and reproduce is longer than the work time of the farmer (Mann and Dickinson 1978). One thus needs a work force that can be pulled into the production process and pushed out as the work requirements change. A second reason is that farming is very risky, because success depends not only on good management and production practices but also on the cooperation of nature (Pfeffer 1983). Small family farms can continue with "underconsumption and overwork by the whole family," while government programs for family farms may aid those in the middle to large range (Sachs 1983:66–67). One suggestion is that corporate agriculture and family agriculture today are not competing with each other, in part because family farms make investments not attractive to large-scale capital.

Pfeffer (1983) has outlined the development of U.S. agriculture in different regions of the United States, showing how differences in the availability of labor affected the organization of production. In California, he points out, capitalist agriculture did develop, since that state has had a constant stream of exploitable labor. (Wells 1984, though, points out that other forms of agriculture have appeared or reappeared as this stream has been dammed.) In the Midwest, where there was a shortage of wage laborers, the family farm developed after an unsuccessful attempt to institute large-scale corporate farming. Also Friedmann (1982) showed that in the nineteenth century, for wheat farming in the United States (and in parts of Europe), the use of wage labor and managers by outside investors gave way to family farming as the dominant form of agricultural production. One could see the ascendance of family farming even in the development of agricultural machinery, as scale shifted down after larger equipment was first introduced for corporate farms. Thus in many parts of the United States family farming was not an anachronism left over from a previous era, but a form of production that won out over "capitalistic" farming.

Table 1.1. *1978 U.S. Farm and Ranch Business Organization*

	Numbers of Owners (1,000s)	Percent Owners	Percent Acreage
Form of organization			
Sole proprietor	3,032	44.1	35.8
Husband-wife	3,016	43.9	35.7
Family partnership	423	6.2	12.1
Family corporation	107	1.5	6.6
Nonfamily partnership	97	1.4	2.0
Nonfamily corporation	71	1.0	3.9
Other	131	1.9	3.9
Total	6,877	100.0	100.0

Source: Department of Commerce, Statistical Abstract of the United States, 1981, Table 1181.

Statistics on type of farm ownership show the continuing dominance of family farming (see Table 1.1). Most farms are still family owned and run. According to the latest Agricultural Census from which detailed reports were available as of 1984, individuals or couples owned 88 percent of the 1978 farms. Family members usually owned even farms organized as partnerships or corporations. Only 2.4 percent of 1978 farms were nonfamily partnerships or corporations. These few farms, however, are disproportionately large in terms of both acres and, as noted, sales.[6] The 1979 Department of Agriculture report to Congress on the status of the family farm made this prediction with respect to trends in corporate farming (1979:9): "Overall, the output of multiownership farms could account for about half of farm sales before the end of the century. Most of these multiownership farms will likely continue to be multifamily farms. Two decades will probably not bring much dispersion of ownership of present farming corporations. Addition of new corporations will likely result from incorporation of existing farms rather than entry of corporations not now farming. Few nonfarm corporations are likely to be attracted into farming, barring a significant rise in the profitability of farming."

In terms of land ownership there has not been a trend toward increasing tenant farming or manager control, but rather the reverse. Forty-two percent of all farm operators were tenants or managers in 1935 and 20 percent in 1959 (Ross 1982). Between 1975 and 1980 there was a decline in the proportion of the farm population on farms where the operators were tenants or managers, from 11.3 percent to 9.9 percent (U.S. Department of Commerce 1983:650; though see also Wells 1984). However, there has also been an increase in the proportion of operators who are part owners: just between 1974 and 1978 the percent of operators who were part owners went from 27 to 29 (U.S. Department of Commerce 1982: 655).[7] As some have pointed out, when land prices are as high as they are, renting land may be the only way to expand.

While the number of farms in general declined during the last half century and became larger on average, recently there has been an opposing trend: the number of very small farms has actually increased (Gladwin and Downie 1982; Ross 1982). Their owners are more likely to be full owners. People can enter farming when they inherit or buy a small piece of land and then not be able to expand even by renting.

Most farms are still family farms, then, but there are fewer of the middle size, fully owned, family staffed, stereotypic family farms. Farming has tended to polarize into two segments: very large operations and very small, often part-time, farms.

The situation of any particular farm will be affected by the pressures upon it in various markets. Most farms depend on markets for farm inputs, as well as family consumption goods. As already mentioned, the price of land, which is affected by the demand for land for alternative uses as well as for agriculture, has risen and changed the way farms expand: farmers rent land rather than buy it. Expenses for other inputs have risen enormously over past decades at the same time that the input mix has moved toward machinery, chemicals, and other items that have to be bought and away from labor (Martinson and Campbell 1980:234).

Increasing production costs and increasing capitalization have led farmers to increase their use of credit in the last twenty-five years. Interest as a production expense has therefore increased (U.S. Department of Agriculture, OGPA 1979). One young Oklahoma farmer described the extent of the farm's debt in 1981–82: "We purchased a $300,000 farm a year ago, obligating ourselves to payments of $40,000 annually for the next 30 years—a total investment of 1.5 million dollars for two quarters of land . . . that doesn't even include the $130,000 loan to buy cattle last fall or the operating costs of machinery parts, diesel fuel, grain, fertilizer, pesticides, veterinary bills, etc. Yet . . . our land value did not increase enough last year to even meet interest expenses" (Jones-Webb 1982:3). Credit markets, interest rates, and government loan programs are increasingly important to farmers. As has been seen recently, when credit is withdrawn, even formerly successful farms go under.

Product markets have become larger and more likely to be national rather than regional or local (U.S. Department of Agriculture 1979:9). Farmers now depend on smaller numbers of buyers. Given the large proportion of agricultural exports from the United States, farmers' positions as sellers of commodities depend as well on what is happening in world markets and on U.S. foreign policy.

There has been a rise in one kind of marketing that provides an alternative to the direct takeover of farming by nonfamily corporations—contract farming. Production contracts are usually made before production begins. They often specify that the nonfarm corporation provide some of the production inputs and control production practices. The farmer, in turn, agrees to deliver a certain type and quantity of commodity. In 1960, 4.5 percent of all farm operators reported having some sort of contract for production or marketing. In 1974, over 9 percent of operations with sales of $2,500 or more had such contracts (U.S. Department of Agriculture 1979:10). Such arrangements assure the food processor of a given product at a given time without requiring that the processor provide the labor to raise the food. In most cases, it is the nonfarm company that sets the price to be paid for the commodity. The farmer continues to bear most of the risk associated with a crop or other failure. The producer may also lose so much control over the production process as to become little more than an employee. This is especially true with respect to broiler and egg contracts. At the same time, contracting can reduce some of the marketing and price risks faced by the farmer (Davis 1980). Those producing under contract may be able to get credit more easily, or those trying to get credit may be urged to contract.

While market production contracts leave at least the actual production in the hands of the farmer, there is concern that such arrangements favor the larger farmers. Other types of markets for a particular commodity may disappear when contracting is the dominant arrangement. If large farms are better able to get contracts than small ones, then small farmers may find themselves without a market at all for their products (U.S. Department of Agriculture 1979:18).

At least some farmers have tried to increase their market power through cooperatives and commodity associations. Cooperatives are arrangements by groups of farmers to buy inputs, process commodities, or market products. Commodity bargaining associations negotiate contract terms with contractors. In 1974–75, farm cooperatives supplied 35 percent of farm petroleum inputs, 30 percent of fertilizer and lime, and 29 percent of farm chemicals. They accounted for approximately 30 percent of farm level marketing (Martinson and Campbell 1980:232, 237). In 1974, cooperatives were listed as the contractor in 36 percent of all contracts (U.S. Department of Agriculture 1979:16).

While some research suggests that cooperatives increase competition in markets where monopolies would otherwise be present, it is unclear to what extent they actually improve the general position of farmers. Cooperatives, too, may need to deal with other large buyers and suppliers. They themselves may become larger. While the number of cooperatives has gone down over the last two decades, the volume of sales and purchases has gone up tremendously (U.S. Department of Commerce 1983:667). Further, they may help one group of farmers by restricting membership (Martinson and Campbell 1980).

In addition to being tied in with credit, inputs, and product markets, the U.S. farm population has also become increasingly involved with the nonfarm labor markets. A rising proportion of farm income comes from off-farm sources, usually in the form of wages and salaries. The percentage of the farm population's total income from farm sources went from 69 percent in 1950 to 42 percent in 1976 (Carter and Johnson 1978: Table 1). In 1980, 1981, and 1982, 39, 45, and 38 percent of the farm population's personal income came from the farm (U.S. Department of Commerce 1983: 661). According to the 1979 Farm Finance Survey, 45.5 percent of farms in that year received 80 percent or more of their net cash income from activities and investments off the farm. Relatively more farm operators are employed away from the farm. In 1950, 34 percent of all farm operators reported any off-farm work, while in 1978, 58 percent of U.S. farm operators said they had worked off the farm (Sander 1981, 1983).

Among those with off-farm employment in the United States, the time spent on jobs off the farm has also increased. In 1950, among farm operators employed off the farm, 39 percent worked off-farm 200 days or more; in 1978, two-thirds (Sander 1981, 1983).

Greater proportions of farm operators have a principal occupation other than farming: 37 percent in 1974 and 46 percent in 1978 (U.S. Department of Commerce 1983:654.)

Off-farm work can be in agriculture, such as custom work or a job in a feed store. However, there are indications that increasing proportions of farm men and women's off-farm jobs are outside agriculture. Among employed farm women (including unpaid family workers), for example, the percent employed in agriculture went from 44 in 1960 to 29 in 1974 (Beale 1978:2). From the evidence available on the pervasiveness, intensity, and nature of off-farm employment, it is clear that for farm families, there has been an increasing interface between farm and nonfarm labor markets.

These trends fit in with another already mentioned: the increasing number of small farms. While not all part-time farms are small (Buttel and Larson 1982; Coughenour and Swanson 1983), small farms have a greater proportion of income from off-farm employment. Off-farm employment has been important both in keeping small farms operating and in keeping their family incomes at the level of other families (Sander 1981; Hanson 1972; Huffman 1977). The state of the labor market (especially the nonfarm labor market) is increasingly important for farm families, especially those on very small farms.

The modern U.S. family farm, then, is *not* outside the general market economy but rather very much a part of it. While the family or multifamily farm is still the dominant form of operation, farms are larger and more capital intensive than even 30 years ago, and farming in general is more concentrated. At the same time, new kinds of marketing techniques and dependence on credit may be taking some control of production away from the farmer. Even in the trend to larger farms there is considerable heterogeneity in the nature of family farms. At one end of the spectrum is the very large operation that depends on hired labor; at the other is the small farm run directly by family members and dependent on the off-farm income of some of these members as well.

Variations among farms along these dimensions would be expected to affect the ways in which women provide labor, on or off the farm, needed to keep the farm going. At the same time, emphasizing the importance of various market relationships for today's farms points to certain kinds of work critical to a farm's survival. Women might in general be less involved in such tasks, given the general tendency for men to perform important linkage tasks in many situations, while variation among women in performance of these tasks might be especially sensitive to the structure of the family and farm.

Before further specifying these ideas, the next section traces some of the effects of changes in farming on women's work over time. Extrapolation from historical accounts in conjunction with recent research is then used to form hypotheses about the nature and variation in farm women's work today, which is the subject of the rest of this book.

The Place of Women in Agriculture: Trends and Variations

TRENDS IN FARM WOMEN'S WORK

It is difficult to trace changes in the work roles of farm women. Because scholars have not considered women "farmers," we do not have much information about what they did in the past. There have been very few attempts to reconstruct the history of farm women in the U.S.[8] Joyce and Leadley (1977:5–6), in their review of the literature on rural women from 1900–1976, suggest that the roles of farm women may not have changed so much as "consciousness of women and men about the role of women on farms." It may thus be hard to distinguish historical trends from changes in focus with respect to farm women's work.

Not only the focus but also the nature and quantity of the research on farm women has varied over time (Boulding 1979). Many of the accounts from the early 1900s are anecdotal. However, in 1915 the USDA published a series of reports on farm women's social, labor, domestic, education, and economic needs. The 1920s saw at least four studies of farm women's use of time, encouraged by the passage of the Parnell Act in 1925, which apportioned funds for research on rural areas. In the 1930s research went beyond women's domestic roles and focused on the "hard times" and how they affected rural and farm women. Hagood's (1977/1939) study of white tenant farm women in the South, supported by the Institute for Research in Social Science at the University of North Carolina, is an outstanding example of this work. Women disappeared from studies of farming during the war years, to reappear in the 1950s and 1960s mainly as wives performing domestic and supportive functions. Wilkening's work on farm decision making (Wilkening 1958; Wilkening and Bharadwaj 1968; Wilkening and Guerrero 1969) was an exception during this period in seeing women as possible partners in the operation. In the 1970s and 1980s we see more studies that present women as individuals who can contribute to the operation in a variety of ways. In addition to the problems of changing consciousness and changing research, there is the complication that farming has varied and does vary across regions and ethnic groups in the United States (e.g., Sachs 1983; Jensen 1981).

Despite problems with the literature, we can use historical accounts and the research on women and labor to piece together a description of general changes in the nature of farm women's work in the home (both paid and unpaid), on the farm, and off the farm in both the labor market and voluntary associations.

Over time, farm women have produced less in the home for the family's subsistence and for sale or barter. When women made soap, clothing, candles, and food for the family, money did not have to be spent on these necessities. Butter and egg money could cover other costs. Vanek (1980:425) quotes a 1915 Michigan farm study as showing "that 80 percent of the living expenditures . . . were met by cash earnings of farm wives." Money from cash crops could go to sustaining or improving the farm. At times some of the cash from women's paid in-home work went to the farm as well (Smuts 1959; Bush 1982). For example, "By 1910, women on the plains of Montana were using butter money to buy windmills necessary for survival of farms in the waterless land" (Jensen 1981:108).

Over time, however, many products that women made at home for family use became things the family bought. Bush's (1982: 248) 1974–76 interviews with rural Idaho women ages nineteen to ninety-four contrast women's work now with that earlier in the century: "Instead of sewing the family's clothes, a farm woman now buys them; instead of canning the produce from her garden, she buys food. In fact, it is cheaper for the farm wife to buy case lots of canned peaches than to put up the equivalent amount herself. Cash income, the availability of fresh produce, and good roads have removed the *economic* necessity of her doing anything beyond shopping." Bush may have overstated her case. Still, in general there has been a trend toward buying rather than producing goods for the family, as well as for the farm.

More cash was needed for family expenses, but at the same time women's opportunities to earn money at home were decreasing. Not only were factory produced goods often cheaper, but also legal restrictions limited cottage industry, as discussed earlier. Farm women were caught up in this process, although later than urban women.

Farm women have contributed cash to their families by working off the farm as well as on it. Some of the first factory workers in New England were farm daughters who often sent their wages back to their families. In the post–Civil War South, young white farm women worked in cotton mills, while black women did domestic or field work for pay (Smuts 1959; Janiewski 1979). In South Dakota the young Laura Ingalls sewed button holes in a drygoods store and later taught school, giving her wages to her homesteading family (Zochert 1976). (See also, Wilder 1941; 1943.)

Off-farm employment of farm women has increased rapidly in the recent past although it has still not reached the level of farm men's (Beale 1978:3). Further, as is true for the female work force as a whole, the typical farm woman employed off the farm is no longer the daughter but the wife and mother. Such off-farm employment brings in cash, but may also limit the time these women have for production activities in the home and on the farm (Graff 1982).

On the farm, the increasing need for cash affected people's perception of the value of the home and farm's work done by women and men. Looking at Piedmont tenant farm families before the turn of the century, Janiewski (1979:43, 46) says, "Although women certainly controlled their work in the household, it was clear that farmwork took precedence over housework whenever labor demands conflicted."

Given the precedence of farm work, women would cross over to do "men's" work, but not vice versa. The same was true with respect to capital investments. Money went for farm equipment before household improvements. "Men's work took precedence in the family budget because it provided the family income and satisfied the family creditors. However important women's domestic labor might be to the family well-being, its value was disregarded because it brought no cash into the family economy" (Janiewski 1979:46). A 1911 U.S. Country Life Commission saw the same lack of attention to helping women's work. "Whatever general hardships, such as poverty, lack of labor-saving devices, may exist on any given farm, the burden of these hardships falls more heavily on the farmer's wife than on the farmer himself" (quoted in Sachs 1983:22).

One might expect that women had decreasing contacts with the agricultural markets (although contact with nonfarm *labor* markets increased) as they produced less to sell directly themselves and as farm communities saw cash crops as "men's." Men would be the ones to market products and deal with those who sold machinery and credit. There are hints that this was the case. For example, on the basis of farm couples' time budgets for the first half of this century, Vanek (1980:428) reports, "Women tended to spend more time visiting friends than their husbands . . . But farmers made up for this with trips to market . . . as well as by hunting and fishing."

Mechanization, a component in the increasing capitalization and centralization of U.S. farms, not only meant that cash (and credit) was needed to purchase machinery; it also affected women's work on the farm and in the home. One explanation for women's lower participation in agrarian as compared with horticultural societies' food production is that plowing takes greater strength than hoeing. It is true that women are on average smaller than men and not as strong. Furthermore, plowing is less compatible with child care than hoeing. While it might still be difficult to combine use of machinery with caring for children, mechanization could eliminate the importance of differences in size and strength, so that as farming becomes increasingly mechanized, one would see less difference between the tasks of women and men. In Japan small-scale mechanization led to greater involvement of women (and older men) in farming, whereas working age men found employment off the farm (Kada 1980:48). Research on women in developing countries and on the industries that employ women in the contemporary United States, however, finds that women do the more labor intensive, less capitalized work, even when employed away from home, where caring for children while doing other work is not an issue (e.g., Hodson 1978). When they use machines, they use simpler ones (Form and McMillen 1983). Men, then, seem to do the work that produces more, even when relative strength is not a factor.[9]

If mechanization on U.S. farms has decreased the need for labor, then in the absence of other factors it would not be surprising to find that women are not using the machinery and that their participation in some farm tasks has decreased over time. A quote from a contemporary Ontario farm women makes this point: "I suppose if he needed me to be out there all the time, I would soon learn to use all of those machines, but as long as he can do it himself, I don't have to, do I?" (Graff 1982:10).

If farms do not need women to run machinery, then manufacturers can design machinery for men, but such machines can prevent women from doing certain kinds of work. In her study of women farmers, Sachs (1983) found that the use of larger equipment was a barrier to the women's participation in all aspects of farm work. It was not that women could not run the equipment, but rather that they had problems hooking up pieces of equipment or reaching the pedals. One woman's doctor told her that "a woman wasn't made to drive a tractor." Her response was that "tractors weren't made for women" (p. 98).

If women's use of machinery were necessary for farming as an industry, then manufacturers would develop equipment that fit them as well as allowing them to care for children at some stage while using it. There are farm families for whom a major consideration in buying equipment is whether it is comfortable for the woman and whether she can have her children with her as she runs it. In other industries, such as the telephone industry, when government pressure forced companies to hire women for formerly all-male jobs, the companies redesigned equipment in such a way that it was often easier for both women and men to use.

From her interviews with Idaho farm women, Bush (1982) found that mechanization of farming affected women's household work as well. At least in wheat farming the use of diesel powered tractors meant that fewer hired hands were needed, and that in turn meant that women did not need to cook for as many people. She goes on to note (p. 248) that farm technological advances meant that when labor saving devices were introduced into the houses, they were not as crucial as they would have been earlier. "Farm women did not need new appliances to feed farm workers more efficiently because diesel power had taken the place of horsepower and there were fewer workers to feed."

Another way in which mechanization and decreased labor demands may have affected farm women's work is through an effect on family size (although declining child mortality and increasing cost of child rearing have probably played their parts as well). While farm families are still somewhat larger than nonfarm families, they are much smaller now than earlier in this century (e.g., Okun 1958). With relatively fewer children, farm women spend less time supervising children. In addition, there is a shorter period in women's lives when child care interferes with the use of heavy machinery (if child care is a factor). At the same time, with an emphasis on "higher quality" children, farm women may have increased the amount of time they spend making sure that children participate in activities (e.g., Scouts, ballet lessons) thought to be beneficial for them (see Huber and Spitze 1983).

There are some hints that with the increasing complexity of farming, women have been less likely to take part in decision making. Sachs (1983:29) cites a 1937 study, in which "Beers . . . reported that the family farm was moving away from the patriarchal authority that had existed on pioneer farms. According to his study, women were consulted in some decisions, especially decisions related to borrowing money. However, decisions such as whether to purchase equipment or what crops to plant were usually made by the husband. He suggested that as farms become more commercialized, decision making and the division of labor would become more specialized, with men involved in farm decisions and women involved in the home." The decisions seem to be divided into production decisions versus others, with husbands taking sole responsibility for production decisions. If one believes that women are not included in market transactions, then one might have expected them to be consulted less about things such as borrowing money. On the other hand, while women may not be the ones who make contact with banks, etc., they may still take some part in these decisions since the economic situation of the whole family depends on them (see Jones 1983).

In his 1978–79 data, Wilkening (1981) also found women participating more in decisions about buying or renting land than in production decisions. However, comparing 1962 data with the 1978–79 data and asking couples about changes in their own decision-making practices, he concludes that women over the two decades were somewhat less involved with expansion or reduction decisions or with decisions about borrowing money, but somewhat more involved in production decisions. The increase in discussion of farm management issues within couples, even those farming for over a decade, suggests that at least some women are becoming more like equal partners in their enterprises, perhaps as a result of the spread of ideas from the Women's Liberation Movement. On the other hand, Wilkening speculates that the reason for decreased (though still high) participation of the wife in various business decisions is "that such business actions are more common now and becoming less of a matter for family consideration. If this is true, it indicates that male farm operators are placing a greater emphasis on profit-making, perhaps at the expense of other family goals and considerations" (p. 7). The idea that credit transactions are increasingly routine is consistent with the changes in the nature of agricultural enterprises over the last decades. It is possible, too, that banks, government agencies, and other entities outside the family now influence decisions about expansion, credit, and so on, and that it is the man who deals with these institutions.

The increasing complexity of farming seems to have increased at least one type of work women do for the farm: bookkeeping. Perhaps because women have often had more education than their husbands, they have traditionally kept the books in farm families. With more bookkeeping to do, women do more of it. One Idaho farm woman said (Bush 1982:250): "In the days when I was growing up there were no books kept. There wasn't any income tax in those days. But since we've had books and there's a terrific amount of bookkeeping on a farm nowadays and especially in the partnership my husband is in. . . . Of course we have our income tax done by an accountant but then I have to get the books ready."

Wilkening's (1981) comparison of Wisconsin farm families in 1962 and 1978 also points to an increase in farm women's bookkeeping for the farm. Anecdotal accounts suggest that when a computer is brought in to keep records and accounts, it is often the woman who takes charge of it.

With respect to other sorts of farm tasks, women's work might have remained relatively unchanged. It seems likely that women have continued to fill in when extra labor is needed, for example for harvesting. Mechanization may have freed women from doing field work (Sachs 1983) to some extent. But when a crop is to be harvested, the farm needs extra labor, which often comes from the family. One finds accounts of women not just cooking for extra hands at harvest time but also working in the fields, in the nineteenth century as well as in the 1970s and 1980s (Smuts 1959; Bush 1982). Even on mechanized farms there are still tasks that have to be done by hand. It may be here that women continue to perform farm tasks.

Further, with the increasing off-farm employment of farm men, more women may be filling in on the farm. Gladwin (1982) found in her study of contemporary small farmers in Florida that women would sometimes quit their low-wage jobs to take over farms while their husbands worked off the farm. Historical accounts document well how women have taken over farming, including "men's" work and decision making, when men have been at war or earning cash (e.g., Jensen 1981). As pointed out earlier, it is when there is a scarcity of male labor that one will find women doing valued productive tasks in a society. Bokemeier and Coughenour (1980:5–6) argue that "The importance of farm women as a reserve labor supply has increased in importance as the costs of hired male farm labor increases. With the improvement in farm technology and mechanization, women with little training can participate in farm tasks."

In general, then, farm women's production (paid and otherwise) within the home has probably decreased over the last century. Haney (1983), though, suggests that in the face of more recent pressure on farm incomes, some farm women are increasing their production of food and clothing for home use and turning again to cottage industries for cash. Now that farm families have fewer children, the nature of child care may have changed. Further, domestic chores and other support services may have decreased in terms of scale of effort in any particular task. Women's involvement in the labor market off the farm has increased, although relative to men they may participate less in agricultural markets. With mechanization they do few of the tasks that have been taken over by machines. They may take less part in farm decision making in general as farming has become increasingly complex. Yet they seem to have taken on more of the bookkeeping; they may still be helping out at harvest time and with labor intensive tasks; and they may in some cases be doing more of the farm work (aided by machinery) as their husbands have increased their off-farm labor force participation. I have data from only one year, 1980, and so cannot analyze trends. I will, however, look at women's levels of various kinds of work in 1980 to see whether they are consistent with outcomes of such trends.

So far I have discussed trends in work within the home, in the off-farm labor market, and on the farm. What about unpaid work outside the home, such as participation in voluntary associations?

Several students of farm women's roles portray the women as sustaining networks that go beyond the farm family (Boulding 1980; Hoiberg and Huffman 1978; Kohl 1976; Burge and Cunningham 1983). By at least some accounts, women express neighborliness and service more now through voluntary organizations rather than through informal channels (MacNab–de Vries and de Vries 1982). Advances in transportation and communication have made it easier for family farm members to participate in these organizations. At the same time the increasing off-farm labor force participation of farm women may interfere with the extent to which they do unpaid community work. Volunteer organizations in general have expressed concern that women's increasing labor force participation will make it more difficult to find active members, although more people did volunteer work in the United States in 1974 than in 1965, and those who volunteered put in more hours (Mueller 1975:316).

Farm organizations, cooperatives, and producer associations have become increasingly important for farmers and agriculture over the recent past. When men established general farm organizations before the turn of the century, they often included women. The National Grange, organized in 1867, "realized the importance of the family unit" and had several women officers in its early years (Wiser 1976). Women were encouraged to join and participate in the Farmer's Alliance movement in the 1880s and 1890s. For example, women may have made up as much as a quarter of the North Carolina Alliance's membership in 1891. One woman in an 1891 speech put her feelings about the Alliance as follows: "Words would fail me to express to you . . . my appreciation of woman's opportunity of being co-workers with the brethren in the movement which is stirring this great nation" (cited in Jones 1982:3–4).

Both ideological recognition of women's importance on family farms and also the need for sheer numbers within these movements may have led to the acceptance of women members (Jensen 1981: 145). Other farm organizations at first welcomed women, but later reneged. For example, while women participated in the organization of the American Association of Farmers' Institute Workers, begun in 1895, men later voted that women had to have separate meetings (Wiser 1976). In the twentieth century, although some women were active in various farm organizations, women members were few and concern for women's needs low. Vanek (1980:428) found women were more involved in general community activities, and men in off-farm agricultural organizations.

In many general farm organizations, later twentieth-century women participate through auxiliaries rather than through the main organization (Flora 1981). One sees the same phenomenon in producer organizations: men are the producers; women help increase the demand for their product, educate the public about the farmers' problems, and lobby for favorable legislation through women's auxiliaries. Extension activities have reached out to women in this century, but have often been segregated so that women participate in homemaking activities and men in activities related to farm management (Sachs 1983). At the same time, the last decade or so has seen the rise of general farm women's movements, such as American Agri-Women. The women in these organizations engage in political action to help family farming as a whole while also being concerned with their rights as women in family businesses (Haney 1983).

As a result of improved transportation and communication one might expect to see farm women more involved in community and farm organizations now than in the last century or earlier in this century. The increasing off-farm labor force participation of farm women may have at least dampened the increase, though. Even in the new farm women's organizations one might expect to see an emphasis on women in their role as helpmates rather than producers. Again, while I cannot chart trends, I can see whether and in what ways women did unpaid work off the farm in 1980.

VARIATIONS IN FARM WOMEN'S WORK, 1980

An attempt to chart historical trends in farm women's work roles led to expectations about the kind of work they do today. Beginning with chapter 3, this book will test these expectations, documenting what it is that farm women in 1980 did on the farm, in the home, in the off-farm labor market, and in voluntary organizations and on governing and advisory boards. The book will also use the historical accounts and the general ideas about how to study women's work (the need to look at more than one kind of work, especially family responsibilities, as conditioning other kinds of activities; the importance of the relative availability of male labor and thus the need to look at the work of other household members) to develop hypotheses about how farm women's roles vary across types of operations in the last quarter of the twentieth century.

Farm Size. A number of farm characteristics at least partially measure the relative need for various types of the woman's labor. One would expect to find that what women do on and off their farms differs by the size of their operations at any particular time. The use of larger equipment on larger farms could imply that women are less likely to do field work on these farms. On the smaller farms it might be necessary to call on women's labors even in doing work with equipment and in other "male" tasks, so that not as much difference would appear there. In their study of women in 124 mid-Michigan nuclear family farm operator households, Fassinger and Schwarzweller (1982) found that on larger farms, as compared with hobby or small farms, women spent more hours on farm work. That seemed to be because there were more hours of farm work to do. In terms of the proportion of hours of farm work done by women, there was little variation across types of farms. However, the nature of women's work, if not the amount of it, did change as farm size got bigger. On the larger farms, Fassinger and Schwarzweller found women were less likely to combine, although not less likely to "cultivate fields." While they were more likely to "buy, get machine parts," they were less likely to "buy farm equipment." At the same time, women on larger farms seemed to specialize in what they did, and they did a smaller proportion of farm tasks. In particular, they seemed to specialize more in bookkeeping. This is consistent with what Wilkening (1981) found in his comparison of 1962 and 1978 data on Wisconsin farm women. Thus on smaller farms women seemed to be involved in a larger range of farm work. On larger farms women seemed to specialize more in traditional farm women's tasks. Even though women on smaller farms seem to be doing more varied farm work, one would expect it to be these women who go off the farm for employment (especially if their husbands do not) to bring in cash for the family and farm.

The type of housework and other home tasks women do and the degree to which housework is shared with a husband seem to be stable across farm types. This might have been expected given that housework is women's work, generally unaffected by what other household members are doing. Fassinger and Scharzweller (1982) did not find any great difference in the proportion of home tasks done by farm wives across farms of different sizes. Unpaid work in community and agricultural organizations, though, might vary by farm size, with women from larger farms doing more of this. For them, this might be an extension of specializing in more traditional women's work. They might have both time and money to do organizational work, thus substituting one type of work for another. Further, it might be the larger farms that benefit more from participation in agricultural organizations and thus the women (and men) from these operations who take part.

With respect to decision making, many researchers have found that the woman's role is smaller on larger farms. Some have found a curvilinear relationship, with less involvement on the part of the woman on the smallest farms as well. (Wilkening 1982; Wilkening 1958; Sawer 1973). The explanation for low involvement in the smallest farms is that decisions are relatively few and straightforward, so the man makes them as he goes along. On the largest farms, Joyce and Leadley (1977:12) quote Straus (1960) as suggesting that "technological complexity, perhaps beyond the wife's knowledge or skill, apparently attenuates the possibility for the wife to make a useful managerial contribution." Further, increasing size may make diffuse and shared decision making inefficient (Blau 1972). The man, identifying more as the producer, may then take over. Thinking of decision making as a valued kind of work, one would expect to find women taking part only when there is a relative need for them to do so.

Contract Farming. More farms are involved with contract farming and this has changed the decision making and technology of production (e.g., Sachs 1983). By taking decision making out of the family, it is possible that such arrangements will decrease the woman's part in farm management and marketing. At the same time, women may still do the work to fulfill the contract, although the nature of the work may have changed. Poultry raising, for example, traditionally the farm woman's work, is now largely done under contract. Women still play a role here and "it is often women who receive the shipments of young chicks from the poultry companies and are responsible for the care before they are once again picked up by the poultry companies for slaughter and sale" (Women and Food Information Network Newsletter 7, December/January 1983:2).

Type of Product. In examining what characteristics of farms affect what women do, one must remember that farms are productive units. What is produced on a given farm affects the intensity and timing of farm work and thus how women (and other family members) divide their time among home, farm, and off-farm work (Haney 1983). For example, dairy farming and other livestock operations, which demand constant labor, utilize the woman's work more intensely. Wilkening (1981:15), in his 1978 study of Wisconsin farm families, reports that "On hog and dairy farms, the wife and children are likely to be more involved in farm work than on other types of farms, particularly cash-grain farms." On dairy farms, too, both the husband and wife were less likely to work off the farm.

Family and Family Labor. Many farms are family businesses. Different family members can play different parts. This has implications for the ways in which one looks at the effects of household characteristics on the woman's work. As already mentioned, responsibility for child care can conflict with farm women's ability to do some sorts of farm work, although traditional women's labor intensive tasks may be those compatible with care for children. On farms, however, children are not always simply dependents. They are also a source of labor. The 1964 Census of Agriculture special report on farm labor shows "related household members" contributing slightly more labor than the wives of the male operator: 12 percent of all hours of farm labor versus 10 percent (U.S. Department of Commerce 1967). Hoiberg and Huffman's (1978) analysis showed that children over the age of 10 contributed, on average, 1,821 hours of work per year to the farm. (The average for the farm operator was 2,648.) One needs to think in terms of the labor structure of the farm rather than only in terms of dependents, then, in seeing what affects the woman's work distribution. Indeed, there is evidence that the extent of women's work on the farm does not vary greatly with the stage of the family life cycle (Wilkening 1981; Fassinger and Scharzweller 1982). This may be because progression over the family life cycle corresponds to progression over the farm life cycle. When children are small, the farm may also tend to be small and developing. As the children grow and contribute to the labor supply of the farm, the farm might also have grown and thus require the labor of both children and parents. As the children leave the farm, the operators may decrease the size of their operation as well (Salamon 1978). Thus the size of the farm may be a result of and response to the amount of family labor available to it.

The presence of adult sons, however, may affect the extent of a woman's participation on her operation. As Colman and Elbert (1983:13) found in their study of New York farm families: "A farm wife in the development of family and farm cycles may find her place taken by her son, first in terms of productive labor and then in terms of managerial and ownership power. She has a genuine stake in this intergenerational transfer and often has worked hard and 'managed' to this end, but the cost of her success is her own displacement."

The presence of a husband in the family and his occupation may be especially important for the nature of the woman's work. Sachs (1983) argues that when there is a husband farming, he will be the farmer and the manager, and the woman will be "agricultural helper." Elbert (1982) has even interpreted differences by farm size not as the result of arrangements mandated by technological complexity and efficiency concerns, but as the opportunity for a husband to control production. When the farm is prosperous enough the owner-operator may choose kinds of labor coordination and control that give him more autonomous authority and which exclude the wife. He may even hire labor to replace his wife, since he would have greater control as employer than as husband. Thus Elbert sees husband's control rather than technological complexity or specialization behind a decrease in wife's decision making (and farm labor) with increasing farm size.

In summary, then, I expect the types of work 1980 farm women do to vary by the nature of their families and farms. (1) Women on larger farms are expected to do a smaller range of farm work, to specialize more in tasks traditionally performed by farm women, to be less involved in farm decision making, to be less likely to have off-farm employment, but perhaps to take part in more unpaid organizational work. (2) It is not clear that contract farming affects the range of necessary farm tasks that a woman does, but it may reduce her part in decision making and marketing. (3) Women on livestock, as compared with crop, operations are expected to take part in more of the farm production activities (and perhaps because of this to take part in somewhat more decision making) and to be less likely to have off-farm employment. (4) In families with young children, women may be less likely to take on a wide range of on- and off-farm work. When children are working on the farm, it is not clear that they will be substituting for the woman's work, since this may be a labor intensive stage of the farm life cycle. Hired labor may substitute for the woman, though. Having a husband or son in farming is expected to lessen her involvement in the more "masculine" areas of farm work and decision making.

Individual Characteristics. The recent literature on women's labor force participation demonstrates that women's own characteristics affect their abilities to fill various work roles. For example, those with more education often have more and better employment opportunities. Education that is valuable for off-farm employment, however, may also be useful on the farm. Further, the research on voluntary organization participation has found that those with more education take part in more voluntary organizations. The farm may be a family enterprise, but how this enterprise is organized may affect how particular family members act within it. This point was made with respect to contracting. The woman's *own* relationship to the factors of production may be related to her farm involvement, too. In particular, one may expect women who have their names on rental agreements or deeds, that is, who own or control one of the most important farm inputs, to be those who take a greater part in marketing and in farm decision making.

In the rest of this book I will be looking not just at the kinds of work farm women do but also at variations in their roles by characteristics of their farms, their families, and themselves. It will thus be possible to say something about how different types of women and women on different types of farms and in different types of families vary in the nature of their on- and off-farm work.

Plan of the Book

This chapter contains the general framework and specific hypotheses with which to study farm women's work in 1980. In looking at work one first needs to keep in mind that work is more than paid employment. It can be done with or without pay, within or outside the home. A person's or group's involvement in one type of work can condition involvement in another form. For women, responsibility for unpaid home work, especially child care, can help explain their involvement in other types of work. One thus needs to look at various kinds of work simultaneously, and, especially for farm women, to include unpaid farm and family work for an understanding of other kinds of work.

At the same time, societies value some kinds of work more than others. Such work is often performed by men. In our society work for pay is valued more than unpaid work. On farms, work with large machinery (which costs more and is more productive than other sorts of work) may be more valued. Further, relationships with various kinds of markets are critical for farms' survival. It may be men who are more likely to take on these tasks.

Yet women do perform what are considered "men's" tasks. This is often when not enough men are available to do it. One needs to look at the work of other groups and other family members, therefore, to understand women's work. Because the family provides much of the labor for many farms, one needs to look at how and where other family members contribute labor, as well as at the nature of the farm, in order to understand the woman's contributions.

The rest of this book will examine in more detail the different domains of farm women's work. The next chapter describes the major source of information for this study: the 1980 Farm Women's Survey. Chapter 3 looks at women's work participation in the home and on the farm. It shows how farm, family, and the women's characteristics influence the extent of farm work that they do. Chapter 4 analyzes decision making for the home and farm, and the extent to which women participate in this and share it with their husbands (if they are married). The next topic, in chapter 5, is that of off-farm employment and the division of labor here; what is the nature of women's off-farm employment, what are the patterns of who in a couple goes off the farm to work for pay, and what affects which pattern is followed? The final work domain, covered in chapter 6, is that of voluntary organizations and political bodies—community and farm. Again, I look at the patterns of women's participation as well as at the sexual division of organizational membership. Chapter 7 turns to measures of farm women's attitudes about their work roles. The final chapter summarizes these analyses and draws out their implications. In each chapter I use the substantive literature relevant to the particular topic to expand upon the hypotheses developed in this chapter. While the different types of work are given their separate chapters, within the chapters I will explore the interconnections among participation in the different work domains.

2 The 1980 Farm Women's Survey

This book uses data from the 1980 Farm Women's Survey (FWS). For this survey, telephone interviews were completed with 2,509 women farm operators and wives of farm operators and with 569 male farm operators. These women and men represent people on agricultural operations all over the United States. This chapter first shows the need that existed for this survey and then describes the survey itself.

Background to the Farm Women's Survey

Even though recent years have seen an increasing number of studies that focus on farm women and their work, there is still much that is not known about these women. Most studies use information from relatively small numbers of women from a particular state or even one particular area of a state.[1] Part of the reason for this is that agricultural experiment stations have funded much of the research on farm women and are interested in finding out about people in their states. These studies document the extent and variety of farm women's work. Small but intensive studies provide us with rich and detailed pictures of farm women's lives. The larger ones provide more of a statistical portrait. At the same time, Fassinger and Schwarzweller's criticism holds (1982:5): "Numerous studies claim to represent the characteristic work roles of American farm women, but few provide a solid statistical framework upon which to stake such claims." Even when a study is a good representation of the farm women in a particular region, it is difficult to generalize its conclusions to farm women across the nation.

The usual large national samples social scientists use, such as the General Social Survey, are of little use in studying farm women. Because women in any farm occupation made up less than 2 percent of the population of employed women between 1970 and 1979 (Hayghe and Johnson 1980) and because the proportion of families on farms is small, the number of farm women who would fall into even a large national sample would be minuscule.

The federal government does collect information on all its citizens and residents during the decennial censuses. In between censuses, the Bureau of the Census gets a picture of what is happening through quarterly Current Population Surveys (CPS), surveys of very large samples of the population. The very ways in which the Bureau of the Census defines occupations and employment, however, make it difficult to find women involved in farming even in the very large census and CPS data sets. People are defined as employed if they had a job for pay during the survey week, operated their own business, or put in at least 15 hours as an unpaid family worker in a family operated business. The census week is in early spring, a slack time on many farms. The male may be counted as a farmer, operator, or manager, while the woman may not be counted at all if she worked less than 15 hours on the farm that week. When she is counted, she would often be listed as an "unpaid family worker" or classified by an off-farm occupation if she had one. The recent Current Population Reports on the farm population average responses across quarters but in 1980 still classified 54 percent of the female farm population fourteen years of age and over as "not in the labor force," in contrast with only 19 percent of the males. Only 5 percent of the employed men and almost 20 percent of the employed women were counted as "unpaid family workers" (Banks and DeArc 1981). Even aside from the definitional problem, the information such labels give about what people are actually doing is limited. (See also Scholl 1983, for a discussion of the occupational classification of farm women.)

Since 1840 the Bureau of the Census has carried out special censuses of agriculture. One might expect to get more information about what is happening in farm families from this source. The main thrust of this data collection activity, however, is to get information about U.S. *farms* rather than about U.S. farm people. Until the 1978 Census of Agriculture, the Bureau of the Census did not even ask the sex of the operator. Further, the forms provide for only one operator per farm. In the 1978 Census, "For farm operations where both husband and wife participated, the response [as to who was the operator] was determined by the parties involved" (U.S. Department of Commerce 1981: Census of Agriculture, vol. 1:A-7). In most families, the decision will be to list the man as operator. Some women have complained that this system of one operator per farm, which makes sense if one wants to know only about operations, prevents recognition of their participation. One recommendation from the 1982 Wingspread Seminar on Women's Roles on North American Farms was "that the U.S. Agricultural Census be altered to allow for the designation of multiple operators, or farm partners" (Women and Food Information Network Newsletter 7, December/January 1983:1).

Each year, the Census of Agriculture has special follow-up studies of specialized operations or of subsamples of the farm population. In 1964, as mentioned in chapter 1, a special survey on farm labor did collect information about who performed work on the farm, including unpaid family members other than the operator (U.S. Department of Commerce 1967). In many cases one would suspect that the husband was the one who reported the hours. Whether husbands recognize the extent of their wives' contributions to the farm has been questioned. A 1975 International Harvester poll investigated both husbands' and wives' views of the farm work wives did. It found that "38 percent of the women compared to only 15 percent of the men said the portion of the 'farmwife's' total work time on farm work . . . occupied at least half her time or more. On the other hand, 43 percent of the men said women spend *less* than 10 percent of their time on farm chores while 27 percent of the women said this was true" (cited in Joyce and Leadley 1977:50). Further, the 1964 survey explicitly excluded housework and did not ask about work for pay by the family members. The 1979 Farm Finance special survey did ask about the spouse's off-farm work in some detail, but not about work on the farm or in the home. Thus one can get only fragments of information about family—particularly women's—work roles even from the agricultural censuses.

A need to know more about farm women's work, especially in the face of complaints that women were neither recognized as contributing to agriculture nor given equal access to resources provided to farmers, led the U.S. Department of Agriculture (USDA) in 1979 to undertake steps to reduce the knowledge gap about women's part in U.S. agriculture. In that year the USDA allocated funds for a national survey of women on farms. To my knowledge this is the first national survey directed specifically at farm women and the work they do.

Under an ongoing cooperative agreement with USDA, the National Opinion Research Center (NORC) had done other surveys of the farm population (see for example, Jones et al. 1979; Jones 1980) and thus demonstrated its ability to conduct surveys of this population. In August 1979 NORC submitted a proposal for a cooperative research agreement with USDA to carry out the Farm Women's Survey; this agreement was accepted in October 1979.

Questionnaire Design

NORC designed the questionnaire that was administered to the farm women (and to a subsample of farm men, as described below) with the assistance and cooperation of USDA researchers. During the fall of 1979 the NORC staff for the Farm Women's Survey read letters that had come into USDA from farm women, reviewed the literature on farm women and the government descriptions of program participation, conducted a focus group interview with twelve central Illinois farm women, attended and talked with delegates at the National Young Farmers Educational Institute in Toledo, Ohio, and sent letters to a wide range of researchers, organizations, and policymakers soliciting suggestions and recommendations for the survey. The following spring, members of the NORC group met with USDA personnel and project consultants including several farm women who had been appointed special consultants by the Secretary of Agriculture. Finally, NORC pretested the completed questionnaire on a small number of respondents similar to the ones in the actual sample, using procedures identical to those planned for the full survey. Pretest results guided the final revisions of the questionnaire. Throughout the questionnaire design process NORC's aim was to develop an instrument that would reflect the concern and language of farm women of all types.

The questionnaire covered areas that would give an overall picture of farm women's farm work and management, membership in farm and community organizations, and off-farm employment. It included questions on their operations and families, as well as on their own social and economic characteristics in order to relate these to variation in the women's participation in various spheres.

As well, it devoted a considerable amount of space to questions about the farms' and the women's participation in and contact with various USDA programs, since allegations that USDA denied women access to its services had helped motivate its sponsorship of the survey.

The men were asked about a subset of items on the women's questionnaires. Their data allow comparisons by sex, which help establish women's *relative* levels of participation in various activities and programs. In general, items on the two questionnaires were worded identically. One noteworthy exception is that women were asked about their own involvement in a series of farm tasks and decisions, while men were asked for their perceptions of their wives' involvement. The appendix contains the women's questionnaire and indicates which and how questions were asked of the men.

The Sample

The intertwining of family, market, and farm work is a reason why the definition of "farm women" has been problematic. Who are "farm women"? Wives of farmers? Those running their own farms by themselves? Those doing "significant" amounts of work on their farms? Farm women are not a homogeneous group with respect to their work on the farm. In addition, there are women who do farm work but for whom family and farm do not overlap, that is, those who are working not on *their* family's farm but for someone else. Given the interest of USDA in the roles of women on their own operations and the difficulty of developing a sample of farm women more generally, USDA and NORC decided to use a sample of operations and to survey the women (and a subsample of men) associated with these operations.

A necessary condition for a sampling design that represents the population about which one wants to say something is some sort of exhaustive listing from which to take the sample: a sampling frame. Strictly speaking, one can generalize results from a sample only to the population the sampling frame includes. The sampling frame used for the 1980 FWS was one that the Economics and Statistics Service of USDA had constructed for a 1979 economic survey in the forty-eight contiguous states. It was an area frame based on land use stratification within each state, with the sampling unit being the parcel of land or land area. The 1979 sample consisted of all individuals who qualified as resident farm operators for selected land segments. A resident farm operator was defined as someone who:

(1) was the person responsible for the day-to-day management decisions for the farm or ranch (when there were partners who shared equally in the decision making, then the oldest partner was designated the operator);
(2) raised, produced, or sold at least $1,000 worth of agricultural products in 1978 or spent at least $1,000 on agricultural inputs; and
(3) had headquarters within the sample segment's boundaries (headquarters usually being the farm residence; the total farm did not have to be within the boundaries of the sampled land segment).

Because of budget considerations, the FWS was not able to survey the almost 7,000 operations included in the 1979 sample. Therefore, a random subsample was taken so that about 4,000 farms were included in the FWS sample. These 4,060 farms were selected to provide approximately the same number of anticipated completed interviews in each of four regions, because USDA was interested in regional comparisons. (See Table 2.1 for the list of states in each region.)[2]

The women respondents sampled from this sampling frame were: (1) the 1978 operator, if a woman; or (2) the wife (even if divorced or widowed) of the 1978 male operator. This is not, therefore, a sample of all women who do farm labor (which would include female hired hands and migrant workers) but of women associated with a sample of farms. Most of these were family-run enterprises. However, given the definition of resident farm operators, some of the women could have been farm managers or wives of men managing farms for corporations or other owners.

A 25 percent subsample of the eligible male operators was contacted as well. Interviewing men allows within-household comparisons as well as general comparisons by sex, since most of the men interviewed were husbands of the women respondents.

All designated respondents were screened on whether they were still farming on a commercial basis at the time of the survey. Only those who responded that they (and/or their spouses) were still farming were included. Those who had left agriculture were excluded. Given the nature of the sampling frame, those who entered

Table 2.1. *Regional Definitions for the 1980 Farm Women's Survey*

Region	State
Northeast	Maine, Vermont, New Hampshire, Massachusetts, Connecticut, Rhode Island, New York, New Jersey, Pennsylvania, Ohio, Michigan, Indiana
Northcentral	North Dakota, South Dakota, Nebraska, Kansas, Missouri, Iowa, Minnesota, Wisconsin, Illinois
South	Florida, Mississippi, Alabama, Georgia, South Carolina, North Carolina, Tennessee, Arkansas, Louisiana, Oklahoma, Texas, Kentucky, Virginia, West Virginia, Maryland, Delaware
West	Washington, Oregon, California, Nevada, Idaho, Montana, Wyoming, Colorado, Utah, Arizona, New Mexico

agriculture between 1978 and 1980 were not contacted. Thus generalizations from this sample are limited to the population farming in 1978 and still in business in 1980. While this definition applies to the overwhelming majority of operations in 1980, this population is likely to be older, more stable, and more successful than the total population of agricultural enterprises as of 1980.

Data Collection

Trained and supervised interviewers conducted the survey by telephone from NORC's central office on the University of Chicago campus. About two weeks before the beginning of the field period, all designated respondents were sent an advance letter explaining the purpose of the survey and alerting them to the coming call. In 290 cases the sampling materials supplied to NORC by USDA did not include the telephone number for the operation. Preliminary efforts by NORC interviewers reduced this to about 130 cases. The advance letter to these households included a request that the respondent call a special NORC number collect in order to participate in the interview. By the end of the field period, there were only 75 households that had never been contacted because of a lack of phone numbers.

The field period began on 14 June 1980 and ended on 29 August, just before the Labor Day holiday weekend. Interviews, which

Table 2.2. *Final Status of Cases: 1980 Farm Women's Survey*

	Women	Men
Completed Cases		
Completed without difficulty	2,209	541
Completed after initial refusal	300	28
Total	2,509	569
Not Completed		
Refusal/breakoff	391	118
Other not completed[a]	136	81
Response Rate (Percent)[b]	83	74
Not Eligible		
Deceased/did not exist	326	50
No longer farming	698	182

[a] Includes designated respondents who could not be located, who could not be contacted during the 11-week field period, whose age or health prevented participation, or whose primary language was other than English.

[b] Ineligible cases were excluded from the denominator in calculating response rates.

lasted on average 30 minutes each, were completed with a total of 2,509 farm women and 569 men. In 497 cases both husbands and wives in the same household were interviewed. The response rate was 83 percent for women and 74 percent for men, response rates that are very good in comparison with other phone surveys of farm people (see Jones et al. 1979; Jones 1980). A detailed breakdown of the final disposition for all cases is presented in Table 2.2. (See Jones and Rosenfeld 1981, for further details of the data collection.)

Respondent confidentiality is important in any survey, and particularly so in cases of samples drawn from limited geographical areas. Protection of confidentiality received special attention in all written and training materials developed for this survey. In addition, identifying information for all respondents was kept only on questionnaire face sheets, which were separated from the interview protocols, stored under lock and key in NORC's offices during the period of data preparation, and finally destroyed. Party lines in rural communities with limited telephone service can also threaten confidentiality. Calls for a given phone number may ring on several other lines, raising the possibility of eavesdropping. Anticipating this difficulty, any respondent concerned about privacy was asked to call NORC collect at a time of his or her choosing in order to complete the interview.

Weights

The sample design, a stratified multistage area probability sample with disproportionate selection probabilities, is complex and not self-weighting. USDA supplied case weights (expansion factors) for each farm to NORC with the original sample. The expansion factors were rescaled (on a state-by-state basis) to fractional weights with an average of unity, producing a weighted data base with the number of cases identical to the actual number of completed interviews. Rescaling was done separately for men and women respondents, and also for the data set containing husband-wife pairs (the household file). There is almost no difference in the distributions and associations from weighted and unweighted data. Distributions, cross tabulations, means, and other simple statistics presented in this book are weighted, while multivariate regressions and logits are not.

The lack of information from 19 percent of the sample is a potential source of bias. The question thus arose of whether it would be worth further adjusting the weights for nonresponse. The decision was that such adjustments would not be worth the time and cost involved. In general, nonresponse bias is quite small unless the actual differences in characteristics and opinions between respondents and nonrespondents is very large. Previous analysis of data from farm operators suggested that the extent of difference between respondents and nonrespondents is related to the reason for nonresponse: those who are difficult to contact and interview tend to be similar to respondents who are willing participants, while only those who are reluctant to participate exhibit substantial differences (see Jones et al. 1979). The relatively low refusal rate in FWS suggests that nonresponse bias is not a serious threat to the validity of the data.

Characterizing the Farms, Farm Women, and Families

The review in chapter 1 suggested a number of aspects of the farm, the farm family, and the woman herself that might be associated with how she distributes her work. In this section I will explain how I will measure such characteristics in the rest of this book. The means and standard deviations of these measures are shown in Table 2.3.

FARM CHARACTERISTICS

Size. Changes in the scale of farms suggest that measures of size be included in an analysis of farm women's work. Farm size is often measured in terms of farm sales. Unfortunately, the FWS does not have information on sales. Here I will use literal size, the *acres farmed,* to measure the size of the operation. Other possible measures of size, such as the total value of the farm assets, correlate highly with the number of acres. Further, more women refused or said they were unable to answer other questions about farm scale than gave such responses to the question about acres farmed. To allow for nonlinearities in effects of size, that is, to allow us to see whether there are some farm scales that are particularly likely to affect a woman's work, I divide farms into four categories comparable to other categorizations of farms by size (see U.S. Department of Commerce 1981a; Ross 1982). These categories are: small (less than 50 acres); medium (50–299 acres); large (300–999 acres); and very large (1,000 acres or more). Using this classification, over half of the women in the FWS were connected with small or medium size farms.

Commodities Produced. I characterize the farm as well by a rough measure of what is produced for sale. The categories are more than 95 percent of *gross sales from crops,* less than 5 percent of sales from crops, and mixed sales (between 5 and 95 percent of sales from crops). Those with a greater proportion of sales from crops may be those where labor demands are more seasonal. The FWS did ask women about the particular crops and livestock their farms raised. Ross (1982) used this information to create commodity categories for the operations. While I did not do this, I will refer to Ross's results.

Table 2.3. *Farm, Family, and Farm Women's Characteristics: Means and Standard Deviations*

	Mean	S.D.	N[a]
Farm Characteristics			
Total acres in farm:[b]			2,442
Less than 50	.22	.42	
50 - 299	.39	.49	
300 - 999	.25	.43	
At least 1000	.14	.35	
Gross sales of farm products:			2,253
Less than 5% total sales from crops	.37	.48	
5% - 95% total sales from crops	.33	.47	
More than 95% total sales from crops	.30	.46	
Tenancy:			2,476
Full owners	.57	.50	
Part owners	.32	.46	
Renters	.08	.27	
Neither owners nor renters	.04	.20	
Woman's Legal Relation to Farm			
Own name on deed or rental contract for land	.80	.40	2,509
Decision Makers			
Other than husband and wife	.26	.44	2,504
Region			
Northeast	.26	.44	2,509
Northcentral	.27	.45	
West	.25	.43	
South	.22	.41	
Labor Structure of Farm			
More than 1 hired hand	.30	.46	2,479
No husband	.04	.20	2,509
Husband's work:			
Husband regularly does farm work, has no off-farm job	.49	.50	2,121
Husband regularly does farm work, has off-farm job	.38	.48	
Husband does not regularly do farm work, has off-farm job	.05	.23	
Husband does not regularly do farm work, has no off-farm job	.03	.12	

Table 2.3. *continued*

	Mean	S.D.	Na
Labor Structure of Farm (cont'd)			
Number of sons at least 18 who regularly do farm work	.17	.45	2,509
Number of children ages 6 - 17 who regularly do farm work	.48	.98	2,509
Number of other household members who regularly do farm work	.09	.35	2,509
Number of other, nonhousehold members who regularly do farm work	.55	1.51	2,499
Farm Women's Characteristics			
Education:			2,499
Less than high school	.18	.38	
High school degree	.47	.50	
Vocational school beyond high school or some college	.23	.42	
College degree or above	.12	.33	
Percent of life spent on farm:	62.67	30.42	2,480
Age:			2,497
Less than 31	.10	.30	
31 - 45	.35	.48	
46 - 65	.48	.50	
Over 65	.07	.26	
Dependent Children			
Number of children less than age 6	.23	.58	2,509
Number of children ages 6 - 17 who do not regularly do farm work	.39	.78	2,509

[a]N is less than 2,509 because of missing data.

[b]Means for categorical variables are the proportion in that category.

Control. Family control over the land farmed is measured by whether the woman and/or a husband are *full owners* of their land, *part owners, renters,* or *something else.* Almost 90 percent of the women (and/or their husbands) owned at least some of the land that they farmed. The FWS did not give a clear indication of which operations were simply managed by the woman or her family. It may be that those on farms where land is rented or neither owned nor rented included the farm managers as well as tenant farmers. At the same time at least some of those in these categories might have been farming with or for other relatives. Whether the *woman* herself had *legal control of the farm land* is measured by whether her name was on the deed or rental agreement. In about 80 percent of the cases, it was.

The issue of control also comes up with respect to contract farming. In these cases, while the farm provides at least some capital, other agents participate in the decision making. Again, the FWS did not have a measure of whether the operation had production or marketing contracts. It did, however, ask whether there was anyone other than the woman and her husband who took part in farm and family decision making (question 15). A measure of whether there was *another decision maker* is included in the analyses. About a quarter of the women said that someone else had helped make decisions. In most cases (82 percent of those who said that there was another decision maker) this person was a male relative. Sixteen percent said that a female relative helped make decisions. Only 11 percent said that a male nonrelative and 1 percent said a female nonrelative was one of those involved in the decision making. (These percentages add up to more than 100 percent since people could describe more than one type of outside decision maker.) Thus the response to this question may indicate something about the control the family has over the operation, but in a broader way. Those who rent from mothers or mothers-in-law, for example, may share some decision making with them. It is still likely that the woman's role is affected when someone outside the couple helps make decisions.

Region. The *region* in which the woman lived is also included in the analyses. The categories are those described earlier in this chapter. To some extent region may represent additional farm characteristics, not explicitly included here, such as average rainfall. It could also represent a difference in attitudes toward suitable work for women, as well as variation in off-farm opportunities for women and men.

Labor Structure of the Farm. Another trend is toward a larger proportion of labor on U.S. operations coming from nonfamily members. Family farms have been characterized as those using *no more than one hired hand* (e.g., Ross 1982). This measure is included here. As can be seen in Table 2.3, 70 percent of the women's operations would meet this definition of a family farm. (In fact, 56 percent of the women said that no hired labor was employed, even part-time or seasonally, on their farm.) The use of hired labor may have implications for what women do, as discussed earlier.

Other family members can provide labor as well and either substitute for or complement a woman's farm labor. As Sachs has pointed out, a crucial determinant of what work a woman does is the *presence of a husband farming*. At the same time, the literature suggests that when the husband is employed off the farm, his wife fills in for him. Among the variables measuring the farm labor structure, I include a set of categories indicating the presence of a husband and (if there was a husband) whether he participated in farm and/or off-farm work. The information to construct these categories comes from the questions on marital status (question 2), husband's off-farm income in 1979 (question 50), and household members and their involvement in the day-to-day work of the operation (questions 37 and 38). A woman who said that she was not currently married was categorized as not having a husband. For other women, those who said that a husband was one of those in the household who participated in the regular farm work were categorized as having a husband who did farm work, while those who reported that their husband had a nonzero off-farm income for 1979 were measured as having a husband who did some off-farm work. Very few of the women in the FWS were not currently married—only 4 percent. Of those who were married, most had husbands who regularly did work on the farm, either in place of or in addition to off-farm work.

The questions about household structure were used as well to construct measures of other aspects of the farm labor supply and family composition. It has been suggested that when there is an older son, he and the father work as a team, even if formerly the husband and wife worked as farm partners. An indicator of the *number of sons at least eighteen years of age* in the household *who regularly work on the farm* is thus one of the labor structure variables. Other, younger children may also be supplying farm labor. The *number of children ages six through seventeen who were involved in the day-to-day work of the operation* is measured, rather than simply the number of children those ages. A separate count of *children six through seventeen who did not help with the daily farm work* is included as one indicator of the number of dependent children. A residual category is the *number of other household members*, aside from a husband, older sons, or children under eighteen, *who did farm work*. This can include other relatives living in the household (as well as older daughters) who contribute farm labor.

To round out the measures of the farm labor structure, I use the data from question 40: *how many people living outside the household* (and not hired hands) *took part in the day-to-day work of the operation*. These people could be other relatives living nearby or neighbors who regularly helped out. On 27 percent of the operations, there was at least one such person.

THE FARM WOMAN'S CHARACTERISTICS

The woman's experience and education might also affect the types of work she does. Her *formal education* is measured by the level of schooling she finished: less than high school, high school, postsecondary vocational school or some college, a bachelor's degree or beyond. Most of these women had at least a high school degree. Twelve percent had at least a bachelor's degree. The woman's *experience with farm life* is measured by the percent of her life she lived and (or) worked on farms and ranches. On average, these women had spent two-thirds of their lives in some connection with farms and ranches. *Age,* as an indicator of physical strength as well as cohort differences in attitudes, is measured by a series of categories: under thirty-one years of age, thirty-one to forty-five years of age, forty-six to sixty-five years of age, and over sixty-five. Again, a series of categories is used rather than simply age in years to capture any discontinuities in the relationship between age and various kinds of work. The bulk of the women in the FWS were between the ages of thirty-one and sixty-five. Younger people may not be able to set up their own operations, while women over sixty-five may retire with their husbands or, as widows, leave the farm.[3]

CHILDREN

Child care responsibilities are operationalized by the *number of children under the age of six,* as well as by the count of children ages six to seventeen who were not regularly doing farm work. In part because of their age distribution, 84 percent of the women did not have very young children in the home. In about 80 percent of the families, there were no children between six and seventeen who were not involved in farm work. Thus many of these women were beyond the life cycle stage of heavy child care responsibilities.

Table 2.4. *Ethnicity of FWS Women*

Ethnicity	N	Percent
American Indian or Alaskan Native	30	1.2
Asian or Pacific Islander	6	0.2
Black	27	1.1
Hispanic	35	1.4
White non-Hispanic	2,392	95.3
No response	19	0.8
Total	2,509	100.0

Ethnicity: A Neglected Dimension

The proportion of minority group members in the Farm Women's Survey corresponds closely to that for the farm population as a whole. Overall, 4 percent of the women reported belonging to a minority group (see Table 2.4). The 1980 Current Population Survey estimates the distribution for the farm population as 94.4 percent white, 4 percent black, and 1.9 percent Spanish origin (Banks and DeArc 1981:2). The proportion of whites in the farm population is considerably higher than that in the nonfarm population, which was estimated to be 86 percent white.

The blacks on farms—and black farm women—are worthy of study in their own right. The black farm population has declined at a rate much faster than that of the white farm populations. In 1920 nearly one-half of the black population lived on farms as compared with one-quarter of the white population. In 1980, 1 percent of blacks and 3 percent of whites lived on farms (Banks and DeArc 1981:2). An examination of black farm women would provide an opportunity to look at the intersections of race and sex among those remaining in agriculture.[4]

Looking at farm women in other groups, such as Asians and Native Americans, would offer similar opportunities. One would expect the particular content of the women's experiences to vary across minority groups. Unfortunately, there are too few minority group members to present race and ethnic comparisons.[5]

Conclusion

The 1980 Farm Women's Survey gives us information on women (and men) associated with a national sample of farm operations in existence from at least 1978 to 1980. Given the way in which the data were collected, it is possible to generalize the results with some confidence to all such U.S. agricultural operations, and probably to U.S. farms in general. The FWS provides the major source of data for the analyses to follow. At the same time, I will be referring to research from less representative samples, as well as drawing on various meetings I have had with farm women during the course of working on the FWS and this book. The two kinds of data—from large samples designed to be representative and from more intimate contact with people—are both needed to portray the situation of farm women today.

3
Farm and Home Work

The farm is both home and place of business for many farm families. On the farm, the woman may be doing housework and child care as well as farm tasks. One finding that comes up again and again among studies of farm women is that they work long hours as a result of doing the combination of home and farm tasks. A 1924 book on "Rural Social Problems" "cites the long work day as a major problem for farm women" (Moser and Johnson 173:25). Boulding (1980:267), using a time budget from the May 1975 *Farm Wife News*, calculated that farm women put in a 41 hour week on farm tasks and a 58 hour week on domestic tasks, for a 99 hour work week.

At the same time, there is considerable variation among women in how much work they do on their farms. Wilkening (1981), in his 1978–1979 study of Wisconsin farm families, found that on 14 percent of the farms surveyed the wife or female head had contributed farm work equal to that of a full-time person, while on 10 percent of the farms the wife or female head made no direct work contribution. There is also variation in the types of farm tasks women do. The majority of farm women do such tasks as running errands, while they are less likely to do some other types of farm work, such as plowing. Based on her field work in Colorado, Pearson (1979) suggested that farm women play roles ranging from that of independent agricultural producer to agricultural partner to farm helper to farm homemaker. Lodwick and Fassinger (1979) expanded on this typology, drawing on their study of family farms in two Michigan townships, to include those women who were "agriculturally active" and who played the part of "peripheral helpers." "Agriculturally active" women were not farm partners in the sense of directly managing the farm with a husband, but did farm labor on a more regular basis than farm helpers. "Peripheral helpers" generally only planted a garden and did not even perform the support services of farm homemakers. In studying the work of women on their farms and in their homes, it is important therefore to examine both what it is they do and also the variations among them.

The discussion in chapters 1 and 2 set up expectations for what the 1980 FWS would show about farm women's work in the home and on the farm. Reasoning from the idea that men tend to do the more critical and more literally productive work, it suggested that women would in general be more likely to do labor intensive rather than mechanized work and that they would be relatively less likely to do work that involved contact with agricultural markets. At the same time, because women often help out as needed, they were expected to show a relatively high level of helping with seasonal work, such as harvesting. For the same reason they might perform "helpmate" tasks, such as running errands, more than other sorts of tasks. But they were predicted to do even "male" work when circumstances demanded their labor. Farm size was put forth as one measure of labor need, with women on the larger farms less involved in production and relatively unlikely to deal with farm-related markets. Type of product could also indicate labor needs, with perhaps more labor (including the woman's) needed when animals are being raised. By the same principle, women on operations where there are more people (especially husbands and adult sons) who also perform farm work might be those who do fewer farm tasks, especially field tasks. Because having other people making decisions for the farm or controlling the land would not necessarily affect the amount of labor needed to farm, it was unclear that less family control would mean the woman would do less work, although she again might have less to do with credit, input, and output markets.

It was emphasized that, in studying any particular kind of work, one must take into consideration what other sorts of work a person or group does. It was predicted that farm women's off-farm employment would affect what they did on the farm, because time is a limited resource. Lodwick and Fassinger (1979), for example, found almost all the peripheral helpers were employed off the farm. Family responsibilities are especially important to take into account in examining women's work. One would expect to see most farm women do something in the home for their families. Further, having young children and dependent children might be associated with less participation in farm tasks if such tasks could not be easily combined with child care.

In addition to farm and family structure and work in other domains, variations among the women themselves were expected to affect what they do on (as well as off) the farm. The general literature on women's labor force participation finds more educated women, women with more employment experience, and younger women more likely to have jobs outside the home, in part because better jobs are open to them. One might find younger farm women and those with more experience in farming are also more likely to do more farm tasks. Those with more experience would perhaps be those with both more skill at farm tasks and a greater preference for doing such work. Younger women could be physically more able to do farm work or psychologically more accepting of such work and thus more involved in doing it. The effects of education are somewhat problematic. Women with more education would be more likely to have an off-farm job. This effect will be examined directly in chapter 5. Thus those with more education might have less time for farm work and be less involved in the work of their operation. On the other hand, education could also raise the woman's productivity on the farm (Hathaway and Perkins 1968). A woman who had some accounting courses might be able to get an accounting job off the farm, but she might also be more efficient in keeping the farm books and decide to do that either in addition to or in place of other sorts of work. Or a woman with nursing training might be able to do veterinary work on the operation (Gladwin and Downie 1982). Therefore one can still hypothesize that education would increase the involvement of women in farm work, even net of their off-farm work.

This chapter will use responses from the 1980 FWS to look at the nature of, variation in, and explanations for the types of work women did in their homes and on their operations. In the first section it will examine the range of the women's performance of farm and home tasks and the variability in such performance. It will then check how closely husbands' reports of what their wives did on the farm match their wives' reports, to look for any bias in previous studies that have relied on husbands' responses about the labor input of other family members. Finally, it will see how the variation in women's participation in farm tasks overall and in particular farm tasks can be explained by farm, family, and the woman's characteristics.

Farm and Home Tasks: Patterns and Variability

The Farm Women's Survey asked the women about their involvement in a set of tasks done on the farm and in the home—whether each type of task was a regular duty for them, something they did occasionally, or something they never did. These home and farm tasks are shown in Table 3.1. The responses give measures of the extent of women's participation in these tasks, though not of the hours they devote to them. Also, because men were not asked whether they did these tasks, it is not possible to talk about the sexual division of labor with respect to them.

The women's measured farm task involvement will depend on the exact tasks listed and whether the tasks are even relevant to the operation. For example, a woman who participated in the many tasks necessary for a fruit crop might appear to have low participation if none of those tasks were on the questionnaire. In designing the list of tasks we tried to make it as representative and inclusive as possible (drawing on a number of other studies as well as our conversations with farm women and consultants), while still keeping the list to a manageable length. The percentages for each item in Table 3.1 apply only to operations where the specific task was done. For example, the 562 cases whose farms had no animals (as well as the three cases with no response) were excluded from the percentages for item E in the table.

FARM TASKS

Twelve of the fifteen items specified are farm-related tasks. Items J, N, and O may be done on the farm but are assumed to have little to do with production, marketing, or management of the operation.[1] On average, women reported doing between five and six of the twelve tasks at least occasionally. Of course not all of the tasks were done on every farm. A simple index of the range of a respondent's labor contribution was constructed by first summing the number of farm tasks each woman reported doing (regularly or occasionally) and dividing by the number of tasks performed by someone on her operation (that is, excluding those reported "not done" or for which there was no response). A second, more stringent index was computed by summing only tasks reported as done regularly and dividing by total tasks performed on that farm. On average, women said that of all listed tasks done on their farms

Table 3.1. *Farm Women's Involvement in Farm and Home Tasks*

	Percent Doing Task				
	As Regular Duty	Occasion-ally	Never	Total[b]	N[c]
A. Plowing, disking, cultivating or planting	11	26	63	100	2,257
B. Applying fertilizers, herbicides, or insecticides	5	12	83	100	2,377
C. Doing other field work without machinery	17	25	58	100	2,281
D. Harvesting crops or other products, including running machinery or trucks	22	29	49	100	2,351
E. Taking care of farm animals, including herding or milking dairy cattle	37	29	34	100	1,944
F. Running farm errands, such as picking up repair parts or supplies	47	38	15	100	2,483
G. Making major purchases of farm or ranch supplies and equipment	14	23	63	100	2,455
H. Marketing products--that is, dealing with wholesale buyers or selling directly to consumers	15	17	67	99	2,380
I. Bookkeeping, maintaining records, paying bills, or preparing tax forms for the operation	61	17	22	100	2,489
J. Doing household tasks like preparing meals, house-cleaninga	97	2	1	100	2,499
K. Supervising the farm work of other family members	24	26	51	101	2,060

Table 3.1. *continued*

	Percent Doing Task				
	As Regular Duty	Occasionally	Never	Total[b]	N[c]
L. Supervising the work of hired farm labor	11	25	64	100	1,644
M. Taking care of a vegetable garden or animals for family consumption	74	14	12	100	2,350
N. Looking after children[a]	74	13	13	100	1,846
O. Working on a family or in-home business other than farm or ranch work[a]	33	13	53	99	1,139

[a]Items excluded from indices of farm tasks.

[b]Totals differ from 100 due to rounding.

[c]Total excludes those who say task was "not done" on their operations, who did not respond, or who said "don't know."

they did about 30 percent regularly and about half (53 percent) at least occasionally.

Individuals varied considerably around this mean. However, cases of extreme involvement or complete noninvolvement were few. Most women claimed to be involved at least occasionally with moderate proportions of their farm's work: Half of the women said they did 21 to 80 percent of the types of tasks regularly. Thirteen percent indicated relatively low levels of even occasional contribution (less than 21 percent), while a substantial 17 percent reported performing at least occasionally more than 80 percent of the types of tasks done on their operations.[2]

The proportion of women doing a specific task depended on the nature of the task. Most frequently, women reported regularly taking care of a vegetable garden or animals for the family's food, doing the bookkeeping, and running farm errands.[3] Even though Bush argued it is now cheaper to buy food than to produce it at home, most farms in the FWS raised some of their own food; on these farms women seemed to be continuing unpaid home production. Educational differences between farm women and men could be behind the high proportion of women doing the bookkeeping, as suggested before. Thirty-eight percent of the men had a high school diploma, in contrast with 45 percent of the women, and 33 percent of the men had postsecondary education, in contrast with 35 percent of the women. The prevalence of errand running among farm women was predicted to be part of women's helping out.

Taking care of farm animals (which can include milking) and helping with harvesting were tasks done at least occasionally by over half of the women on farms where these tasks were done. As mentioned before, it is with respect to these tasks that "extra" labor might be needed.

There is some support here for the idea that women are more likely to do labor intensive rather than capital intensive field work. While 17 percent regularly did some field work without machinery (when such work needed to be done on their operation), 11 percent plowed, disked, cultivated, or planted as a regular duty, and only 5 percent regularly applied fertilizers, herbicides, or insecticides, which is often done with machinery. At the same time, one needs to keep in mind that on farms where field work was done, a large proportion of the women reported doing it at least occasionally. However, 83 percent said they never applied fertilizers, herbicides, or insecticides. In a meeting of a group of central Illinois farm women, the women picked out these tasks as particularly dangerous ones that their husbands preferred to do themselves rather than risk the health of other family members.

Women were also more likely to supervise family than hired labor—half of the women on operations where family members worked said they at least occasionally supervised them, in contrast with 36 percent who even occasionally supervised hired labor. As chapter 1 suggested, the husband probably acts as boss when workers are hired rather than members of the family.

Women were predicted to have low contact with agricultural markets. Again, there is some support for that idea here. Only 14 percent of the women said that they regularly made major purchases for the operation, and only 15 percent said they regularly marketed their product. This is in contrast with the proportion regularly running errands, which often includes purchasing parts or supplies needed for some immediate task.

BUSINESS CONTACTS AND INFORMATION GATHERING FROM USDA

As chapter 1 emphasized, farms today are not isolated from the larger economy. Another sort of farm task not listed in Table 3.1 but very important on contemporary farms is that of getting information, cash, credit, and services from outside agencies and institutions. Getting cash by off-farm employment, which in at least some cases is part of keeping the operation going, is the topic of chapter 5. Here, FWS questions asked of both women and men permit examination of sex differences and the sexual division of labor in getting information and having business dealings with several USDA agencies. Respondents were asked whether in the last two or three years they themselves had had any business contacts with personnel of the Agricultural Stabilization and Conservation Service (ASCS), the Soil Conservation Service (SCS), the Farmers' Home Administration (FmHA), and the Cooperative Extension Service (Extension). They were also asked if in the last two or three years they had discussed specific problems of their operation with Extension agents or staff members or gotten information from Extension personnel about USDA programs other than Extension.[4] Because these questions are about activities any time in the last few years and because they do not allow discrimination of operations where no one did these activities, information gathering and business dealings were not part of the indices of range of farm women's tasks but receive separate analysis here and in the next chapter.

While the FWS does not have data on information gathering and farm business contacts more generally, links with USDA are certainly among the potentially most important for farms today. As Jones (Jones and Rosenfeld 1981:80–81) puts it: "In an increasingly complex, rapidly changing agricultural economy, farm operators must devote ever more time and energy to coping with the market environment and the web of government. With its multibillion dollar budget and an immense variety of economic, technical, and educational programs, no single environmental factor is of greater *potential* importance to farm families than USDA. Whether through information distribution or through direct intervention in commodity and credit markets, the impact of the Agency is so great that producers can no longer afford to tolerate restrictions in any form on access to federal benefits or services."

Critical contacts with a department such as the USDA are likely

Table 3.2. *Business Contacts with and Information Gathering from USDA Personnel by Sex*

	Women	Men
Percent who, in last 2 - 3 years:		
Had business contacts with ASCS, SCS, FmHA, or Extension personnel	44	72*
Discussed specific farm problems with or got information about other USDA programs from Extension personnel	23	40*
(N)	(2,509)	(569)

*χ^2 test of independence significant at <.01.

to be ones in which men predominate. People expect that such business will be between men. Further, if the man is listed as owner or operator of a farm or ranch, then for legal reasons he may need to sign the forms. Such contacts then may perpetuate the ability of the man to get information, services, and credit. On the other hand, getting information and dealing with agency officials could be part of the errand running that farm women do. One complaint that came up in discussions with central Illinois farm women was that they had to carry back and forth forms for their husbands to sign. They made the contacts, but were not able to enter formally into contracts. Thus, women might take part in these activities, but not in such a way that they are likely to be integrated into information networks or be eligible for future credit or services.

In Table 3.2 one finds that a sizable proportion of women had business contacts with USDA personnel from at least one of the four agencies about which questions were asked. Further, almost a quarter had gotten advice or information from Extension agents or staff. But the proportions of men with such activities are even higher.[5]

Table 3.3 uses the information on the 497 households in which both the husband and the wife were FWS respondents to look at the family's sexual division of labor for these activities. In approximately a quarter of the FWS households neither the husband nor the wife had had any business contacts with agency personnel in the preceding two to three years, and in just over half of the households neither spouse had gotten information or advice from Extension personnel. When the couple had had business dealings with

Table 3.3. *Husbands' and Wives' Information Gathering and Business Contacts with USDA (percentages)*

	In last 2 - 3 years had business contacts with ASCS, SCS, FmHA, or Extension personnel	Discussed specific farm problems with or got information about other USDA programs from Extension personnel
Neither husband nor wife	22	51
Husband only	35	26
Wife only	6	9
Both husband and wife	37	14
Total	100	100
(N)	(497)	(497)

the programs or gotten advice and information from Extension agents, it was rarely the wife on her own who did so. While in some families both husbands and wives had some sort of interaction with agency staff, in at least as many families the husband alone had these links.

In terms of actual participation in application to ASCS, SCS, and FmHA programs, women were underrepresented relative to men. Approximately 20 percent of the operations had applied for the ASCS Commodity Loan program and for the SCS Conservation Operations, and just under 15 percent had applied for some FmHA loan. Of the men who reported that their farms had applied for the respective programs, only 9 percent said that they were not named on the ASCS application, and 5 and 3 percent said that they were not named on the SCS and FmHA application forms. But among women who said that their operation had applied, 63 percent said that they were not on the application for the ASCS price support program, 55 percent for the SCS program, and 28 percent for the FmHA loan. Differences among programs in whether women were formal applicants may have to do with the nature of the programs and their legal and other requirements. The Commodity Loan program required that applicants be listed as owners, operators, or producers for their enterprise. Among those who said their farms were on file at the ASCS office almost all of the men said they were

Table 3.4. *Having Own Name on Application Form for USDA Program by Business Contact with Personnel (percentages)*

	ASCS		SCS		FmHA	
	Women	Men	Women	Men	Women	Men
Name on application form, no business contact with agency personnel	19	10	19	8	31	14
Name on application form, some business contact with agency personnel	19	83	27	88	42	84
Business contact with agency personnel, name not on application form	14	3	11	1	4	2
Name not on application form and no business contact	47	4	43	3	23	0
Total[a]	99	100	100	100	100	100
(N)[b]	(492)	(120)	(436)	(124)	(331)	(71)

[a]Totals differ from 100 due to rounding.

[b]Based only on those in the total sample who reported their operation had applied for a given program and who knew whether their name was on the application.

so listed, in contrast with only 45 percent of the women. SCS programs involved no such formal requirement but, perhaps because of their technical nature, involved family members who were more likely to manage production. FmHA loans, on the other hand, often require collateral such as land. Eighty-eight percent of the women who reported that their farms owned some of their land had their own names on the deed or title and so might have had to cosign FmHA loan papers when land was used as collateral.

The discrepancy between men's and women's formal part in the application procedure for production related programs fits with the picture of women running errands for such applications but being excluded from formal participation. Table 3.4, however, suggests that women did not usually serve just as go-betweens. In only 4 to 14 percent of the cases where an operation had applied for a particular program did the woman have only business contact with the agency. But men were even less likely to have *only* business contact. In more than 80 percent of the cases where an application had been made, they combined business contacts with being a formal applicant. (See Jones in Rosenfeld and Jones 1981, for further discussion of the USDA programs.)

OTHER FAMILY BUSINESS

Turning back to Table 3.1, an intriguing category is O: working in a family or in-home business other than the farm. Forty-five percent of the women said that this sort of work did apply to their operation, and of these, a third said that they regularly worked in such a business. Boulding (1980:280) has provided some examples of the types of nonfarm businesses farm women run, from craft shops and sheepskin-vest mail order firms to dog grooming and teaching music. In some cases, work in a family nonfarm business would overlap with off-farm employment, since a family business could be a feedstore, grocery, or other concern located away from the farm. Unfortunately, the FWS did not inquire further about the nature of these concerns. Women's cash-generating work within the home is a type of work that deserves further study. The ways in which farming and other family businesses are combined would be another area for investigation. Given the lack of detail about this type of work (for example, who in the family worked in the business in place of or in addition to the woman and whether it was an in-home or off-farm enterprise), such work will not play a further part in this book, but must wait for further research.

DOMESTIC WORK

While not all women did farm tasks, almost all had responsibility for housework. In fact, item J (doing household tasks) was included in the list of farm and home tasks so that women who indicated no involvement in farm tasks and who might, as a result, feel their work was not being fairly evaluated would have something to which they could say, "Yes, I do that." Ninety-seven percent of all the women in the sample said that they regularly had household tasks as a duty. Only 1 percent said that they never did such tasks, and these could be women in households where some other woman (such as a daughter, daughter-in-law, or mother) did the work. For example, one Kansas farm woman interviewed by another author commented, "The last couple, three years, Peggy [the teenage

Table 3.5. *Relationship between Child Care Responsibilities and Presence of Children in the Household*

Children Under Age 18 in Household?[a]	Woman Looks After Children (percentages)				
	Regularly	Occasionally	Never	Total	N[b]
No	35	30	35	100	623
Yes	94	4	2	100	1,224

[a]Includes children other than sons and daughters.

[b]Includes responses only of those who said this task was done on their operation.

daughter] does most of the washing; when we are out in the fields, she fixes the meals for us" (Boucher 1982:22). There is almost no variation in whether a woman did housework to be explained here.

Child care is another activity for which women throughout history have taken primary responsibility. About three-quarters of the women said that looking after children was something that applied to their farm. Of these women, 74 percent said that *they* regularly cared for the children, with another 13 percent saying that they did this occasionally. While this is a high level of participation in child care, it might seem low given expectations about women's mothering role. If the question had been whether the woman had *ever* had regular responsibility for child care, the answer would probably have been "yes" for most women. Ninety-five percent said that they had had at least one child (including adopted and foster children), but 35 percent said they currently had no sons or daughters at home. Further, not all of the women who said that looking after children was done on their operation had children in their own home. Table 3.5 shows that 94 percent of the women with some children (sons, daughters, nephews, nieces, grandchildren, etc.) in the household under the age of eighteen regularly cared for them. When presence of children in the home is controlled, there is very little variation in child care responsibilities left: Almost all women do it when there are children in the household.

The women who say that they look after children even when there are no children in their own home may be doing so for pay or helping relatives or neighbors. Such child care could free other women to do farm work or to find off-farm employment. The same Kansas woman whose daughter was taking over household responsibilities so that she could do farm work also explained, "When the kids were really small and someone had to stay with them, they was usually over with my mother-in-law while I was out in the field" (Boucher 1982:22).

Because of the almost universal participation of women in these kinds of work, I will not attempt to relate variation in women's participation in housework and child care to their own, farm, and family characteristics.[6]

Husbands' Perceptions of Their Wives' Task Involvement

One concern raised in chapter 2 was that husbands may underestimate their wives' contribution to the operation. If husbands are the ones who answer surveys or fill in census forms, and if they do not fully recognize their wives' work contributions, then results from such surveys may underrepresent the amount of work that farm women do. To see how husbands viewed the work their wives did on the farm and in the home, the FWS asked married men in the sample which tasks their wives did regularly, occasionally, or never, using the same list of tasks that had been presented to the women. Although from this it is not possible to compare estimates of hours spent on different sorts of work, it is possible to get a sense of whether husbands saw their wives as regular participants in the same tasks that women reported as regular duties.

Among the 497 couples in our survey, the women on average said they regularly did 29 percent of the listed farm tasks done on their operations, while the husbands said on average that their wives did 26 percent of the tasks regularly—a statistically significant but small difference. Although men tended to underestimate slightly the percent of tasks their wives did regularly, they and their wives agreed on the proportion of tasks wives did at least occasionally: husbands said on average, 51 percent, while their wives reported, on average, 50 percent. The amount of agreement varies by task but the largest discrepancy is only 8 percentage points (see Figure 3.1). Within couples, 60 to 70 percent (depending on the task) of the husbands agreed with their wives on the wife's task involvement.

Figure 3.1. *Comparison of Husbands' and Wives' Reports of Wives' Involvement in Home and Farm Tasks*

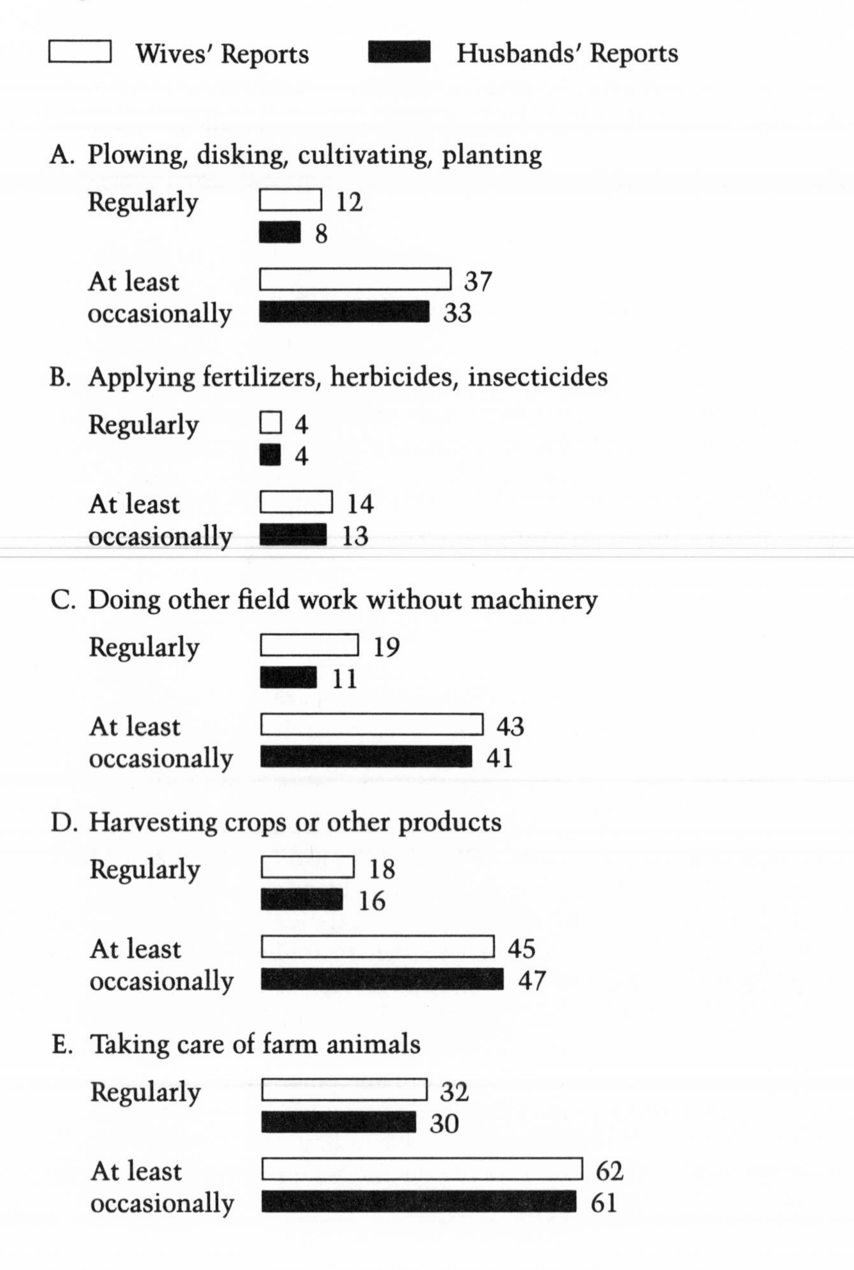

Figure 3.1. (*Continued*)

F. Running farm errands

G. Making major purchases of farm or ranch supplies and equipment

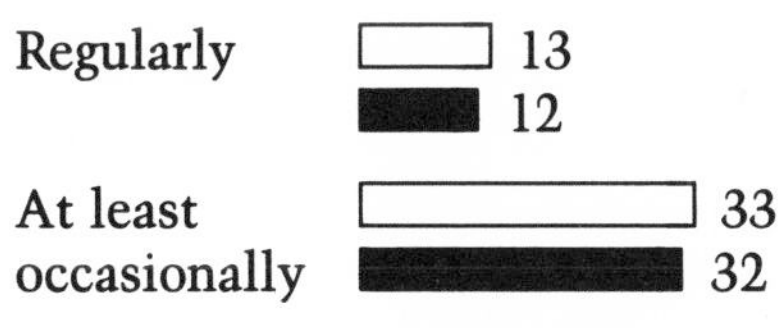

H. Marketing products

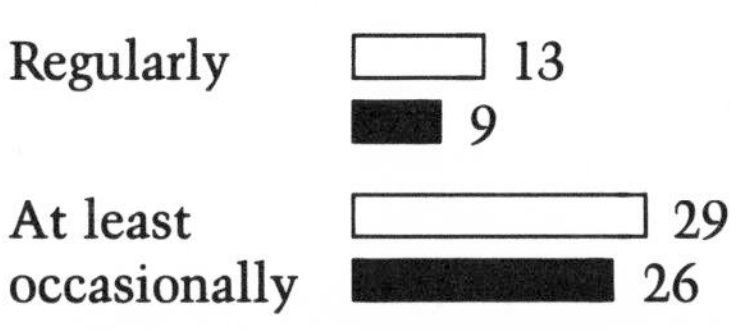

I. Bookkeeping

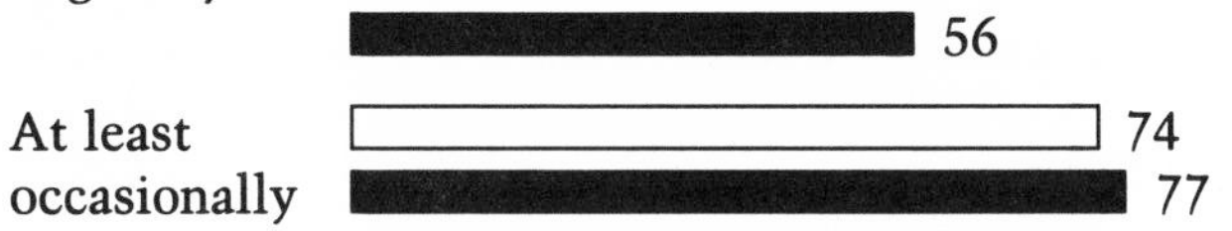

J. Doing household tasks

K. Supervising farm work of family member

Regularly 26
24

Figure 3.1. (*Continued*)

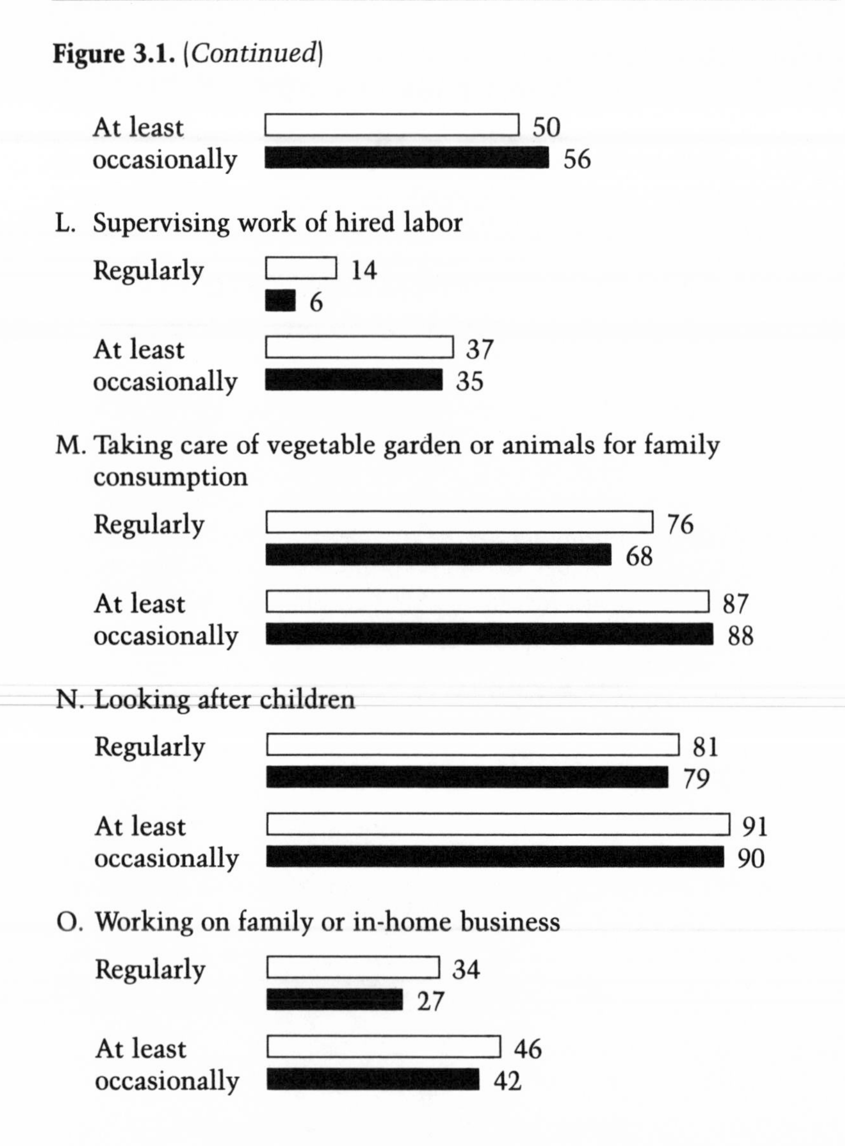

From 16 to 25 percent of the wives reported doing more than their husbands' said they did, but 10 to 20 percent of the husbands reported their wives doing more. In general, there is only slight support for the idea that husbands consistently underestimate their wives' work on the operation.

Farm Task Involvement and Farm, Farm Women, and Family Characteristics

As has already been demonstrated, variation in at least one sort of work—caring for children—is related to variations in family structure—whether there are children in the home. In this section I will see how variations in farm tasks performed are related to farm, farm women's, and family characteristics. I will look first at what explains variation in the overall range of task involvement. Then I will see what predicts whether a woman does particular sets of tasks.

The technique I will use for the first part of the analysis is ordinary least squares (OLS) multiple regression and for analysis of particular tasks, logistic regression. One wants to use multivariate techniques in order to separate out the effects of some given characteristic while controlling for all the others considered. Suppose one found that age influenced the range of tasks a woman did. Age is associated with the number of young children. It could also be associated with the size of the operation. Unless one controlled for young children's presence and farm size, one would not know whether it was one of the variables associated with age or age itself that affected the woman's farm work. Multiple regression permits one to talk about the effect of a given variable, net of all the others, or (to put it another way) as if women were average on every characteristic except the one under focus. Logistic regression, while having a slightly different interpretation, also allows one to separate out net effects. Of course the results of such a technique will be affected by the completeness of the set of variables used to explain a particular outcome. Here I have included fairly specific measures of the characteristics of the women, their farms, and their families, all of which might affect the extent and nature of women's farm work.

TECHNICAL PROBLEMS

There are two technical problems with which to deal before going on to the results. The first has to do with missing data. As can be inferred from Table 2.3, many women did not give responses for two sets of variables to be included in the analysis. The first is percent of sales from crops. Thirteen women refused to reply or just did not respond, and 242 women said that they did not know the sales mix. The women who did not, or could not, give an answer to this question do not seem to be a random subsample of the farm women. Among other things, they were involved in a smaller range of tasks on their farms than the women who answered the question. Lack of response here, then, is an indicator of the extent of the woman's participation on her farm. To exclude such women would be to bias the results because it would limit the analysis to those with higher levels of participation. To include all except refusals or blanks, here and in the next chapters I add a "don't know" category to the set of categories measuring product mix.

The second variable for which a large amount of information is missing is husband's off-farm income, which was used to decide whether the husband had an off-farm job in 1979. While 108 women either refused to answer or did not give a response for some other reason, 208 said they did not know what this income was. (These nonresponses do *not* include those of unmarried women.) Again, exclusion of these women could bias the results. To check on the extent of this bias, I first performed all the analyses, in this and the following chapters, excluding the cases lacking husband's income data. I then did the analyses a second time, making the somewhat heroic assumption that a woman who said that she did not know how much her husband made off the farm probably had a husband who did some off-farm work, following the reasoning that a woman is more likely to know whether her husband did some off-farm work than to know the exact amount that he was paid for that work. In the second analysis, then, a "don't know" response for husband's off-farm income was taken to indicate some off-farm employment, and the husband's work category assigned accordingly. In general, this change did not greatly affect the results. Therefore, I will not present the second set of results but only indicate what differences there were between analyses with and without the "don't know husband's off-farm income" responses included.

The second technical problem has to do with the direction of causality. Multiple regression assumes that the dependent variable (the variable to be explained) is caused by the explanatory variables. If this is not the case, the results may be biased. There is reason to suppose here that in some cases causality is reciprocal. The farm, for example, might be the size it is because of the woman's work as well as affecting the range of her involvement at the moment. This sort of problem is most serious with respect to the labor structure of the farm and the woman's other work. The husband may be free to work off the farm because of his wife's involvement on the farm. In this case, it is not that the husband's work affects his wife's, but rather vice versa. While this may be the case, the discussion of women as the people who provide a flexible work force for the family, the farm, and the economy suggests that the wife's work is in general a response to her husband's work distribution. It is more difficult to sort out the direction of influence among the different sorts of work that the woman herself does. As mentioned in the introduction to this chapter, Fassinger and Lodwick found that those women participating the least in farm production activities were also almost all employed off the farm. It is not clear what comes first: does the woman do less on the farm *because* she is employed off the farm or does she find employment either because her labor is not needed on the farm or because she is not interested in farm work?

Usually, testing the direction of causality involves finding some variable that affects the one outcome only indirectly through the other. For example, one would need to find some family, farm, or individual characteristic that affected the woman's farm work only indirectly through the probability that she held an off-farm job. It is almost impossible to think of such factors, because the family work structure is so affected by the characteristics and attitudes of all the members and because work on the farm is likely to be influenced by the same variables that influence the extent of work off the farm. I was, therefore, not able to deal with this problem directly. Rather, to check the robustness of the results, I estimated the equations first without and then with the woman's off-farm employment included. I also estimated the basic task involvement equation without any of the labor structure variables, results from which will be discussed below. Because association among the various independent variables is in general low, results are much the same with the different sets of variables. (For more discussion of reciprocal causation, see, for example, a standard text such as Hanushek and Jackson 1977, chapters 8–10.)

RESULTS: RANGE AND REGULARITY OF FARM TASK INVOLVEMENT

The regressions for the percent of farm tasks done regularly and at least occasionally are shown in Table 3.6.[7] This table shows that the nature of the operation does affect the range of farm tasks that a woman did. On larger farms, as compared with those of less than 50 acres, women did a significantly smaller percentage of the tasks regularly or at least occasionally. The biggest difference comes in comparing the very small with the largest operations. On operations of at least 1,000 acres, women did 6 percentage points fewer of the relevant farm tasks regularly and 9 percentage points fewer at least occasionally. This is consistent with the idea that women are excluded from the farming itself on larger operations. However, this finding is also consistent with the idea that women are not spending less *time* on farm tasks on larger operations but are specializing in what they do. Looking at determinants of whether women do specific tasks in the next section will help decide whether this is the case.

Controlling for size and other variables, the general product mix affects women's task participation. Women reporting that almost all sales on their operations were from crops did a significantly smaller range of tasks than those on mixed-sales farms, while those on farms with almost all sales from livestock did more (as expected), perhaps because of a more regular need for labor. As was also expected, those who said they did not know the sales mix of products did a significantly smaller range of tasks regularly and at least occasionally.

It was not clear that differences in control of the land or production would affect the woman's work for the operation. Yet there is some effect of tenancy here, though it is not consistent with the image of women being excluded from production when others own the land. Where the farm was fully owned in contrast with partly owned, women did 3 percentage points fewer of the farm tasks at least occasionally. When participation is measured by the percent of tasks done regularly, women did 5 percentage points more tasks when the farm was wholly rented. This latter effect, though, is not significant when those who did not know their husband's income are included. No other contrast is statistically significant. When there were other decision makers for the operation, the woman did a smaller range of the tasks regularly or at least occasionally.

On the other hand, when the woman had *her* name on the deed or rental contract, she did almost 5 percentage points more of the tasks regularly and 4 percentage points more at least occasionally. Legal control of land may spur a woman to contribute to a wider range of the work for the farm, although it is also possible that those women who put their names on a legal document having to do with the operation are those who in general are more active in the operation. This is another case where the possibility of reversed causality exists.

Women in other regions did a wider range of farm tasks than women in the South. This is especially true for women in the Northeast. As mentioned in chapter 2, region may represent a number of factors. Some of its effects may be due to differences in women's involvement in the production of certain kinds of crops. For example, women did a smaller range of tasks in the production of tobacco and cotton in comparison with other kinds of products (Ross 1982). Regional effects could represent other differences in the organization of production. They might also represent attitudinal differences. Sex role attitudes in the South are more conservative (and in the West perhaps somewhat more liberal [Sachs 1983]) than those in other regions. Further, it is possible that the regional variables are proxies for the woman's off-farm employment. Women in Southern rural areas have had and do have higher levels of labor force participation than women in other areas (Brown and O'Leary 1979; Sweet 1972). Controlling for whether the woman was employed off the farm, however, does not change this effect.

There are no significant effects on range of women's farm work from having more than one hired hand. The effects of having other people working on the farm are mixed. It depends on who was doing the work. Further, some of the effects are directly contrary to expectations. The effect of having a husband who did farm work is clear and as expected. Women who did not have a husband, in contrast with other women, did almost 20 percentage points more tasks regularly and 12 percentage points more at least occasionally. When a woman was married to someone employed off the farm and not regularly in farm work, she also did a somewhat greater range of tasks, although the contrast here is not as great as that for women with no husbands at all. The lack of effect for the last category—husband did not farm or have off-farm employment—may be due to the very small number of cases that fall into this group. There is a hint that when the husband was both farming and employed off the farm, the woman had a somewhat more extensive involvement with the operation. This effect, however, vanishes when one includes the "don't know husband's off-farm income" respondents. The general impression, then, is that when a husband did not regularly take part in production, the woman was involved in a wider range of farm activities.

Although women did a smaller percentage of tasks when they

Table 3.6 *OLS Regression for Percent of Farm Tasks Performed by Farm Women*

	Dependent Variables			
	Percent of Farm Tasks Done at Least Occasionally			
	Excluding Women's Off-Farm Employment		Including Women's Off-Farm Employment	
Independent Variables[a]	Unstandard-ized Coefficient	Standardized Coefficient	Unstandard-ized Coefficient	Standardized Coefficient
<u>Farm Characteristics</u>				
Total acres in farm relative to less than 50 acres:				
50-299 acres	-4.44	-.09**	-4.42	-.09**
300-999 acres	-5.37	-.09**	-5.68	-.10**
> 1,000 acres	-8.56	-.12**	-9.18	-.13**
Sales relative to mixed crops and livestock:				
Less than 5 percent total sales from crops	1.56	.03	1.48	.03
Greater than 95 percent total sales from crops	-7.56	-.13**	-7.56	-.13**
Don't know percent of sales from crops	-7.96	-.08**	-8.19	-.09**
Tenancy relative to part owners:				
Full owners	-2.99	-.06*	-3.02	-.06*
Renters	2.39	.03	2.48	.03
Neither owners nor renters	-3.18	-.02	-3.23	-.02
<u>Woman's Legal Relation to Land</u>				
Own name on deed or rental contract for land	4.22	.07**	4.12	.06*
<u>Decision Makers</u>				
Include other than husband and wife	-4.26	-.07**	-4.11	-.07**
<u>Region</u>				
Relative to South:				
Northeast	8.65	.15**	8.43	.15**
Northcentral	5.82	.10**	5.64	.10**
West	8.24	.14**	7.94	.14**

Dependent Variables			
Percent of Farm Tasks Done Regularly			
Excluding Women's Off-Farm Employment		Including Women's Off-Farm Employment	
Unstandard-ized Coefficient	Standardized Coefficient	Unstandard-ized Coefficient	Standardized Coefficient
-3.98	-.09**	-3.95	-.09**
-3.97	-.08*	-4.40	-.09**
-6.06	-.10**	-6.89	-.11**
3.18	.07**	3.06	.06*
-3.74	-.08**	-3.74	-.07**
-4.73	-.06*	-5.03	-.06**
-1.61	-.04	-1.65	-.04
4.50	.05*	4.63	.06*
2.33	.02	2.27	.02
4.67	.08**	4.54	.08**
-3.50	-.07**	-3.30	-.07**
6.48	.13**	6.20	.12**
4.19	.08**	3.96	.08**
6.04	.12**	5.63	.11**

Table 3.6. *continued*

	Dependent Variables			
	Percent of Farm Tasks Done at Least Occasionally			
	Excluding Women's Off-Farm Employment		Including Women's Off-Farm Employment	
Independent Variables[a]	Unstandardized Coefficient	Standardized Coefficient	Unstandardized Coefficient	Standardized Coefficient
Labor Structure of Farm				
More than 1 hired hand	1.55	.03	1.37	.03
Husband's work relative to husband who regularly does farm work and has no off-farm job:				
No husband	11.59	.09**	11.99	.10**
Husband regularly does farm work and has off-farm job	3.28	.06**	4.00	.08**
Husband does not regularly do farm work and has off-farm job	8.56	.07**	8.71	.08**
Husband does not regularly do farm work and has no off-farm job	2.08	.01	1.88	.01
Number of sons at least 18 who regularly do farm work	.06	.001	-.11	-.002
Number of children ages 6-17 who regularly do farm work	2.35	.09**	2.13	.08**
Number of other household members who regularly do farm work	2.66	.04	2.66	.04
Number of other non-household members who regularly do farm work	-.43	-.02	-.44	-.03
Farm Woman's Characteristics				
Education relative to high school graduate:				
Less than high school	-2.99	-.04	-3.14	-.04*
Postsecondary vocational or some college	2.77	.05*	3.29	.05*
College degree or above	2.08	.03	3.28	.04
Percent of life spent on farms or ranches	.09	.11**	.09	.11**

Dependent Variables			
Percent of Farm Tasks Done Regularly			
Excluding Women's Off-Farm Employment		Including Women's Off-Farm Employment	
Unstandard-ized Coefficient	Standardized Coefficient	Unstandard-ized Coefficient	Standardized Coefficient
-.30	-.006	-.54	-.01
17.95	.17**	18.49	.17**
1.56	.03	2.53	.06*
11.00	.11**	11.20	.11**
4.45	.03	4.18	.03
-.87	-.02	-1.09	-.02
1.71	.07**	1.41	.06*
1.81	.03	1.82	.03
-.85	-.06*	-.86	-.06**
-.53	-.009	-.73	-.01
2.51	.05*	3.22	.06**
.31	.005	1.94	.03
.06	.08**	.06	.08**

Table 3.6. *continued*

Independent Variables[a]	Dependent Variables			
	Percent of Farm Tasks Done at Least Occasionally			
	Excluding Women's Off-Farm Employment		Including Women's Off-Farm Employment	
	Unstandard-ized Coefficient	Standardized Coefficient	Unstandard-ized Coefficient	Standardized Coefficient
Farm Women's Characteristics (cont'd)				
Age relative to over 65:				
less than 31	21.69	.26**	23.80	.28**
31-45	19.95	.38**	21.95	.42**
46-65	12.54	.25**	13.67	.27**
Dependent Children				
Number of children less than age 6	-2.20	-.05*	-2.91	-.07**
Number of children 6-17 who do not regularly do farm work	-1.84	-.06**	-2.09	-.06**
Off-Farm Work				
Woman currently employed off-farm	-	-	-4.77	-.09**
Constant	22.52		13.71	
R^2	.17		.18	
N[b]	2,031			

* .01 < p < .05

** p < .01

[a]For categorical variables, 1 = yes, 0 = no

[b]Ns differ from 2,509 because of missing data

Dependent Variables			
Percent of Farm Tasks Done Regularly			
Excluding Women's Off-Farm Employment		Including Women's Off-Farm Employment	
Unstandard-ized Coefficient	Standardized Coefficient	Unstandard-ized Coefficient	Standardized Coefficient
13.57	.18**	16.42	.22**
12.49	.27**	15.19	.33**
8.63	.19**	10.16	.23**
-2.18	-.06*	-3.14	-.08**
-1.54	-.05*	-1.88	-.07**
-	-	-6.47	-.14**
5.87		-6.06	
.14		.15	
2,031			

had a husband doing day-to-day chores, they actually did a greater percentage when there were children regularly involved in the farm work. Women did about 2 percentage points more of the tasks for each additional child between six and seventeen years of age who regularly contributed work to the farm. More family members working may mean more involvement in supervision of labor, a possibility I will explore in the next section of this chapter. In addition, I had suggested that the number of household workers represented the farm's degrees of labor intensity, something that cannot be tested directly.

On the other hand, controlling for the other variables, the number of sons over seventeen and other household members have no significant effect. The only suggestion that people other than the husband substituted for the labor of the farm women is in the relatively small effect of the number of other people (aside from hired hands) from outside the household who regularly helped. For each additional person (who might be a neighbor, a son living outside the household, a brother—the survey did not ask who these people were), the woman did less than 1 percentage point fewer of the farm tasks regularly.[8]

One would expect children, especially young children, to constrain women's work on the farm. The results in Table 3.6 suggest that this is true. For every child under six years of age, women did 2 to 3 percentage points fewer tasks regularly or occasionally, while for every dependent child ages six to seventeen they did 2 percentage points fewer. These effects of younger children are larger than the effects of school age children.

There are thus two ways in which children ages six to seventeen affect the range of a woman's at least occasional tasks: more children of this age helping on the farm increases the range, while more children of this age who are not helping decreases it. If one did not make the distinction between the two groups, one would conclude that having children in this age range had no effect on the range of a woman's work. This was indeed the result when all labor structure variables were excluded from the equation for at least occasional farm task performance.

Looking at the effects of the human capital variables, one finds that women with more education, especially some vocational education or college beyond high school, did a wider range of tasks. More experience in farming, in the sense of having spent a greater proportion of one's life on a farm or ranch, increases the percent of tasks with which a woman was involved. Age has one of the largest effects. Women forty-five or below did about 20 percentage points more tasks at least occasionally (and 13 to 16 percentage points more regularly) than women over sixty-five, while those between forty-six and sixty-five did 13 percentage points more tasks at least occasionally (and 9 to 10 percentage points more on a regular basis). The effect of age could represent differences among women born in different periods in their preference for doing such work or their habits with respect to doing them. Older women might have always done fewer of the farm tasks because of ideas about women's roles or because of the greater demands on their time within the home, given the past absence of modern household conveniences. Comparing the effects of age on doing specific more and less physical tasks may shed light on this.

The last variable to consider is the woman's employment. Not surprisingly, controlling for all the other variables, a woman who was employed off the farm did 5 percentage points fewer types of tasks at least occasionally and 6 percentage points fewer regularly. The effect is relatively small, but the measure of off-farm employment is simply of employment or not, not of the number of hours employed. There is, though, the possibility that even this effect is overestimated because the simultaneous effect of doing farm work on employment has not been taken into account.

RESULTS: DOING SPECIFIC SETS OF FARM TASKS

The discussion in chapter 1 on the work farm women do and the results from the preceding section raise questions about how the nature of the farm and the family may affect whether a woman did specific sets of farm tasks. Some of the particular hypotheses from the discussion are:

1. Women on larger farms, on farms that have hired labor, and with male family members farming are less likely to do field work. This hypothesis is derived from the observation that women tend to do field work only when necessary and do not do it when the farm can afford to do without their labor.
2. Women with more young children are less likely to do field work with machines. This would be the case if working with machines were not compatible with caring for children.
3. Older women are less likely to do physical tasks such as field work, while age has no effect on activities such as labor supervision or bookkeeping. One interpretation of age is as physi-

cal ability to work. If this interpretation is correct, then one would expect to see age affecting performance of physical tasks but not of nonphysical ones.

4. Women on larger farms and on farms where other people own the land and make decisions will be less likely to market products or make major purchases. This follows from the reasoning that women are excluded from market activities when the farm has other decision makers and perhaps when, on larger farms, farm men keep more of the important decisions under their own control.

5. Women on larger farms are more likely to keep the books. The preceding discussion suggests that it is possible women on larger farms do a smaller range of tasks because they specialize in particular tasks, with bookkeeping one of the areas of specialization.

6. Women with more children who do farm work are more likely to report supervising labor. One explanation for the finding that women with more child helpers did a wider range of tasks was that this larger range reflected their greater likelihood of overseeing their children's labor.

7. Women whose husbands also farm are less likely to get information and advice from USDA agencies. One possible reason that women are less likely to have contacts with government agencies is that such contacts are expected to be between men. If this is correct, then when a husband is there to make these contacts, he, rather than the woman, would do so.

In this section I use the same independent variables as in the previous section to predict whether a woman regularly: (1) plowed, disked, cultivated or planted, or harvested; (2) did other field work without machinery; (3) marketed products or made major supply or equipment purchases; (4) kept the books; (5) supervised family or hired labor; and (6) got information or advice from Extension personnel in the 2–3 years before 1980.

The variables to be explained are now a dichotomy in each case. A woman does a given type of task or she does not. For statistical reasons, ordinary least squares is not appropriate for such dependent variables. An alternate multivariate technique, which is appropriate for categorical dependent variables, is used: logistic regression. In logistic regression, the dependent variable is transformed into the natural logarithm of the odds of being in one category versus the other. Here, the dependent variable is the log of the odds that a woman did a given task.[9] The results of the logistic regression are shown in Table 3.7.

Field work with and without Machinery. On larger farms, women were less likely to do field work without machinery, supporting the first hypothesis that when the farm can afford it, women do not work in the fields. Of course, men, too, could be less likely to do manual work on larger farms, where scale makes the use of machines more feasible and profitable. There is no effect of farm size, however, on whether women did field work (including harvesting) regularly with machines. When one looks just at plowing and disking, one finds that being on the very largest farms as compared with other size categories decreases the probability that a woman did this task. Women without a husband farming were more likely to do field work than other women, consistent with hypothesis 1, but having other people helping with farm work did not decrease the woman's performance of this kind of work. In fact, having more children helping is associated with a greater chance that the woman did field work without machines. Having young children does not seem to be incompatible with using machinery, contrary to the second hypothesis. It is only with respect to doing field work *without* machinery that the number of children under six has a significant effect. The decreasing probability with age of doing this sort of task supports the third hypothesis that older women pull out of the physical part of farming.

Marketing. On smaller farms, on those where there was no husband regularly doing farm work, on those depending on livestock for sales, and on those where the woman had some legal control of the land, the woman had a greater probability of purchasing inputs and marketing the farm products. The results with respect to farm size and a husband farming are predicted by the fourth hypothesis. Having other people controlling the land or having others involved in the decision making, however, does not significantly decrease the probability of doing this sort of task, contrary to what was expected. There is not a monotonic decrease in the probability of doing this task with age: Those in their middle years (thirty-one to forty-five) were those most likely to do this task. This is consistent again with the argument that the age effect on the range of tasks represents in large part the association of age with involvement in physical tasks.

Table 3.7A. *Logistic Regression for Whether Woman Performs Specific Type of Farm Task (logit coefficients)*

	Dependent Variables	
	Plowing, Applying Herbicide, Harvesting, etc.	
Independent Variables[a]	Excluding Women's Off-Farm Employment	Including Women's Off-Farm Employment
Farm Characteristics		
Total acres in farm relative to less than 50 acres:		
50-299 acres	-.09	-.09
300-999 acres	-.008	-.04
> 1,000 acres	.07	.007
Sales relative to mixed crops and livestock:		
Less than 5 percent total sales from crops	-.18	-.19
Greater than 95 percent total sales from crops	-.18	-.18
Don't know percent of sales from crops	-.20	-.23
Tenancy relative to part owners:		
Full owners	-.24	-.24*
Renters	.60**	.62**
Neither owners nor renters	.18	.16
Woman's Legal Relation to Land		
Own name on deed or rental contract for land	.36*	.35*
Decision Makers		
Include other than husband and wife	-.30*	-.29*
Region		
Relative to South:		
Northeast	.19	.17
Northcentral	-.05	-.08
West	.14	.10

Dependent Variables			
Other Fieldwork without Machines		Marketing and Purchasing	
Excluding Women's Off-Farm Employment	Including Women's Off-Farm Employment	Excluding Women's Off-Farm Employment	Including Women's Off-Farm Employment
-.56**	-.55**	-.40*	-.40**
-.58**	-.62**	-.58**	-.62**
-.95**	-1.00**	-.52*	-.58*
-.08	-.09	.38**	.38**
.07	.08	-.12	-.12
.08	.07	-.30	-.32
-.16	-.17	-.06	-.06
.42	.41	.64*	.65*
.56	.55	.54	.53
.43*	.42	.57**	.57**
-.38*	-.37*	-.005	.005
.09	.07	.46**	.45**
.28	.27	.19	.19
.41*	.39*	.29	.27

Table 3.7A. *continued*

Independent Variables	Dependent Variables: Plowing, Applying Herbicide, Harvesting, etc. — Excluding Women's Off-Farm Employment	Including Women's Off-Farm Employment
Labor Structure of Farm		
More than 1 hired hand	.03	.02
Husband's work relative to husband who regularly does farm work and has no off-farm job:		
No husband	1.05**	1.11**
Husband regularly does farm work and has off-farm job	.20	.28*
Husband does not regularly do farm work and has off-farm job	.72*	.73**
Husband does not regularly do farm work and has no off-farm job	-.43	-.44
Number of sons at least 18 who regularly do farm work	-.001	-.02
Number of children ages 6-17 who regularly do farm work	.10	.07
Number of other household members who regularly do farm work	.23	.23
Number of other non-household members who regularly do farm work	-.08	-.08
Farm Woman's Characteristics		
Education relative to high school graduate:		
Less than high school	-.05	-.07
Postsecondary vocational or some college	.15	.21
College degree or above	-.41*	-.28
Percent of life spent on farms or ranches	.004*	.005**

Dependent Variables			
Other Fieldwork without Machines		Marketing and Purchasing	
Excluding Women's Off-Farm Employment	Including Women's Off-Farm Employment	Excluding Women's Off-Farm Employment	Including Women's Off-Farm Employment
.04	.03	.14	.13
.98**	1.02**	1.56**	1.61**
.14	.20	.12	.17
.49	.50	.50*	.51*
-.57	-.57	.92**	.92**
-.10	-.11	-.05	-.07
.16*	.14*	-.001	-.02
.15	.15	.06	.05
-.04	-.05	-.05	-.05
.28	.27	.03	.02
.12	.15	.27	.32*
-.22	-.12	.57**	.67**
.004	.004	-.001	-.001

Table 3.7A. *continued*

Independent Variables	Dependent Variables: Plowing, Applying Herbicide, Harvesting, etc. — Excluding Women's Off-Farm Employment	Including Women's Off-Farm Employment
Farm Women's Characteristics (cont'd)		
Age relative to over 65:		
less than 31	.93**	1.16**
31-45	.82**	1.04**
46-65	.67**	.79**
Dependent Children		
Number of children less than age 6	-.13	-.21
Number of children 6-17 who do not regularly do farm work	-.07	-.10
Off-Farm Work		
Woman currently employed off-farm	-	-.53**
Constant	-2.69	-3.70
D	.05	.06
N[b]	1,984	
Observed probability	.29	

Dependent Variables			
Other Fieldwork without Machines		Marketing and Purchasing	
Excluding Women's Off-Farm Employment	Including Women's Off-Farm Employment	Excluding Women's Off-Farm Employment	Including Women's Off-Farm Employment
1.98**	2.17**	.36	.53
1.67**	1.85**	.54*	.71**
1.42**	1.51**	.38	.47*
-.28*	-.35*	-.20	-.26*
-.09	-.11	-.12	-.14
-	-.40**	-	-.39**
-4.12	-4.88	-2.28	-3.03
.06	.06	.07	.08
1,835		2,021	
.18		.31	

Table 3.7B. *Logistic Regression for Whether Woman Performs Specific Type of Farm Task (logit coefficients)*

	Dependent Variables	
	Bookkeeping	
Independent Variables[a]	Excluding Women's Off-Farm Employment	Including Women's Off-Farm Employment
Farm Characteristics		
Total acres in farm relative to less than 50 acres:		
50-299 acres	.14	.14
300-999 acres	.16	.14
> 1,000 acres	.01	-.03
Sales relative to mixed crops and livestock:		
Less than 5 percent total sales from crops	.13	.12
Greater than 95 percent total sales from crops	-.24	-.24
Don't know percent of sales from crops	-.52**	-.54**
Tenancy relative to part owners:		
Full owners	-.19	-.19
Renters	-.22	-.22
Neither owners nor renters	-.33	-.33
Woman's Legal Relation to Land		
Own name on deed or rental contract for land	.001	-.004
Decision Makers		
Include other than husband and wife	-.47**	-.46**
Region		
Relative to South:		
Northeast	.63**	.62**
Northcentral	.30*	.29*
West	.62**	.61**

Dependent Variables			
Supervising Farm Labor		Getting Information or Advice from Extension	
Excluding Women's Off-Farm Employment	Including Women's Off-Farm Employment	Excluding Women's Off-Farm Employment	Including Women's Off-Farm Employment
-.23	-.23	.15	.15
-.54**	-.58**	.29	.27
-.97**	-1.05**	.27	.24
.03	.02	-.25	-.26
-.36*	-.35*	-.32*	-.32*
-.57*	-.60*	-.73**	-.74
-.00	-.01	-.15	-.16
.32	.31	.15	.16
.78*	.79*	.17	.16
.51**	.51**	.61**	.61**
-.13	-.11	.07	.07
.16	.14	.16	.15
.14	.14	.12	.12
.22	.20	.25	.24

Table 3.7B. *continued*

Independent Variables	Dependent Variables	
	Bookkeeping	
	Excluding Women's Off-Farm Employment	Including Women's Off-Farm Employment
<u>Labor Structure of Farm</u>		
More than 1 hired hand	.11	.10
Husband's work relative to husband who regularly does farm work and has no off-farm job:		
No husband	.42	.44
Husband regularly does farm work and has off-farm job	-.01	.04
Husband does not regularly do farm work and has off-farm job	.18	.19
Husband does not regularly do farm work and has no off-farm job	.52	.51
Number of sons at least 18 who regularly do farm work	-.07	-.08
Number of children ages 6-17 who regularly do farm work	.07	.06
Number of other household members who regularly do farm work	-.18	-.19
Number of other non-household members who regularly do farm work	-.10**	-.10**
<u>Farm Woman's Characteristics</u>		
Education relative to high school graduate:		
Less than high school	-.36*	-.37**
Postsecondary vocational or some college	.11	.14
College degree or above	-.35*	-.27
Percent of life spent on farms or ranches	.005**	.005**

Dependent Variables			
Supervising Farm Labor		Getting Information or Advice from Extension	
Excluding Women's Off-Farm Employment	Including Women's Off-Farm Employment	Excluding Women's Off-Farm Employment	Including Women's Off-Farm Employment
.19	.17	.16	.15
1.31**	1.35**	.22	.24
.12	.20	.01	-.04
.48	.50*	.26	.26
.65*	.64*	-.06	-.07
-.03	-.04	.13	.12
.47**	.45**	.12	.11
.27	.28	.26	.26
.01	.01	.01	.01
-.04	-.06	-.75**	-.76**
.25	.30*	.36**	.38**
-.08	.05	.93**	.98**
.003	.003	.001	.001

Table 3.7B. *continued*

	Dependent Variables	
	Bookkeeping	
Independent Variables	Excluding Women's Off-Farm Employment	Including Women's Off-Farm Employment
Farm Women's Characteristics (cont'd)		
Age relative to over 65:		
less than 31	-.11	.02
31-45	.21	.34
46-65	.17	.24
Dependent Children		
Number of children less than age 6	-.06	-.11
Number of children 6-17 who do not regularly do farm work	-.17**	-.19**
Off-Farm Work		
Woman currently employed off-farm	-	-.30**
Constant	-.78	-1.34
D	.06	.06
N	2,015	
Observed probability	.66	

* .01 ≤ p < .05.

** p < .01.

[a] 1 = yes, 0 = no.

[b] Ns differ from 2,509 because of missing data.

Dependent Variables			
Supervising Farm Labor		Getting Information or Advice from Extension	
Excluding Women's Off-Farm Employment	Including Women's Off-Farm Employment	Excluding Women's Off-Farm Employment	Including Women's Off-Farm Employment
1.27**	1.49**	.17	.26
1.10**	1.32**	.35	.43
.84**	.97**	.21	.26
.-.07	-.15	-.07	-.10
.19*	.16*	-.15	-.16*
-	-.50**	-	-.20
-3.21	-4.17	-2.16	-2.53
.11	.12	.07	.07
1,850		2,031	
.26		.24	

Bookkeeping. Contrary to what was expected in the fifth hypothesis, women on the larger farms were not more likely to keep the books. This may be because the measure used is simply whether a woman regularly did a task, not how much time she spent on it. Bookkeeping is a common farm woman's task that she may do regardless of the size of the operation but that might take more of her time as the operation grows. Further, larger enterprises may be those more likely to have a professional accountant. Also, large farms more often engage in credit futures buying and selling in which the man is more likely to be dealing with the officials and agencies (Wilkening, personal communication). The effects of presence of other decision makers and other nonhousehold help also suggest that the less the immediate family controls and works the farm, the more likely someone else is to take the woman's place as bookkeeper. That this is a task routinely assigned to the woman in the family is borne out by the lack of any effect of a husband's farm involvement on the chances of doing the bookkeeping. Because doing books is not a physically taxing task, it is not surprising that a woman's age has no significant effect here.

Supervising Labor. Having more children helping with farm work increases the probability that the woman supervised farm labor, as expected in the sixth hypothesis. Her chances of supervising labor, however, were less on larger farms and not related to the number of hired hands. These results and the positive effect of the number of children ages six to seventeen who do not do farm work suggest that women are less farm managers than supervisors of children.

Getting Information and Advice from Extension Personnel. There are no hints here that women are excluded from this part of farm management when there is a husband present, contrary to what the last hypothesis predicted. Rather than farm characteristics and husband's work, education and the interest of the woman in the operation (as indicated by her name appearing on rental contracts and deeds and by her knowledge of the percent of sales from crops) affect whether she had gotten advice or information from Extension staff. The lack of age effects is again consistent with the idea that age represents involvement in the physical work of the operation rather than attitudinal differences among cohorts.

Conclusions

This chapter examined the range and variation in women's farm and household work. Very few women participated in none of the farm tasks on their operations. On average, women at least occasionally did more than half of the inventoried farm tasks done on their farms. The tasks that they were most likely to do at some time were those the literature shows to be the common ones for farm women, for example, bookkeeping and doing errands, although at least some women did field work and other less traditional work as well. Almost all women did housework, and they cared for children, when children were in the house. In general, husbands seemed to report what their wives were doing just as their wives did.

Multivariate analysis showed that the type of operation affected the range and the specific types of tasks in which a woman took part. In particular, those on larger farms and ranches reported involvement in a smaller range of tasks. There was evidence that women were excluded or exempted from doing some field work, from market contacts, and from supervision of labor on the larger enterprises. The analysis of whether a woman did the bookkeeping did not provide support for the hypothesis that women specialize in such tasks on larger farms, but it must be kept in mind that the measure of task involvement did not allow for differing levels of time spent on a given task. What was produced also affected the range of women's work. On farms selling mostly crops, women reported doing a smaller range of farm tasks.

In general, family control of land had no consistent effects on the nature of women's farm work, although women with their own names on deeds and rental contracts were more likely to be involved in most farm tasks. The presence of other decision makers generally restricted the probability that a woman did a particular task, although unexpectedly it did not lessen her chances of marketing and purchasing or of contacting Extension agents.

The interactions of family and farm characteristics were shown by the effects of husbands and children. When a husband was farming, the woman did a smaller range of tasks and was less likely to do all but the often female task of bookkeeping. The other exception here was contacting Extension agents for information or advice, a task measured with a different time referent and without controlling for whether anyone on the enterprise did the task. While having young and school-age children who did not help on the farm regularly decreased the range of tasks which the woman did (although the effects varied over specific types of tasks), having school-age children helping with the farm increased the overall range and the chance that the woman supervised farm labor and did field work without machinery.

Women's own characteristics, such as their age, education, and experience with farm life, also affected the extent of their involvement in farm tasks, in much the same way that these variables have been found to affect women's labor force participation in general. Looking at the separate types of tasks indicated that age was a measure of participation in the more physically demanding tasks of the operation and that education was more important for tasks involving other than physical labor. The woman's market work, too, affected the extent of her work on the farm. In general, those employed off the farm did a smaller range of tasks and were less likely to do any particular task. (An exception, again, is with respect to getting help from Extension personnel.) The results for women's employment, however, must remain tentative because of the statistical problem discussed in this chapter.

Thus the nature of the farm work that women do seems to depend on the need for their labor, if larger operations, those with a greater dependence on livestock for sales, and those without a full-time farm husband are those with a greater need for the woman's labor. Women do not seem to substitute for other people, however. The presence of children, even small children, does not always inhibit women's participation in farm tasks, because some tasks, such as bookkeeping, can be combined with child care, and because children may also be part of the farm work force. At the same time that family and farm characteristics affect the extent and specifics of women's participation in farm tasks, the woman's own characteristics and other work roles also exert an influence.

4
Farm and Household Decision Making

Crucially influencing the long-range success of an agricultural operation are basic decisions about what commodities to produce, on what scale, with what level of technology, and with what marketing strategy in mind. To take a role in these decisions is to share in the clearest sense the ultimate responsibility for the enterprise. Most farm families will be making decisions about the home and nonfarm activities of family members as well. This chapter will examine the sexual division of labor in making farm and household decisions.

Following from the idea that men take on the more critical tasks in any important economic activity, one would expect to see men making most of the farm decisions. The literature on farm family decision making, though, suggests that we will find considerable sharing of decisions between the farm husband and wife (e.g., Sawer 1973; Wilkening and Bharadwaj 1967; Wilkening 1981). At the same time, Wilkening and Bharadwaj, who looked at both farm and home decisions, did report some tendency for women to take more responsibility for home decisions and men for farm decisions. The pattern of decision making, then, sounds much like the pattern of task performance, with women having greater responsibility in the home domain. This chapter shows the results from the FWS with respect to women's and men's parts in home and family decisions. It will further examine farm family decision making by comparing husbands' and wives' reports and by showing women's satisfaction with the patterns with which they live.

This chapter will explore, too, factors that explain variations among farm families in patterns of farm and home decision making. In chapter 1, women were predicted to be excluded or exempted from farming in families and on farms that had less need for their input. This might be more true for decision making than for actually performing labor. Thus, when the husband is active in a given domain, when there is an adult son, when the land is owned by someone else, or when someone outside the couple routinely helps make decisions, one might expect the woman to be less involved in the decisions herself. The evidence for such hypotheses comes mainly from a few case studies (e.g., Hagood 1977/1939, on tenant farmers; Colman and Elbert 1983:13, with respect to sons). There is, however, consistent empirical evidence about the effect of one farm characteristic, size, on women's part in decisions, as discussed in chapter 1. Women seem to have lower levels of decision-making participation on larger farms. While this result has been interpreted as indicating that women cannot or do not wish to understand the technical complexities of larger operations, it has also been taken to show that when men can afford to take control, they do or that on larger operations hierarchical decision-making processes are necessary, and men dominate these hierarchies in their roles as producers.

Rather than talking about the need for the woman to play a part, the general literature on family decision making has suggested that levels of resources (education, connections with the broader society) affect the distribution of decision making. It explains the greater part employed women play in family decisions, for example, by the greater financial resources they bring to the family, and by the social networks and skills relevant to decision making that women form in the labor market (e.g., McDonald 1980). Such hypotheses have been tested to some extent in the literature on farm decision making. Looking only at the correlations of decision-making shares with education, income, and wife's social participation, Wilkening and Bharadwaj (1968) and Sawer (1973) failed to find support for the resources hypothesis. As Scanzoni and Szinovacz (1980) point out, what may be important in determining who makes decisions is the relative, rather than absolute, resources of the wife as compared with the husband. In this chapter I will use both approaches to test the effects of resources on decision-making patterns.

There is, however, evidence of decision-making effects by other variables that could be taken as measures of resources (or lack of them). Ownership of land is one. In her interviews Boulding (1980) noted that women who owned the land themselves took a bigger part in making farm decisions. The fact that a woman owned land might give her greater power in deciding how the farm should be run.

Another variable is children. Sawer's (1973) data showed a constraint of children on the wife's involvement in farm decision making. She takes number of children to represent direction of the wife's resources away from the farm and to act as a proxy for the general sex role orientation of the family: having more children could mean both that the woman has less attention to devote to the farm and that the husband and wife have more traditional ideas of family roles. According to Sawer (1973: 420), other nonfarm studies also provide evidence that in families with larger numbers of children decision making is husband dominated.

Further, Wilkening and Bharadwaj (1968) and Sawer (1973), among others, provide evidence that the women who do more types of farm work are likely to take a greater part in decision making, although the association is far from perfect.[1] Experience with the work and in seeing the results of alternative methods of doing things could be seen as a resource brought to decision making (e.g., Elbert and Colman 1975). As was seen in the last chapter, farm women are involved in a wide range of activities on their farms and if nothing else contribute domestic work.

Sawer (1973:417) highlighted the job of seeking agricultural information as related to taking a part in farm decision making: "Since decision-making patterns appear to evolve as husbands and wives participate according to their interests and abilities . . . , it follows that wives who become knowledgeable about farm matters will likely increase their chances of making a useful contribution in farm decision-making." She found that the level of the wife's overall information seeking activities was significantly associated with her part in farm decision making, although number of contacts with Extension agents in the past year was not.

Doing farm tasks does not necessarily mean controlling how and when the tasks are done, as implied by the less than perfect correlation between the two. Lodwick and Fassinger (1979:16), in fact, classified 21 percent of their sample as "agriculturally active." These women are active daily farm participants. They perform much of the same work that agricultural partners do, some even to the extent of a reported 40 hours per week of farm work. They tend not, however, to engage in management functions or decisions directly.

The results of this chapter are generally consistent with the previous results on farm family decision making. At the same time, the chapter extends the previous research by using multivariate techniques to predict both home and farm decision-making patterns with variables representing the farm's need for the woman to take part in production and the resources she brings to decision making.

Patterns of Farm and Household Decision Making

The FWS asked all respondents about family decision patterns for nine specific areas—six basic farm management decisions and three types of household decisions (question 14). For each type of decision, interviewers asked respondents whether they usually made the final decision themselves, their spouses (or, for unmarried respondents, someone else, such as a son, sister, manager, or partner) made the final decision, or they reached the final decision jointly with their spouses (or with someone else if they were not married).

On the face of it, this measure is one of the division of decision-making labor, in contrast with the measure of task performance. The categories here are coarser than the usual ones in decision-making studies, where there is often an attempt to measure the extent to which husband and wife take part in joint decision making (with categories of "husband always," "husband more than wife," "both equally," "wife more than husband," "wife always"). Reliability (consistency of response) might be higher here since respondents did not have to choose among as many categories. Some joint decision making might be missed, however, because in the three categories there is no place for the case where one spouse dominates but the other occasionally decides a given type of issue. Further, it asks only about who makes the "final decision," not about how people participate in other ways in making the decision. This is an issue that will be discussed later in this chapter. The impression of women's participation in decision making, especially for the farm, is likely to be a conservative one.

Table 4.1 lists the decision areas and displays the percentages of women who reported each arrangement for each type of decision. (Respondents who indicated that a particular decision had never come up and the very few who did not give a response or said "don't know" are eliminated from the percentage for that item.) Only a very small minority (2 to 4 percent) indicated that they alone had final authority for the six types of farm decisions. Substantial proportions, however, reported sharing decision responsibility in these areas. For example, 58 percent said they shared in decisions about land purchase or sale, and 50 percent shared land rental decisions. Similarly, just under half participated in final decisions about the purchase of major equipment. When it came to trying a new production practice, producing something new, or selling products, fewer women were involved—around 60 percent said someone else usually made the final decision.

These results parallel Wilkening and Bharadwaj's (1967) report of two farm decision-making dimensions: one for decisions about major farm resources (e.g., about buying more land) and the other about farm operation (e.g., whether to try a new production practice). They found somewhat higher participation by wives in the former. Beers in the 1930's, discussed in chapter 1, and Sawer (1973) had similar findings. Wilkening discusses the difference in women's participation in these two types of farm decisions in terms of allocation of family resources: the woman is more involved in decisions that directly affect the family's well-being. "She is more concerned with practices that are observable and affect immediate cash outlay as well as returns, whereas the husband is somewhat more concerned with the management aspect of the land and livestock. The consequences of these management practices for economic return, for prestige, or farm labor-saving may not be as apparent to the wife" (Wilkening and Guerrero 1969:193, quoted in Joyce and Leadley 1977:14). In addition, husbands would normally need to consult women as the farm bookkeepers before they made large outlays of cash. On the other hand, Salamon and Keim (1979:115) argue that in U.S. farm families, as in other societies, "retention of control of production and of distribution of what is produced allows men to be dominant in the family and in the wider community because they gain prestige from these acts." Men control the decisions about production and marketing just as they are more likely to have actual contacts with markets. Further, as reported in chapter 1, while there is some evidence for an increase in women's participation in management decisions, Wilkening (1981) has suggested that women's participation in expansion and reduction decisions has decreased as the credit transactions that can follow from these decisions have become more common.

In contrast with decisions about the farm, more women made decisions about the house (whether to buy major appliances and when to make household repairs) alone (22 percent and 24 percent)

Table 4.1. *Farm Women's Involvement in Home and Farm Decision Making (percentages)*

	Usually respondent	Usually husband/ someone else	Both Together	Total[a]	N[b]
Who usually makes final decisions about:					
A. Whether to buy or sell land	3	39	58	100	2,166
B. Whether to rent more or less land	3	48	50	101	1,915
C. Whether to buy major household appliances[c]	22	4	73	99	2,481
D. Whether to buy major farm equipment	2	52	46	100	2,426
E. Whether to produce something new such as a new crop or a new breed or type of livestock	3	58	39	100	2,175
F. When to sell products	4	60	37	101	2,350
G. When to make household repairs[c]	24	14	62	100	2,468
H. Whether to try a new production practice	3	63	35	101	2,125
I. Whether respondent takes a job off the farm/ranch[c]	41	7	53	101	1,959

[a]Totals differ from 100 due to rounding.

[b]Total excludes those who reported that a particular type of decision had never come up, who did not respond or said "don't know."

[c]Not included in indices of farm decision making.

or with their husbands or someone else (73 percent and 62 percent). Husbands rarely made final decisions alone with respect to the home, suggesting some division of decision-making labor. When it came to something that affected the woman herself most directly—whether to take a job off the farm—women were most likely to say they decided themselves, although over half made the decision with their husbands. As will be seen in Figure 4.1, however, the woman's off-farm employment is more of a couples' joint decision than is the man's employment. Among the men in couples who answered the FWS, 60 percent said they alone usually made the final decision about whether they took an off-farm job.

Indices were created to measure the range of women's decision making similar to those for range of task performance. Decisions were classified as farm (items A, B, D, E, F, and H) or household (items C, G, and I). For each category of decision, two indices were formed: one for the proportion of types of decisions actually relevant to the farm or family that the respondent made alone; the other for the proportion of types of decisions that the respondent made jointly with someone else.[2] A third index measured overall participation in terms of percent of decision types that had come up in which the woman had a final say either alone or jointly.

As was true for the task involvement measures, these indices capture the diversity of respondents' involvement in the listed types of decisions but do not explicitly include how often a respondent made a given type of decision nor the proportion of all specific decisions in which a respondent took part. Thus a respondent who is involved in 75 percent of the *types* of decisions cannot automatically be assumed to make 75 percent of all final decisions. At the same time, there is probably a reasonably strong correspondence between the decision diversity measure and a more specific index of decision-making participation.

The women on average made only 3 percent of the listed types of farm decisions relevant to their operations by themselves, but made 45 percent with their husbands or someone else; 94 percent made none of the types of decisions for their operations by themselves, and 26 percent made none jointly. At the same time, of the types of farm decisions we asked about, almost one-fifth of the women made 100 percent of the decisions jointly or alone.

As would be expected from the responses to questions about the individual types of decisions, the women had the final say in a greater range of the household decisions. On average, they made over one-quarter of them alone and almost two-thirds together with someone else. Nine percent of the women made the final decision for 100 percent of the relevant listed household decisions alone, while almost 40 percent took part in joint final decision making for all of the relevant types of household decisions. On the other hand, 50 percent of the women said that in matters relevant to the home they made none of the final decisions alone, while 16 percent made none jointly. Even with respect to household decisions, there is some variation among women in the extent of their participation.

ASSOCIATION AMONG DIMENSIONS OF DECISION MAKING

In order further to describe farm women's managerial responsibilities, this section looks at the association between making farm and household decisions. Table 4.2 shows these correlations for the FWS. The higher the Pearson correlation coefficient, the more strongly being high on one variable is associated with being high on the other. A coefficient of 1 would indicate a perfect ordering between the variables being compared. Zero indicates no association. A negative coefficient means that someone high on one variable is likely to be low on the other.

Table 4.2 shows that final decision making on one dimension (home or farm) is related to the pattern of final decision making on the other. Women who make larger proportions of types of farm decisions alone tend to make a larger proportion of types of household decisions alone (the correlation equalling .30). Women in households where farm decisions are made jointly also tend to be part of joint household decisions. Rather than home and farm being independent decision-making dimensions, patterns in each area seem to reflect general family decision-making practices. At the same time, the correlations are far from perfect.[3]

Comparison of Husbands' and Wives' Responses

A number of studies of general family decision making have found that when one asks the husband who makes a given decision one does not always get the same answer as when one asks the wife (e.g., Wilkening and Morrison 1963; Filiatrault and Ritchie 1980; Davis 1976; Duncan and Duncan 1978; Douglas and Wind 1978; Huber and Spitze 1983). The FWS also asked the sample of men who made the various decisions. The results from men's responses are similar in overall frequencies to those from women's (see Figure 4.1). (In reading this figure, keep in mind that the response "alone" refers to the wife making the decision alone, except for item I.) There is no consistent evidence of husbands as a group undervaluing their wives' parts in decision making: if anything, they see women playing a greater part than do the women. This is consistent with the results from general research on husband/wife comparisons for household decisions: in the *aggregate* one gets the same picture from husbands as from wives.

Table 4.2. *Pearson Correlations between Dimensions of Decision Making*

	Percent Farm Decision Types Woman Makes Alone	Percent Farm Decision Types Woman Makes Jointly	Percent Farm Decision Types Woman Makes Alone or Jointly
Percent Household Decision Types Woman Makes Alone	.30**	-.27**	-.15**
Percent Household Decision Types Woman Makes Jointly	-.25**	.38**	.28**
Percent Household Decision Types Woman Makes Alone or Jointly	.03*	.24**	.24**

* One tail test, .01 < p < .05.

**One tail test, p < .01.

Within couples here, too, there was a high degree of agreement for household decisions. For the two decisions other than taking an off-farm job (which was asked with a different referent for the women and the men), 57 percent of the couples agreed on the exact percent of types of decisions that the wife made alone and 73 percent agreed on the percent in which the woman participated either alone or jointly. The average difference within couples in the percent of types of household decisions made by the woman alone or with someone else as reported by the husband and the wife of a couple was just about 0. For farm decisions there was less agreement: 28 percent of the couples agreed on the exact percent of types of decisions in which the wife participated. Husbands tended to overestimate the wife's participation as compared with her report (with husbands on average reporting the wife involved in almost 3 percentage points more of the farm decisions types), though this difference is not statistically significant.

Other researchers looking at family decision making have also found that when there are disagreements between husbands' and wives' reports of decision-making patterns, they tend to be in this direction. For example, in a study of decisions about vacationing, Filiatrault and Ritchie (1980:137) report, "In all cases of noncon-

Figure 4.1. *Comparison of Husbands' and Wives' Reports of Wives' Involvement in Home and Farm Decision Making*

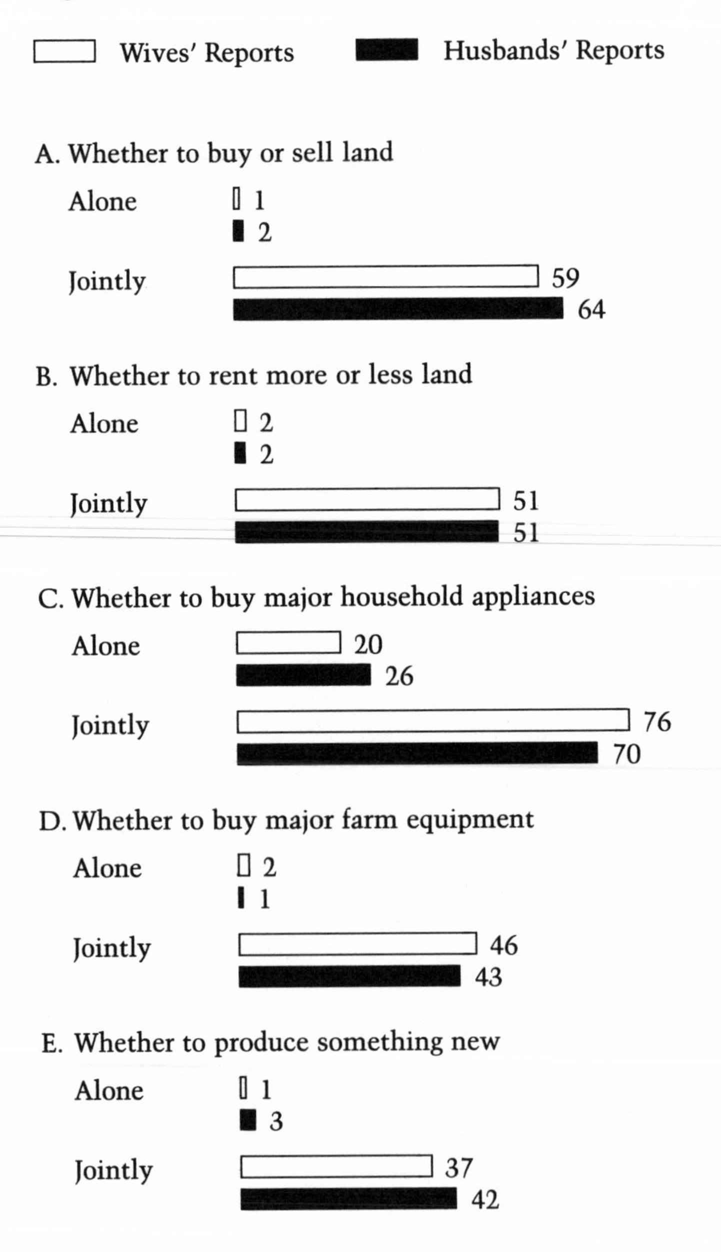

Figure 4.1. (*Continued*)

F. When to sell product

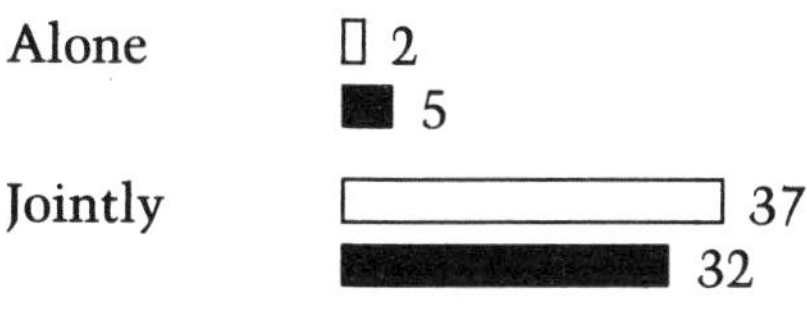

G. When to make household repairs

H. Whether to try new production practice

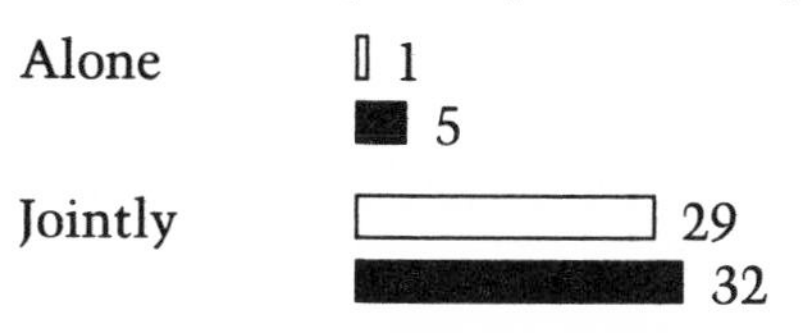

I. Whether husband/wife takes job off-farm

gruency for family responses, the source of role disagreement was found to derive from 'modesty' or 'concession' on the part of the husband." In their study of differences in reports of decision making among farm families, Wilkening and Morrison (1963:350) suggest that one spouse might be giving the socially respectable or expected answer while the other gives a response indicating more the reality. It is difficult, though, to know which spouse is giving which answer. It is possible that women are more likely to report the reality, while men react with the norm of equality. But it could also be true that women report on the basis of the norm of women deferring to men, while their husbands recognize their wives' actual part in decision making.

The goal of using the results from questions on decision making such as those in the FWS is to describe the "objective" situation. One could argue that husband-wife discrepancies are simply mistakes in "correct" reporting on the part of one or the other, and thus it is simply a matter of taking care of such error. One needs to keep in mind, however, that such survey questions give people's *perceptions* of reality, and that different types of people (e.g., wives versus husbands) may experience reality differently. (See the discussion in Douglas and Wind 1978:35–36; Huber and Spitze 1983, chapter 3; and Berk and Shih 1980.) The "real" process of decision making is rarely clearcut. Decisions about the farm, especially, are often made in such a way that it is difficult to assign final responsibility for the decision. The husband may consult a number of people and information sources, and the decision may grow out of these consultations. When husbands consult with their wives, they may see the process as joint decision making, even when their wives report it as the husband making the final decision.

Given the focus of this book on farm women (rather than farm men) and because much of the analysis includes unmarried women and married women whose husbands were not respondents, I will consistently use the women's perceptions of final decision making in the rest of this book, remembering that these make up only one possible set of impressions of what happens.[4]

Farm Women's Satisfaction with Responsibility for Decision Making

Scanzoni and Szinovacz (1980:95) argue that the outcome is an important part of the family decision-making process, with outcome defined not as the objective decision, but "how the decisioning parties evaluate the present status of their discussions, negotiations, or arrangements regarding a certain matter." With their relatively high average involvement in a range of farm tasks, but general lack of autonomous decision making, how did the farm women evaluate their share in the decision-making process? The FWS asked women, "In general, thinking about the part you have in making decisions for the operation of this (farm/ranch), do you feel that you have too much responsibility for these decisions, or would you like to take a greater part in making these decisions?" Despite question wording that offered no choice indicating satisfaction with the amount of decision-making responsibility, a great majority (87 percent) said that they thought the responsibility was about right. Three percent thought they had too much responsibility, 9 percent too little, and 1 percent said they didn't know.

Scanzoni and Szinovacz (1980) predict that there will be a high degree of satisfaction with decision making in couples where husband and wife share the same sex role attitudes. Where both members of the couple believe in traditional sex roles, the wife may have less of a say in the final decision, but be content with such an arrangement. Given reports of widespread attitudes favoring traditional sex roles among farm families, it is possible that this is what is behind these data. Illinois farm women, in our exploratory interviews, said that they often influenced decisions indirectly, leaving the ultimate choice to their husbands, because "he should feel that he is making the decision." Further, Boulding (1980:275) points out that the decisions farmers make involve a great deal of risk. "Many women genuinely do not want to share the risk. Some women reported that their husbands were always bugging them about whether today was a good day to start planting; some men were really begging their wives to share that risk." There are also the "new breed" of young farmers (e.g., Jones-Webb 1982), who believe that the husband and wife are equal partners. To the extent that these couples also share sex role ideologies, they too may find their joint decision making satisfactory. Keep in mind, though, that three times as many women who did not feel their responsibility was about right wanted *more* rather than less responsibility.

Explaining Range of Women's Decision Making

How can one explain the variation among women in their decision-making shares? In this section, multiple regression will be used to examine the range of women's autonomous decision making and the range of women's participation in final decision making (alone or jointly) for the farm and household. As the previous sections of this chapter showed, relatively few women gave the extreme response that they alone were responsible for various types of farm decisions, although more women said they made final household decisions alone. Perceptions of autonomy in making a final decision may have different predictors from a more general measure of farm and home decision-making participation, although perceptions of having any part in coming to a final decision are of interest in their own right.

The analysis will first use the set of farm, family, and the woman's characteristics that was used in the previous chapter to predict women's range of farm and home decision making. As a second step, it will include variables measuring the nature of women's farm, off-farm, and home work. The question of the direction of causality for the work variables is less ambiguous here than it was for analysis relating work in different spheres. Doing the work usually leads to making the decisions, rather than vice versa. While it is possible that someone who does not do the work makes decisions about how the work should be done (e.g., when a person is a farm manager), it is less likely that decision making itself would lead a person to doing tasks. The exception is the task of gathering information. As Sawer (1973) says, it is easy to imagine how someone who makes decisions will as a consequence seek further information. For that reason, results will not be shown with a variable measuring whether a woman got information from Extension. Results including this variable, though, will be discussed in the text.

FARM DECISIONS

Table 4.3 shows the results from regressions of the percent of farm decision types that a woman made alone and that a woman made alone or jointly. The most important variable for autonomous farm decision making is whether a woman was married. Unmarried women made 37 percentage points more farm decision types alone than other women, not controlling for the work a woman did. When the husband was not farming, a woman was somewhat more likely to make decisions alone for the farm. These results support the need hypothesis. The size of the operation also has an effect. Women on larger farms made proportionately fewer types of farm decisions alone. There is no evidence here of a curvilinear relationship with size found by some other analysts, as discussed in chapter 1. However, having other people making decisions for the farm does not affect the percent a woman made alone, net of the other variables. Control of the land, either by the woman herself or by the operation, also has no effect on making decisions alone.

There is little support here for the resource theory of decision making, with the exception of the effect of the farm task variable (and perhaps the crop mix variable). More education, more experience with farm living, older age, and fewer children make no difference. Women, however, who did a wider range of farm tasks regularly did tend to make more farm decisions alone. A woman who did 50 percentage points more types of farm tasks regularly, controlling for everything else, would make 7 percentage points more types of farm decisions alone. Women also made fewer types of solo decisions on farms that produced a mix of livestock and crops or all crops, perhaps because when animals were being raised, women often worked with them. Crop mix, then, may be a proxy for the nature of women's farm work. Getting information from the Extension Service, though, when included, did not change the value of the other coefficients and was not statistically significant. Nor was off-farm employment or involvement in housework important.

Marital status and nature of a husband's work also affect the percent of farm decision types in which a woman reported having a final say either alone or jointly. These effects are similar to those for autonomous farm decisions before adding the work variables. Once the range of work a woman did on and off the farm is controlled, only the absence of a husband has a statistically significant effect. Controlling for the nature of the work a woman did, she would have made 10 percentage points more types of final decisions on the farm if she were unmarried.[5]

The negative effect of size on general participation in final farm decisions is even stronger, however, than on the percent of farm decision types that the woman made alone. The control of land and decision making here affect the woman's part. Although tenancy patterns have no effect on the extent of a woman's joint decision making, women who legally controlled their operation's land shared in 6 percentage points more types of farm decisions, when their various kinds of work were controlled. When other people helped make the decisions, the woman was less likely to take part, although this effect disappears when her work roles are controlled.

There is some support here for the idea that the level of social resources that a person brings to decision making affects how decisions are made: A college education increases somewhat the proportion of farm decision types in which a woman shared. Age again has no effect. The lack of a regular association between age and decision making suggests that the association of age with doing farm tasks is more likely to be one of physical than of sex role ideological inclination.

Table 4.3. *Explaining Variation in Farm Decision-Making Patterns: OLS Regression*

	Dependent Variables			
	Percent of Farm Decision Types Woman Makes Alone			
	Excluding Women's Work Variables		Including Women's Work Variables	
Independent Variables[a]	Unstandard-ized Coefficient	Standardized Coefficient	Unstandard-ized Coefficient	Standardized Coefficient
Farm Characteristics				
Total acres in farm relative to less than 50 acres:				
50-299 acres	-3.40	-.11**	-2.84	-.09**
300-999 acres	-3.83	-.11**	-3.27	-.10**
> 1,000 acres	-5.03	-.12**	-4.21	-.10**
Sales relative to mixed crops and livestock:				
Less than 5 percent total sales from crops	2.20	.07**	1.76	.05*
Greater than 95 percent total sales from crops	.04	.001	.55	.02
Don't know percent of sales from crops	-.05	-.00	.54	.01
Tenancy relative to part owners:				
Full owners	-.56	-.02	-.34	-.01
Renters	2.01	.04	1.44	.03
Neither owners nor renters	1.99	.02	1.54	.02
Woman's Legal Relation to Land				
Own name on deed or rental contract for land	.62	.02	-.16	-.00
Decision Makers				
Include other than husband and wife	.38	.01	.84	.02
Region				
Relative to South:				
Northeast	.60	.02	-.22	-.006
Northcentral	-.21	-.006	-.75	-.02
West	.61	.02	-.17	-.005

Dependent Variables			
Percent of Farm Decision Types Woman Makes Alone or Jointly			
Excluding Women's Work Variables		Including Women's Work Variables	
Unstandardized Coefficient	Standardized Coefficient	Unstandardized Coefficient	Standardized Coefficient
-12.31	-.16**	-9.50	-.13**
-13.90	-.17**	-11.12	-.13**
-20.84	-.20**	-16.71	-.16**
4.67	.06*	2.48	.03
-6.04	-.07**	-3.45	-.04
-7.37	-.05*	-4.28	-.03
-2.54	-.03	-1.43	-.02
.06	.000	-2.83	-.02
-3.66	-.02	-5.64	-.03
9.45	.10**	6.25	.07**
-5.52	-.07**	-3.17	-.04
11.32	.13**	7.04	.08**
7.72	.09**	4.91	.06*
11.35	.13**	7.32	.09**

Table 4.3. *continued*

	Dependent Variables			
	Percent of Farm Decision Types Woman Makes Alone			
	Excluding Women's Work Variables		Including Women's Work Variables	
Independent Variables[a]	Unstandard-ized Coefficient	Standardized Coefficient	Unstandard-ized Coefficient	Standardized Coefficient
Labor Structure of Farm				
More than 1 hired hand	.74	.02	.77	.02
Husband's work relative to husband who regularly does farm work and has no off-farm job:				
No husband	37.09	.51**	34.55	.47**
Husband regularly does farm work and has off-farm job	-1.02	-.03	-1.20	-.04
Husband does not regularly do farm work and has off-farm job	6.65	.10**	5.10	.07**
Husband does not regularly do farm work and has no off-farm job	7.51	.09**	6.81	.08**
Number of sons at least 18 who regularly do farm work	-1.03	-.03	-.91	-.03
Number of children ages 6-17 who regularly do farm work	-.28	-.02	-.51	-.03
Number of other household members who regularly do farm work	-.58	-.01	-.81	-.02
Number of other non-household members who regularly do farm work	.18	.02	.29	.03
Farm Woman's Characteristics				
Education relative to high school graduate:				
Less than high school	.17	.004	.28	.007
Postsecondary vocational or some college	1.49	.04*	1.20	.03
College degree or above	1.66	.04	1.64	.04
Percent of life spent on farms ranches	-.005	-.009	-.01	-.02

Dependent Variables			
Percent of Farm Decision Types Woman Makes Alone or Jointly			
Excluding Women's Work Variables		Including Women's Work Variables	
Unstandard-ized Coefficient	Standardized Coefficient	Unstandard-ized Coefficient	Standardized Coefficient
-1.73	-.02	-1.54	-.02
22.90	.13**	10.31	.06**
3.31	.04	2.31	.03
11.19	.07**	3.44	.02
9.05	.04*	5.67	.03
-2.66	-.03	-2.03	-.03
-.53	-.01	-1.70	-.04*
3.87	.04	2.70	.03
-.95	-.04	-.36	-.01
.47	.005	.96	.01
5.02	.06*	3.52	.04
7.53	.07**	7.43	.07**
.07	.06*	.03	.03

Table 4.3. *continued*

	Dependent Variables			
	Percent of Farm Decision Types Woman Makes Alone			
	Excluding Women's Work Variables		Including Women's Work Variables	
Independent Variables[a]	Unstandard-ized Coefficient	Standardized Coefficient	Unstandard-ized Coefficient	Standardized Coefficient
Farm Women's Characteristics (cont'd)				
Age relative to over 65:				
less than 31	2.27	.05	.58	.01
31-45	3.17	.10*	1.52	.05
46-65	2.13	.07	1.00	.03
Dependent Children				
Number of children less than age 6	-1.14	-.04	-.87	-.03
Number of children 6-17 who do not regularly do farm work	-.13	-.007	.08	.004
Woman's Work				
Woman currently employed off-farm	---	---	-.23	-.007
Percent farm tasks woman does regularly	---	---	.14	.20**
Involvement in housework[b]	---	---	-1.64	-.02
Constant	1.73		-1.42	
R^2	.31		.35	
N[c]	2,027			

* .01 < p < .05.

** p < .01.

[a]For categorical variables, 1 = yes, 0 = no.

[b]1 = Never does housework, 2 = does occasionally, 3 = regular duty.

[c]N's less than 2,509 because of missing data.

Dependent Variables			
Percent of Farm Decision Types Woman Makes Alone or Jointly			
Excluding Women's Work Variables		Including Women's Work Variables	
Unstandard-ized Coefficient	Standardized Coefficient	Unstandard-ized Coefficient	Standardized Coefficient
.81	.007	-7.90	-.06
5.06	.07	-3.34	-.04
.34	.005	-5.44	-.07
-1.98	-.03	-.54	-.009
-2.58	-.05*	-1.52	-.03
---	---	-.86	-.01
---	---	.70	.42**
---	---	-5.10	-.03
28.40		16.62	
.13		.29	
2,027			

Again, the percent of types of farm tasks a woman did regularly increases the part she played in decision making, and is the most important variable here. Getting information from the Extension Service, when included, has a significant effect on decision-making participation as well. Those who sought advice or information from Extension Service personnel in the preceding 2 to 3 years, net of all other variables, made 9 percentage points more types of final farm decisions alone or jointly. Product mix has an effect: Women from farms where sales were almost totally from crops took part in a smaller percent of types of farm decisions. But here there is evidence that this *is* a result of the range of tasks women did, since controlling for this variable wipes out the effect of product mix.

Whether women made decisions alone or jointly varies by region. A common saying, "the South is different," applies to these results. It is not possible, though, to say in what way the difference between the South and other regions influences women's part in making farm decisions; it may be differences in the structure of operations, in sex role attitudes, or something else.

In these results there is some support for the idea that both the need for the woman's input and her own resources affect decision-making patterns, although most operationalizations of these concepts have no effect. Overall, the nature of the operation, especially its size, the work a woman did on it (but not in the home or off the farm), and the presence of a husband influence the woman's part in final farm decision making more than any other of her, her farm, or her family's characteristics.

HOUSEHOLD DECISIONS

Table 4.4 presents the analysis of women's share in types of household decisions. Again one sees marital status, operation characteristics, and the nature of a woman's work predicting the woman's part in household decision making. For decisions made alone, marital status plays the strongest part. When a woman was not married, she made more decisions alone. When she had a husband (employed or not off the farm) who did not regularly do farm work, she alone made somewhat more of the types of household decisions (effects that are consistently significant when the respondents who did not know their husbands' incomes are included). Not playing a continuing regular part in the farm work seems to take the husband away from household decision making, perhaps because he is not as concerned with home-farm resource allocation or is not physically around the house as much.

The characteristic of the operation that has the largest effect here is whether the farm had more than one hired hand. When it did, the woman made about 6 percentage points more types of household decisions by herself. No other labor structure variable makes a difference. It is possible that farms with more hired hands were those where the husband or someone else acted as a farm manager and had less time or interest for family decisions. It may also represent situations in which household decisions were less contingent on farm resource decisions. On larger farms women made more types of household decisions alone (effects that are statistically significant when the respondents who did not know their husbands' off-farm incomes are included), perhaps again representing the demands of managing the operation on a husband or someone else with whom a woman might have discussed family decisions, as well as the separation of farm and household resources.

There is very little evidence that social resources and constraints affect farm women's autonomous household decision making, with the major exception of the effects of the employment variable. To the extent that having an off-farm job represents social resources, it pays off in increasing the range of household decision types that a woman made alone.

Farm, family, and women's characteristics are able to explain very little of the variance in the percent of household decisions in which women had any say, whether alone or with someone else. The R^2 is .04, meaning that 4 percent of the variance is explained by the independent variables, a statistically significant but substantively small amount. Probably one reason for this is that such a high proportion of women took some part in almost all of the household decisions about which the FWS asked: there is very little variation to be explained.

The labor structure characteristic that has a significant effect here is the number of sons in the household doing farm work. One might expect such an effect on women's part in farm rather than household decisions. One could speculate that, because resources for the home are often also potential resources for the farm, when an adult son is present women are not as likely to have a say in how the resources are divided. Or adult sons may have wives who are in charge of household decisions. Of course, this significant result could have occurred by chance. The farm characteristic that ap-

Table 4.4. *Explaining Variation in Household Decision-Making Patterns: OLS Regression*

	Dependent Variables			
	Percent Household Decision Types Woman Makes Alone			
	Excluding Women's Work Variables		Including Women's Work Variables	
Independent Variables[a]	Unstandardized Coefficient	Standardized Coefficient	Unstandardized Coefficient	Standardized Coefficient
Farm Characteristics				
Total acres in farm relative to less than 50 acres:				
50–299 acres	3.12	.05	3.35	.05
300–999 acres	2.92	.04	3.45	.05
> 1,000 acres	3.59	.04	4.47	.05
Sales relative to mixed crops and livestock				
Less than 5 percent total sales from crops	-.37	-.005	-.37	-.005
Greater than 95 percent total sales from crops	-2.09	-.03	-2.05	-.03
Don't know percent of sales from crops	-.76	-.006	-.59	-.005
Tenancy relative to part owners:				
Full owners	-2.53	-.04	-2.45	-.04
Renters	.53	.004	.29	.002
Neither owners nor renters	-5.60	-.03	-6.12	-.03
Woman's Legal Relation to Land				
Own name on deed or rental contract for land	-.14	-.002	-.20	-.002
Decision Makers				
Include other than husband and wife	2.74	.04	2.67	.04
Region				
Relative to South:				
Northeast	-5.12	-.07*	-4.92	-.07*
Northcentral	-4.29	-.06*	-4.09	-.06
West	-2.05	-.03	-1.75	-.02

Dependent Variables			
Percent Household Decision Types Woman Makes Alone/Jointly			
Excluding Women's Work Variables		Including Women's Work Variables	
Unstandard-ized Coefficient	Standardized Coefficient	Unstandard-ized Coefficient	Standardized Coefficient
-1.65	-.04	-1.47	-.04
-.95	-.02	-.51	-.01
-1.46	-.03	-.64	-.01
-.66	-.02	-.85	-.02
-2.46	-.06*	-2.11	-.05*
-6.92	-.10**	-6.22	-.09**
-.79	-.02	-.64	-.02
3.15	.05	2.77	.04
-3.33	-.03	-3.04	-.03
2.37	.05	2.08	.05
1.89	.05	2.08	.05
1.82	.04	1.30	.03
3.39	.08**	3.06	.07*
2.51	.06*	2.10	.05

Table 4.4. *continued*

	Dependent Variables			
	Percent Household Decision Types Woman Makes Alone			
	Excluding Women's Work Variables		Including Women's Work Variables	
Independent Variables[a]	Unstandardized Coefficient	Standardized Coefficient	Unstandardized Coefficient	Standardized Coefficient
Labor Structure of Farm				
More than 1 hired hand	6.28	.09**	6.36	.09**
Husband's work relative to husband who regularly does farm work and has no off-farm job:				
No husband	48.76	.31**	47.30	.30**
Husband regularly does farm work and has off-farm job	1.58	.02	.93	.01
Husband does not regularly do farm work and has off-farm job	5.30	.04	4.67	.03
Husband does not regularly do farm work and has no off-farm job	8.05	.04*	7.82	.04
Number of sons at least 18 who regularly do farm work	-.52	-.007	-.32	-.004
Number of children ages 6-17 who regularly do farm work	-1.53	-.04	-1.37	-.04
Number of other household members who regularly do farm work	-.93	-.01	-1.00	-.01
Number of other non-household members who regularly do farm work	.007	.00	.03	.001
Farm Woman's Characteristics				
Education relative to high school graduate:				
Less than high school	2.59	.03	2.84	.03
Postsecondary vocational or some college	2.84	.04	2.29	.03
College degree or above	3.20	.03	2.00	.02
Percent of life spent on farms or ranches	.001	.00	.001	.00

Dependent Variables			
Percent Household Decision Types Woman Makes Alone/Jointly			
Excluding Women's Work Variables		Including Women's Work Variables	
Unstandard-ized Coefficient	Standardized Coefficient	Unstandard-ized Coefficient	Standardized Coefficient
.68	.02	.93	.02
.54	.01	-.66	-.007
-.24	-.006	-.97	-.03
-2.71	-.03	-3.52	-.04
.25	.002	.31	.003
-3.07	-.08**	-2.90	-.07**
-.67	-.04	-.64	-.03
1.06	.02	.92	.02
-.31	-.02	-.23	-.02
-2.17	-.04	-2.11	-.04
1.42	.03	.82	.02
2.11	.04	1.24	.02
.01	.02	.006	.01

Table 4.4. *continued*

	Dependent Variables			
	Percent Household Decision Types Woman Makes Alone			
	Excluding Women's Work Variables		Including Women's Work Variables	
Independent Variables[a]	Unstandard-ized Coefficient	Standardized Coefficient	Unstandard-ized Coefficient	Standardized Coefficient
Farm Women's Characteristics (cont'd)				
Age relative to over 65:				
less than 31	-.41	.004	-2.68	-.02
31-45	.53	.008	-1.76	-.03
46-65	1.81	.03	.50	.008
Dependent Children				
Number of children less than age 6	-2.68	-.05	-1.95	-.03
Number of children 6-17 who do not regularly do farm work	-.26	-.006	.04	.00
Woman's Work				
Woman currently employed off-farm	--	--	4.23	.06**
Percent farm tasks woman does regularly	--	--	.04	.03
Involvement in housework[b]	--	--	-5.48	-.03
Constant	29.32		30.70	
R^2	.13		.13	
N[c]	2,027			

* $.01 \leq p < .05$.

** $p < .01$.

[a]For categorical variables, 1 = yes, 0 = no.

[b]See Table 4.3.

[c]N's are less than 2,509 because of missing data.

Dependent Variables			
Percent Household Decision Types Woman Makes Alone/Jointly			
Excluding Women's Work Variables		Including Women's Work Variables	
Unstandard-ized Coefficient	Standardized Coefficient	Unstandard-ized Coefficient	Standardized Coefficient
3.46	.06	.72	.01
3.11	.08	.68	.02
3.63	.10*	2.11	.06
-.08	-.003	.64	.02
.20	.009	.49	.02
--	--	3.82	.10**
--	--	.07	.08**
--	--	4.89	.05*
91.32		103.53	
.04		.06	
2,027			

pears significant in these equations is the dependence of the operation on crops for sale. When almost all sales came from crops, women made 2 percentage points fewer of the final household decisions on the FWS. This might have been an effect of the type of work the woman did on the farm, though the effect decreases only slightly when the range of farm work is included. There are also some regional effects, although this time it is the Northcentral region that stands out as an area in which women made relatively more household decisions.

All three measures of work roles are significant (although when women who did not know their husbands' off-farm income are included, involvement with housework is not statistically significant). Having an off-farm job again increases women's say in household decisions, whether she took part autonomously or jointly, consistent with results of nonfarm family decision-making studies. But having housework as a regular duty and doing a greater range of farm tasks also increase women's participation in making household decisions. These effects are consistent with the notion that decisions for the household are not always separate from decisions about the farm, an idea supported by the earlier results showing some association between decision-making shares across the two dimensions. Women who did housework might have had more of an interest in what was bought for the house and when things were repaired. But, controlling for everything else, women who were more active on the operation, especially with the bookkeeping, might have been able to help more with final decisions about the allocation of resources between house and farm. The negative effect of not knowing the percent of sales from crops fits in with this explanation. (Getting advice or information from Extension personnel, though, was not significant when included.) Doing farm work pays off in terms of decision making for both the farm and home while doing work in the home affects decision making only in the domestic realm. When those with missing data on husbands' off-farm income were included, another type of resource—education—significantly affected household decision making: Those with less than a high school degree took part in fewer household decisions.

In general, farm characteristics, a male presence, and the woman's work roles affect women's part in household decision making more strongly than other measures of their resources or of the make-up of their families. While the particular variables differ from those affecting decision making for the farm, the overall similarity in the types of factors reinforces the idea that for farm families, farm and household are not separate domains.

RELATIVE RESOURCE LEVELS WITHIN COUPLES

For both farm and household decision-making patterns, the usual measures of social resources and constraints have only a minor influence. As mentioned in the introduction to this chapter, however, some students of family decision making argue that the relative resources of husbands and wives within families are important, not the absolute levels.

To see whether this was the case for farm couples, the analysis of patterns of farm and household decision making was repeated including comparisons of the age, farm experience, education and off-farm income of the spouses rather than simply using the woman's characteristics. While women were asked about such variables for themselves, they were not asked about most of them for their husbands. Men who were part of the FWS, though, were asked about their own level of education, etc. By using the data on couples in which both spouses were FWS respondents, it is possible to compare husband's and wife's resources. In this section only the regressions for farm decision-making patterns are shown, since the overall regressions for household decision patterns were not statistically significant when estimated with the couples' data.[6]

As can be seen in Table 4.5, when the husband had higher off-farm income than the wife, the wife made a larger range of farm decisions by herself. This variable may represent the husband's employment per se rather than the relative resources that the spouses bring to decision making. There is no other support here for the hypothesis that spouses' relative resources affect decision-making patterns. The husband's and wife's farm work roles play the largest part. When the husband regularly did farm work, the woman made a smaller percent of final decisions about the farm alone, and when the wife did a greater range of farm tasks, she made a larger proportion of the final decisions herself.

In the analysis of the extent to which the wife played a part either alone or with her husband in making final decisions about the operation, there is some support for the idea that spouses' relative resources affect their patterns of decision making. When the husband had spent a smaller proportion of his life living and working on farms than had his wife, she took part in a wider range of farm

Table 4.5. *Explaining Variation in Farm Decision-Making Patterns: FWS Couples and Relative Resources, OLS Regression*

	Dependent Variables			
	Percent of Farm Decision Types Wife Makes Alone			
	Excluding Wife's Work Variables		Including Wife's Work Variables	
Independent Variables[a]	Unstandard-ized Coefficient	Standardized Coefficient	Unstandard-ized Coefficient	Standardized Coefficient
Farm Characteristics				
Total acres in farm relative to less than 50 acres:				
50–299 acres	-1.32	-.09	-.81	-.06
300–999 acres	-2.43	-.15*	-1.92	-.12
> 1,000 acres	-3.71	-.20**	-2.78	-.15*
Sales relative to mixed crops and livestock:				
Less than 5 percent total sales from crops	1.49	.09	1.91	.12*
Greater than 95 percent total sales from crops	-1.08	-.07	-.57	-.04
Tenancy relative to part owners:				
Full owners	-2.15	-.15**	-1.92	-.13*
Renters	.47	.02	.82	.03
Neither owners nor renters	-2.48	-.05	-2.72	-.06
Woman's Legal Relation to Land				
Wife's name on deed or rental contract for land	-.32	-.02	-.27	-.01
Decision Makers				
Include other than husband and wife	1.13	.07	1.82	.11*
Region				
Relative to South:				
Northeast	.96	.06	.34	.02
Northcentral	1.37	.09	.72	.05
West	2.22	.13*	1.50	.09

Dependent Variables			
Percent of Farm Decision Types Wife Makes Alone or Jointly			
Excluding Wife's Work Variables		Including Wife's Work Variables	
Unstandardized Coefficient	Standardized Coefficient	Unstandardized Coefficient	Standardized Coefficient
-5.33	-.07	-2.37	-.03
-11.35	-.14	-8.30	-.10
-17.07	-.17*	-11.31	-.11
-4.44	-.05	-1.90	-.02
-10.72	-.13*	-7.46	-.09
-3.35	-.04	-1.80	-.02
-8.62	-.06	-6.55	-.05
-8.83	-.04	-9.97	-.04
3.77	.04	4.01	.04
-5.63	-.06	-1.03	-.01
5.70	.07	1.54	.02
2.47	.03	-1.87	-.02
9.26	.10	4.39	.05

Table 4.5. *continued*

	Dependent Variables			
	Percent of Farm Decision Types Wife Makes Alone			
	Excluding Wife's Work Variables		Including Wife's Work Variables	
Independent Variables[a]	Unstandardized Coefficient	Standardized Coefficient	Unstandardized Coefficient	Standardized Coefficient
Labor Structure of Farm				
More than 1 hired hand	.95	.06	1.17	.08
Husband regularly does farm work	-5.96	-.23**	-5.16	-.20**
Number of sons at least 18 who regularly do farm work	-.37	-.02	-.11	-.007
Number of children ages 6-17 who regularly do farm work	.25	.03	.07	.009
Number of other household members who regularly do farm work	.45	.02	.40	.02
Number of other non-household members who regularly do farm work	.17	.02	.21	.03
Couple's relative Characteristics[b]				
Relative education	-.34	-.06	-.27	-.05
Relative age	-.03	-.02	-.02	-.01
Relative income	.07	.14**	.06	.12*
Relative percent of life spent on farms	-.02	-.10*	-.01	-.05

Dependent Variables			
ercent of Farm Decision Types Wife Makes Alone or Jointly			
Excluding Wife's Work Variables		Including Wife's Work Variables	
Unstandard-ized Coefficient	Standardized Coefficient	Unstandard-ized Coefficient	Standardized Coefficient
-4.28	-.05	-2.77	-.03
5.12	.04	10.17	.07
-4.28	-.05	-2.66	-.03
-1.33	-.03	-2.46	-.06
-5.90	-.04	-6.31	-.05
-2.89	-.08	-2.58	-.07
1.45	.05	1.89	.06
-.75	-.08	-.71	-.08
-.19	-.07	-.27	-.10
-.24	-.19**	-.16	-.13**

Table 4.5. *continued*

	Dependent Variables			
	Percent of Farm Decision Types Wife Makes Alone			
	Excluding Wife's Work Variables		Including Wife's Work Variables	
Independent Variables[a]	Unstandard-ized Coefficient	Standardized Coefficient	Unstandard-ized Coefficient	Standardized Coefficient
Dependent Children				
Number of children less than age 6	-.49	-.04	-.43	-.04
Number of children 6-17 who do not regularly do farm work	-.04	-.004	-.03	-.003
Woman's Work				
Percent farm tasks woman does regularly	—	—	.10	.30**
Involvement in housework[c]	—	—	-.54	-.02
Constant	9.98		6.51	
R^2	.17		.24	
N[d]	404			

* $.01 \leq p < .05$.

** $p < .01$.

[a]For categorical variables, 1 = yes, 0 = no.

[b]These variables are formed by subtracting the wife's value from the husband's: H-W.

[c]See Table 4.3.

[d]N's less than 497 because of missing data.

Dependent Variables			
Percent of Farm Decision Types Wife Makes Alone or Jointly			
Excluding Wife's Work Variables		Including Wife's Work Variables	
Unstandard-ized Coefficient	Standardized Coefficient	Unstandard-ized Coefficient	Standardized Coefficient
1.69	.03	1.99	.03
-1.95	-.04	-1.82	-.04
--	--	.61	.36**
--	--	-.05	-.00
48.28		30.46	
.13		.24	
404			

decisions. The wife's current involvement in the operation, however, is the most important variable predicting her participation in farm decision making.[7]

Thus actual work roles, which may be affected by the other characteristics of a couple, seem to be more important in the participation of the wife than relative resources, although relative farm experience plays some part.

"Pay" for Farm Work

In this and the previous chapter, I have looked at the woman's work both in doing tasks and in making decisions on her operation and in her household. In the next chapter I take up the issue of off-farm work. Generally, for this work the women received a wage. This is not always the case for women doing farm work on their own operations and is almost never the case for their doing housework in their own homes. The FWS data set has no way to measure whether a woman received a regular payment for doing the housework. It also did not explicitly ask whether the woman received a wage for her farm work. It did, however, ask whether the woman was the payee on the checks received for any of the products the operation sold. Having one's name on a check could be seen as representing the woman's control over the product of her operation and as rewarding her for her labor. One-third of the FWS women said that they had had their own names on a product check. The first hypothesis about who these women are would be that they are those who did a wider range of work on their farms and who participated more in the decision making. A second hypothesis would be that, net of the woman's participation on the operation, whether her name was on the check was affected by the nature of the operation. Larger farms may be incorporated and have the name of the corporation (rather than an individual) on a check.

To test these hypotheses, I did a logistic regression on whether the woman had her name on a check for the operation's products (results not shown). I included first the percent of farm task types that the woman did regularly and the percent of farm decision types in which she participated. I next added the measures of farm, the woman's, and family characteristics that appear in the other models. Both task and decision-making participation increased the likelihood that a woman had her name on a product check. However, the predictive ability of these two variables was fairly low, as indicated by a D of only .09. To see whether adding the other variables improved the fit of the model, I compared the chi-square statistic for the more inclusive model with that for the more parsimonious one. The difference between the two chi-squares is distributed as chi-square with degrees of freedom equal to the differences in the degrees of freedom between the two models. Here the chi-square for the difference was 28.81, with thirty-two degrees of freedom, which is not statistically significant. Adding the other variables did not significantly add to the model.

The parameter estimates for the larger model did not show effects of operation size, although having an operation more dependent on crops for its sales decreased the likelihood of the woman's name being on the check, perhaps reflecting a greater involvement of women in rearing livestock. Being single and having one's name on a deed or rental agreement significantly increased the chance that a woman had her name on a check. This analysis suggests that legal arrangements relating to the operation probably affect whether the woman is officially recognized as a producer (in the sense of getting paid directly for the product) more than other aspects of the farm. Further, in some cases it might be to the financial advantage of the family not to have the woman's name on a check. While in some families traditional ideas about who is the farmer may play a part in whose name is on the check, in others one would expect practical and legal concerns, rather than purely symbolic ones, to be the deciding factor (see also Salamon and Markan 1984).

Conclusions

This chapter has examined patterns of farm and household decision making. A large proportion of the types of decisions made for the farm and the home were made jointly by the farm woman and another person, usually her husband. There is some association, too, between the proportion of farm and home decision types that are made jointly, perhaps reflecting general patterns of joint decision making among farm couples. At the same time, women were more likely to take sole responsibility for household decisions, while men were more likely to make farm decisions on their own. Further, among the types of farm decisions, men were more likely to keep control of production decisions. There is evidence, then, of some sexual division of labor with respect to decision making, with men dominating in the farm area, especially in production, and women dominating in the household arena.

Husbands, if anything, overestimated the parts their wives played in farm and home decision making, as compared with their wives' reports of how things were decided. And the women were in general satisfied with the amount of responsibility that they had for decisions. As was discussed in this chapter, such results may indicate that men hold norms of joint decision making while still making many of the final decisions themselves, while their wives are satisfied with this situation because they share traditional sex role ideologies with their husbands. At the same time, one needs to keep in mind the large extent of joint decision making. When women were *not* satisfied with how much responsibility they had, they wanted more rather than less.

Doing tasks was related to making decisions in a given domain. The wider the range of a woman's farm tasks, the greater the proportion of types of farm decisions she made. Women more involved in doing housework took part in more types of household decisions. However, with respect to household decisions, doing other sorts of work—bringing in money from off the farm and doing a wider range of farm work—had even stronger effects. Cross-societal research has emphasized that labor contributions are only a necessary but not sufficient condition for women to have higher status and power (e.g., Blumberg 1978; Friedl 1975). Control of production and distribution and of scarce resources are necessary as well. Farm decision making could be seen as a measure of control of production and distribution. Doing economically important work affects such control, although it certainly does not explain all variations in enterprise decision-making patterns, and the influence of doing such work seems to spill over into decision making about other areas as well.

Net of their own work contributions, at least some of the women's part in decision making depended on what their husbands were doing. A woman seemed to take more or less part in farm decision making depending on whether her husband was less or more engaged in farming. Those with no husbands were much more likely to make farm decisions on their own, even controlling for the range of their farm task performance. Those with no husbands also made more types of household decisions alone. Again, there is a sense that women fill in when a husband is not present. The nature of the operation also affected how the decision making was divided.

Women on larger farms and on farms that received most of their revenue from crops did a smaller range of farm decision making. The labor structure of the farm, as measured by whether there were two or more hired hands, affected household decision making, too. On farms with hired help, the woman made more household decisions on her own. When an adult son farmed, she took part in fewer household decisions alone or jointly. These labor structure effects were also interpreted as indicating women taking over decision making or being displaced depending on the presence of men to make decisions. The family's (and woman's) measures of control over land and other decision making played very little part, contrary to what was expected. There was only limited evidence that the women's absolute or relative resources (aside from those measured by the work variables) affected patterns of decision making for the farm or home, and no evidence that having young children was any constraint. Given that the range of farm work done also depended on the presence (and activities) of a husband and on the size of the farm (perhaps representing the degree of the enterprise's hierarchical control), these results suggest that future research on farm family decision making should focus more on family power relationships than on resources or extrafamily control.

Playing a part in decision making, as well as in doing the tasks of a farm, increased the chances that a woman was directly paid for the farm's products, in the sense of having her name on the check. This association, though, was relatively weak. Whether the woman's name is on a check probably reflects a host of other legal, practical, and family arrangements as well.

The analysis of this chapter can take us only so far in understanding families' decision making. If nothing else, the results are limited by focusing only on women and men operators. While some of the independent variables tap other decision makers or potential decision makers, the influence of such actors is not explicitly traced. Beyond this, there is the problem of using final-say measures rather than examining the decision-making *process* (McDonald 1980). This process includes defining something as an issue about which a decision is to be made. A considerable amount of control over a situation can be exercised in terms of deciding what is and what is not to be on the decision-making agenda. Further, while those studying family power relationships often use decision making to measure the power structure, power is not always exerted by making decisions. Sometimes it is exercised through delegating decision-making power or by letting another make decisions by default. Husbands might delegate household decisions to their wives, for example. Salamon and Keim (1979), in their study of landholding and women's power in a central Illinois farm community, explicitly recognized that women could concede decision making to men and exert power by the choice of the men to whom they gave use of the land. As a decision is made, there may be a process of negotiation, influence, and compromise, perhaps affected by the nature of decisions made in the past. Even when a decision is made, it may be implemented in a way different from that decided upon (McDonald 1980; Scanzoni and Szinovacz 1980). When tracing a particular decision through these stages, though, one does not always get a good sense of how the characteristics of a family and farm affect and are affected by the decision-making process.

It is difficult to capture the whole process of household decision making in a general survey such as the FWS, although some modifications of the final-say questions would be possible. Of more use are longitudinal studies such as Elbert and Colman's, which used a variety of techniques to get a sense of how different members of a family perceived the decision-making process and their part in it over time. But combining results of different sorts of studies can at least give us some idea of where to look to understand family power relationships and the roles women play in decision making both for their homes and for their farms.

5
Off-Farm Employment

The phenomenon of people in farming doing at least some off-farm work is of importance all over the world. "The bare statistics state that in Germany, 55 percent of all farms are part-time farms, producing about one-third of the total farm output; in the UK some 24 percent of farmers, partners and directors of farm businesses are classified as part-time; in Japan over 87 percent in 1974 of farm households had other sources of income and employment. In Norway only one third of the farms were the sole source of income for the farmers working them" (Fuguitt et al. 1977:i). As discussed in chapter 1, increasing proportions of people in the United States are going off the farm for at least some of their income while continuing to farm. In developing countries, too, farming simultaneously with another job is, or is becoming, a way of life. Wherever significant proportions of those in agriculture also engage in other sorts of work, there is "an interface between policies for agriculture, policies for non-farm employment in rural areas and social policies for rural families" (Fuguitt et al. 1977:1).

The discussion of off-farm employment is often couched in terms of "part-time farming." This term is one about which there is much ambiguity and debate (Coughenour and Wimberley 1982; Frauendorfer 1966; Fuguitt et al. 1977; Mage 1976; Kada 1980). Sometimes part-time farming is defined by time employed off the farm but in other cases in terms of relative off-farm income. Too often the discussion is about part-time *farmers*, usually meaning the male operator who also works off the farm, rather than about part-time farms, on which any household member could bring the farm into the part-time category. If an operation were classified as part-time when over half of the family's income (as measured by net farm income plus spouses' off-farm incomes) was from off-farm sources, then about 37 percent of the FWS respondents would come from part-time farms (Ross 1982). This chapter will examine the off-farm work of the women and men in the Farm Women Survey. Because the focus is on women's work and the sexual division of labor, I will look at the extent and nature of off-farm employment directly, rather than using it as a basis for categorizing farms or farm people as part-time or not. Before turning to the FWS data, however, I will discuss in more detail the issues associated in the United States with off-farm employment and with farm women's versus farm men's employment.

Off-Farm Employment Issues

The meaning and implications of off-farm employment depend on who is doing it, for how long, and with what impact on the farms. At least some of the increase in the percentage of farm operators with a primary occupation other than farming could signify an increase in "hobby" farmers, those who farm as a sideline out of preference or for a tax break, with a primary commitment to another occupation. Part-time farming can also be part of the process of leaving or entering farming (Hathaway and Perkins 1968:348; Kada 1980:88–89). In still other cases, taking off-farm jobs may be an intermittent way of supplementing family income. Looking at part-time farm operators (working off the farm at least 100 days a year) in Kentucky in 1973, Coughenour and Gabbard (1977) found remarkable stability in combining farming with another occupation: on average, these farmers had been part-time over 8 years, and a majority intended to continue that way. Whereas earlier part-time farming may have been part of a transition into or out of farming, it now seems to be a permanent way of life for many families (Simpson and Wilson 1983).

As mentioned in chapter 1, the proportion of income from off-farm employment is greater on smaller farms, and off-farm employment not only keeps small farms operating but also keeps their family incomes up (Sander 1981; Hanson 1972; Huffman 1977). Expansion would be an alternative way to increase income on small farms because larger operations can be more efficient by invoking economies of scale unavailable to smaller farms (Quance and Tweeten 1972, Fig. 2.1; Madden and Partenheimer 1972; though see also Lodwick and Morrison 1982; Greene 1978). But expansion usually takes cash. Wilkening (1981) found that for at least some farmers in Wisconsin, off-farm work was a substitute for expansion. Of course, the cash from off-farm employment may provide the capital for later expansion.

It is not just the level of actual earnings from a given activity, such as farming, but also the certainty of getting that income that can affect the choices people make. Farming is risky. A farmer cannot be certain of high earnings even with high productivity, given fluctuation in farm prices. In the face of risk in one activity, one can diversify into other activities with lower risks or with risks that are not affected by the same factors as those associated with the first activity. At least one sort of diversification in farming is in product. For example, at least in the past, hogs were a fairly low-risk venture and were raised as a source of cash on farms with some other major product. Diversification, like expansion, however, may take capital that is not available. Another way to diversify is by going off the farm for employment, especially nonagricultural employment where the risk of unemployment is less dependent on the booms and busts of agriculture. (See the discussions in Sumner 1978, and in Hannan 1973.) The form of diversification will depend on the relative gains from diversifying on the farm versus the wages off the farm. In the few cases where measures of diversity have been examined, greater on-farm diversity has been found to decrease significantly the probability of working off the farm (e.g., Sumner 1978).

Pull factors, in addition to push forces, may be increasing off-farm employment. Jobs have expanded in rural areas. "Jobs in every major industry increased faster in nonmetropolitan counties than in metropolitan areas during the 1970s. Between 1970 and 1976, rural employment grew by 12 percent compared to 8 percent in metropolitan counties" (Brewer 1981:8). The greater labor force participation of men and women in the South, where there have been more nonagricultural industrial jobs in rural areas, also suggests that availability of jobs is a factor influencing whether at a particular time a farm person has an off-farm job (Brown and O'Leary 1979; U.S. Bureau of the Census 1980; Sweet 1972; Jones and Rosenfeld 1981). It is even possible that at least some farmers are better able to compete in the nonfarm labor market than the often less-educated agricultural wage laborers, and that off-farm employed farmers receive salaries that enable them to hire cheaper labor to substitute for them on the farm (Sander 1981). One study of changes in source of labor on part-time farms, though, found that most additional labor came from the family or was from the outside just for specific tasks (Kada 1980:103).

At the same time that part-time farming increases the levels and stability of farm family incomes and reflects expansion of employment opportunities, there is concern about what such activity might mean for agricultural productivity and for the level of farm prices and rural incomes. Employment off the farm may take hours that would have been spent on the farm. Kada (1980) reported that of the Wisconsin operators who went from full-time farming to part-time farming, or who had started out part-time farming, 37 percent said that they had reduced the labor needs of the operation by changing type of production or by reducing acreage or number of livestock. Taking people and time away from agriculture could hurt agricultural productivity in general (e.g., Low 1981; Coughenour and Wimberley 1982:352–53; Gladwin and Downie 1982). If the farm does not provide enough net income, however, there may be no choice but to seek off-farm employment. In the Rural Income Maintenance Experiment, in which some samples of rural families received transfer payments, if necessary, to maintain a given minimum income level, those in the experimental groups reported more hours of on-farm work and less of off-farm work than those who were in the control groups. The decline in off-farm work was especially noticeable for wives. However, this increase in on-farm work did not seem to increase productivity, farm profits, or technical efficiency. (See Saupe 1977:20–22.) Even when overall productivity is not affected, farm prices and rural wages might be. If farm incomes are subsidized by off-farm wages, then farm prices can remain low without losing as many families from farming as would otherwise occur. Further, off-farm wages can remain low, because they are subsidized by farm income. To the extent that farm wages were set relative to off-farm wages, they too would remain depressed.

One thing that is often missing from discussions of off-farm employment is the farm family. Yet farms are usually family enterprises, and the strategies to keep them going are strategies that involve all the family members. Who does how much of what kind of work depends on the relative opportunities for the different household members as well as the needs of the home and farm. Cross-culturally and historically, there is no one pattern that predominates. As mentioned in chapter 1, in nineteenth-century Europe and New England, daughters often went to the factories and were expected to send money back to their families (Scott and Tilly

1975; Baker 1964). In South Africa (Thadani 1981) and in Colorado (Moen et al. 1981:22), men went to work in the mines while women continued the agricultural work. In some situations, part-time farming has meant that both husband and wife are employed off the farm (Gladwin and Downie 1982; Coughenour and Swanson 1983; Kada 1980). Sweet (1972) found that wives with farm residences whose husbands had both farm and nonfarm incomes had slightly above-average employment rates themselves. With respect to all U.S. farms, little is known about the distribution of off-farm employment within families. This chapter will look at the division of labor between members of the farm couple with respect to off-farm employment and at the nature of off-farm employment according to who in the couple is employed off the farm.[1]

Patterns of farm work and off-farm work are, of course, intertwined. Coughenour and Swanson (1983) suggest that going from only the wife to only the husband to both members of the couple employed off the farm represents "successively greater disruptions of the farm labor process" (assuming that both husband and wife contribute farm labor, with the husband's contribution greater than the wife's). The association of the different patterns of couples' off-farm employment with attitudes toward farming, with farm characteristics, and with spouses' farm work involvement will be examined in this chapter in a search for the causes and implications of couples' off-farm employment.

When women find employment off the farm, it is often as part of a strategy to maximize family income. In Kada's (1980) study, a large majority of both husbands and wives gave "financing farm investment" as one reason for off-farm employment. The nature of women's off-farm work and the forces affecting whether they go off the farm, however, differ from men's. The labor market is extremely sex segregated (England 1981). The employment opportunities that have come to rural areas are often for predominantly one sex. Firms have gone to Southern rural areas, for example, to find pockets of cheap, ununionized labor, and labor with these characteristics is very often female, as well as black male (Bokemeier et al. 1983). The jobs that women obtain usually pay less than comparable jobs for men (England and McLaughlin 1979). The nature of the labor market of a particular area, then, can determine whether it is the woman, the man, or both who seek off-farm employment. Further, the labor market can constrain the amount of income a woman earns for her family.

In addition, there are more intrafamily pressures affecting a woman's decision to seek employment. For a man, the relevant factors may be the gain from wages earned off the farm relative to the loss from his absence and his interest in farm versus other work. For a woman, not only may her relative earnings and her own inclination and skills be important, but also what her husband is doing and the extent of her home responsibilities. As discussed in the introductory chapter, women are often those who fill in as needed. It was hypothesized in chapter 1 that relative need for women's contributions would affect their off-farm employment. In particular, women from larger farms and from those selling mainly livestock would be less likely to have off-farm employment, in the first case because of less need for the women's income from work outside the home and in the second because of a greater, more constant need for the woman's farm labor. (Of course, as just suggested, *men* from smaller and less diverse farms would also be expected to have higher off-farm employment.) Women's decisions about off-farm employment might follow those of their husbands about what farm and off-farm work is needed, however. As seen in the previous chapter, among the FWS farm couples there is less autonomous decision making about off-farm employment for women than for men. One might expect that women with husbands employed off the farm are less likely to have off-farm jobs themselves and also that the husband's work status mediates the effects of farm characteristics. Farm characteristics may have stronger net effects for men than for women. Even if they have a work life separate from the farm such that farm needs are not a consideration, women making employment decisions often have to take into account their work in the home and the cost in terms of time and money of delegating or condensing such work. Because men rarely have primary responsibility for household work and child care, such responsibilities are unlikely to affect their off-farm employment (and indeed, some studies, for example, Sumner 1978, and Huffman and Lange 1982, find much smaller effects, if any, of numbers of children on men's than women's employment off the farm).

Elbert and Colman give examples of such constraints on women's employment decisions from their interviews with farm families. "Jane Root actively supported her husband's decisions. She worked at the local GLF, an agricultural purchasing and marketing cooperative, as bookkeeper and secretary prior to her marriage and for a year afterwards but decided that full-time participation in farm work was necessary to their success. When asked about the possibility of working elsewhere, she stated firmly, 'It can't be done on a successful family farm. You have to work together.' This view is shared by her husband" (Elbert and Colman 1975:1–2).

When the pressure on income builds up and when home responsibilities allow it, the decision can go differently. "For many years, Emma [Crocker] mentioned that it would be financially beneficial if she were to get an off-farm job (as her husband had in 1963), but she was reluctant to do so. She felt needed at home. She thought it important to be present in the morning when the children went to school and in the evening when they returned. In addition, she knew the services she performed on the farm were helping maintain the farm operation. As the two older daughters began to assume more responsibility toward the house and toward caring for the younger children, and as the family income . . . dwindled, Emma became less reluctant to work. . . . Thus, in 1973, Emma became employed for thirty-five hours a week as office manager and bookkeeper, a position which utilizes her skills" (Colman et al. 1979:7–8).

Even though this report states that "it was Mrs. Crocker's decision to go back to work" (p. 8), it is obvious that her decision was more affected than her husband's by the combination of farm needs (some of which may have resulted from her husband's off-farm employment) and family needs. Before looking at couples' off-farm employment jointly, then, this chapter will look at women's and men's employment separately.

Description of Farm Women's and Farm Men's Off-Farm Employment

In the 1980 FWS, 31 percent of the women were employed off the farm at the time of the survey; another 6.4 percent had had a job in the last year. Among the men 42 percent were currently employed and 6.3 percent had had recent employment. In order to avoid picking up simply seasonal employment (especially because the FWS does not give information that would allow a meaningful distinction between seasonal and other work), I will describe the work characteristics of those people who were either currently employed in the summer of 1980 or had been employed in 1979 or later.[2]

It is usually assumed that men seek employment because they need to earn the money. Such an assumption is not automatically

Table 5.1. *Reasons for Women's Off-Farm Employment*

Reason	Percent
A. Main reason for having an off-farm job:[a]	
Keep up, use skills	17
Get out of house, see people	17
Need the money	57
Other	9
Total	100
(N)	(910)
B. For those who said "Need the money," money needed for:	
Farm-related expenses	19
Other things	57
Both equally	24
Total	100
(N)	(520)

[a]Those currently employed in 1980 or employed since 1979.

made for women. The FWS reflects this common attitude about women's employment in that it asked the women but not the men the main reason they had an off-farm job. Among the 1979–80 employed women, a quarter said that they had an off-farm job at least partially for money for farm-related expenses, and another 33 percent said it was because they needed the money for other reasons (see Table 5.1). This, of course, does not mean that those giving other reasons could not use the money when they earned it.[3]

Table 5.2 uses data from the FWS couples' subsample to show the implications for family incomes of husbands' and wives' off-farm earnings.[4] The wife's and husband's off-farm earnings together were, on average, almost equal to the net income from the farm (47 percent versus 53 percent of the total income). Although family income varied across farm income categories, it was kept up at the lower end by off-farm earnings of both the husband and wife, consistent with the general impression that off-farm earnings support the family income level on small farms. Women, on average, made a smaller contribution than men (both because of their lower em-

Table 5.2. *Average Family Income and Contributions to Family Income by Net Farm Income*

1979 Net Farm Income[a]	Average Percentage contribution from:[b] Wife's Off-Farm Jobs	Husband's Off-Farm Jobs	Net Farm Income	Average Family Income[c] (s.d.)	N
0	25	75	0	$18,171 (14,317)	95
> 0–$4,999	17	51	31	$17,164 (11,609)	89
$5,000–9,999	13	25	62	$16,361 (11,945)	48
$10,000–19,999	7	16	77	$24,475 (20,604)	70
≥ $20,000	2	4	94	$55,248 (55,992)	94
Total	13	34	53	$27,628 (33,938)	398

[a]Family income is calculated as the sum of wife's 1979 off-farm earnings, the husband's 1979 off-farm earnings, and 1979 net farm income.

[b]Excludes 19 families with 0 calculated family income.

[c]Includes 19 families with 0 calculated family income.

ployment rates and their lower earnings when employed, as will be shown below), although their contribution was more important the lower the family's farm earnings. Further, in cases where only the woman was employed off the farm, she may have been providing important nonwage benefits to the family, such as health insurance (Salant 1983).

Among those who had 1979 earnings, the women earned only about 40 percent of the men's off-farm income, $8,242 as compared with $20,305. Earnings depend on the wage one is paid and on the hours per week and weeks per year one works for pay. The farm women employed off the farm were more likely than the men to be employed part-time (40 percent versus 16 percent), although it is still true that a majority of them worked off the farm full-time.[5] The FWS does not give any other information on time spent working off the farm, but the 1979 Farm Finance Survey shows a larger proportion of operators (the majority of whom are men) than of their spouses (the majority of whom are women) working off the farm full year: 63 percent versus 54 percent (Department of Commerce 1982a: Table 90). Therefore at least some of the difference in earnings between farm women and men is probably due to differences in the intensity of their off-farm work, such a difference perhaps reflecting the constraints of farm and home needs on women's off-farm work time. At the same time, this difference is surely due at least in part to the segregation of women into lower paying jobs. The lower returns that women are able to get in the labor market may be one reason why the men have higher off-farm employment rates than the women.

The extent of occupational differences in the types of jobs farm women and men hold off the farm can be seen in Table 5.3. Here, to get a sense of the way the farm population differs in its off-farm occupations from the U.S. occupational structure as a whole, I also show the U.S. distributions by sex.[6] Almost one-third of the off-farm employed farm women were in clerical occupations (bank tellers, bookkeepers, cashiers, secretaries, teacher's aides), about one-quarter were in professional and technical jobs (teaching, nursing), and 16 percent were service workers (including nurse's aides, cooks, janitors, practical nurses, hairdressers, health aides). These women tended to be in "typical" women's jobs, which are mostly white-collar (70 percent are in the first four categories). Among the farm men, on the other hand, there were concentrations in the crafts occupations, as well as in professional and managerial and the operative occupations. In contrast with the women, only 44 percent of the men were in white-collar occupations, whereas 51 percent were in the blue-collar categories of crafts, operative, and nonfarm labor. Such differences are typical of the occupational structure as a whole. Relatively few women or men worked as farm managers or laborers. Those who operate their own farms do not seem especially likely to go to work on other people's.

One way of summarizing the relative standing of a person's occupation is by its prestige rating, which ranges from 0 (low) to 100 ("best" occupation) and measures the perceived goodness of an occupation (Siegel 1971). Although there are striking differences between the occupational distributions, the average occupational prestige of the women and men is the same. This sort of misleading equality has been noted for the general U.S. population as well. (See England 1979, for a discussion of this.)

The difference between the types of jobs farm men and women

Table 5.3. *Occupational Distributions by Sex: FWS Respondents Employed 1979–80 and U.S. 1979 Employed Population (percentages)*

	Women		Men	
	Farm Women Employed Off-Farm, 1979-80	U.S. Employed Women, 1979[a]	Farm Men Employed Off-Farm, 1979-80	U.S. Employed Men, 1979[b]
Professional, technical	24	16	17	15
Managerial, administrative	9	6	19	14
Sales	7	7	4	6
Clerical	30	35	4	6
Crafts	2	2	28	22
Operative	10	12	18	18
Non-farm labor	1	1	5	7
Farm	1	1	2	4
Service	16	20	3	8
Total	100	100	100	100
Average Prestige (s.d.)	42.0 (13.5)		41.7 (13.3)	
N	916		262	

[a]Source: Hayghe and Johnson, Perspectives on Working Women: A Databook.

[b]Source: U.S. Department of Commerce, Statistical Abstract of the U.S., 1980.

hold is even more striking when one looks at the industries of these jobs (see Table 5.4). Over 40 percent of the women held jobs in professional service industries (e.g., hospitals, schools, libraries, accounting offices), and another 14 percent were in retail trade. Among men there is a more even distribution over industries, with 10 to 20 percent in each of five categories: construction, durables manufacturing, nondurables manufacturing, professional service, and public administration. Agricultural industries were not big employers of either farm women or men. One gets a sense from these figures of the extent to which women, as compared with men, are dependent on a smaller range of occupations and industries for their employment, another factor that could contribute to the somewhat lower employment rate of the farm women as compared with the men.

There has been concern about rural areas as "periphery" labor markets where workers can find only lower level, lower paying jobs (Bokemeier et al. 1983; Brown and O'Leary 1979). Although this may be the case for the rural population as a whole, it does not seem to describe the situation of these farm operators and their families. The women were actually overrepresented in professional, managerial, and technical jobs. The farm men were overrepresented in professional and managerial positions also, as well as in the higher level blue-collar crafts occupations. Other researchers have also found that rural farm women, in contrast with rural nonfarm women (and even with urban women), have relatively more professional positions (Bokemeier et al. 1983; Flora and Johnson 1978). It may take in general a better position to bring a farm, as compared with a rural nonfarm, person into the off-farm labor force, because this position might have to compensate in part for decreased time spent on the farm.

Although there are these differences between the distributions of the farm women and men and U.S. job-holders as a whole, there is overall similarity. Salant (1983) and Bokemeier and Coughenour (1980) also found the off-farm jobs held by farm people very much like those of other people in the local area or state. Thus, as Coughenour (1980:5) concludes, "the occupational (and income) welfare [of those farm people with off-farm jobs] will respond to developments affecting the non-farm economy in much the same way as for non-farm . . . workers generally."

Determinants of Women's and Men's Off-Farm Employment

To see how farm and personal characteristics are related to the probability of having off-farm employment for women and men, I estimated logistic regressions for off-farm employment. The full sample of men does not have information on all the farm and family variables. In addition to discussing results from the full sample of women, therefore, I use the couples' subsample, in which

Table 5.4. *Industrial Distributions by Sex: FWS Respondents Employed 1979–80 and U.S. 1979 Employed Population (percentages)*

	Women		Men	
	Farm Women Employed Off-Farm, 1979-80	U.S. Employed Women, 1979[a]	Farm Men Employed Off-Farm, 1979-80	U.S. Employed Men, 1979[a]
Agriculture, forestry	3	1.7	6	4.9
Mining	1	0.3	1	1.4
Construction	1	1.2	16	10.3
Manufacturing-durables	6	16.9	19	27.1
Manufacturing-nondurables	8		12	
Transportation, communication	3	3.9	6	8.6
Wholesale trade	2	2.4	2	5.0
Retail trade	14	20.0	6	13.8
Finance, insurance	7	8.2	3	4.3
Business & repair services	1	2.8	3	4.3
Personal services	4	6.9	1	1.8
Entertainment, recreation	1	1.0	1	1.1
Professional, related	42	30.5	15	11.5
Public administration	7	4.3	10	5.9
Total[b]	100	100.1	101	100.0
(N)	(910)		(261)	

[a]Source: U.S. Department of Commerce, Statistical Abstract of the U.S., 1980.
[b]Totals differ from 100 due to rounding.

one can use the wife's report on things about which the men were not asked, for comparisons by sex.

Because it is possible that farm characteristics, as well as personal job-relevant variables, affect the nature and intensity of work off the farm when it is found, OLS regressions for hours worked per week, occupational prestige of the 1979–80 job, and 1979 off-farm income were also estimated for the women in the full sample and for husbands and wives who had been employed 1979–80. To look at influences on the nature of off-farm jobs, it makes sense to look only at those employed. If one were to estimate, for example, regressions for hours worked for the full sample, one would have over half "0" on the dependent variable. To a large extent, effects of the independent variables would be picking up the distinction between any hours worked and none. Although it is conceptually interesting to examine only those with off-farm employment, doing so introduces a statistical problem—selectivity bias. Selecting on entrance into the off-farm labor market means inability to generalize the results to the whole population, which includes those who in the future might be employed (see Berk and Ray 1982). To control for selectivity, I followed the procedure suggested by Ray et al. (1981), in which one calculates the probability of being in the subgroup of interest (here, of being employed off the farm) using a logistic regression, and then uses the predicted probability for each person who is selected as one variable in the analyses of interest.[7]

There is another statistical problem with which I have not dealt. As discussed at the beginning of this chapter, taking up off-farm employment is sometimes one of many strategies for raising family income. In the analyses to follow, sales mix will provide a measure of on-farm diversity as well as perhaps farm labor needs.[8] Yet the off-farm employment decision and the diversification decision may be made simultaneously, in which case one would have simultaneity bias. Further, as discussed briefly, off-farm employment can lead to changes in the operation and its labor structure to accommodate such employment. Once such changes are made they may affect the continuation of off-farm employment. Without a history of the operation and of the household's employment (or more variables about farm characteristics to use as instruments, e.g., Sumner 1978), it is difficult to disentangle the effects of operation characteristics on off-farm employment from effects of off-farm employment on the nature of the operation. Here I am essentially assuming that the needs of the farm and the family facilitate or hinder family members in seeking off-farm employment and that any adjustments in the nature of the operation were made earlier. To the extent that this assumption is incorrect, and to the extent that the simultaneity bias is of a different magnitude for women and men, the comparisons by sex of effects of farm characteristics will be misleading. These results, then, should be taken as tentative.

EMPLOYMENT

Table 5.5 shows the logistic regressions for women's off-farm employment in the full sample. As is true in other analyses of women's employment in general and farm women's in particular, there are strong effects of education, age, and number of children. (See, for example, Sumner 1978; Sweet 1974; Huffman and Lange 1982.) Women with more education, and especially with a college education, were more likely to have had off-farm jobs, perhaps because they had better jobs open to them as a result of their education. Older women were less likely to have off-farm employment, with the drop especially sharp after age 65, the usual retirement age. The more children, especially young children, the less likely the woman was to have work off the farm. The usual explanation (discussed in chapter 1), of course, is that a woman's responsibility for children makes it more difficult for her to work away from home. Whether children did farm work seems to make little difference: the number of school-age children who helped with farm work also has a negative effect on the woman's off-farm employment possibility. This suggests that the substitution of children's farm work for the mother's is incomplete or that having more children working signifies a more intense stage of the farm life cycle. There is even a significant negative effect of the number of sons over eighteen in the family, perhaps again representing greater household responsibilities of the woman or a more traditional attitude toward the farm or some other aspect of the operation's management. (This effect continues to be significant after including the husband's work status when one corrects for the exclusion of those who did not know their husband's off-farm income.)

There are regional effects as well. In contrast with women in the South, women in the West (and in the Northeast, after including husband's work status) were less likely to have off-farm employment. Opportunities for such employment may be fewer outside the South, or there may be unmeasured regional characteristics of farms that keep women out of the off-farm labor force.

The nature of the operation does have some effect on the employ-

Table 5.5. *Logistic Regression for Whether Farm Woman Had Off-Farm Job 1979–80 (logit coefficients)*

Independent Variables[a]	Excluding Husband's Work Variables	Including Husband's Work Variables
Farm Characteristics		
Total acres in farm relative to less than 50 acres:		
50–299 acres	.02	.07
300–999 acres	-.40**	-.29
> 1,000 acres	-.74**	-.60**
Sales relative to mixed crops and livestock:		
Less than 5 percent total sales from crops	.05	.003
Greater than 95 percent total sales from crops	.07	.06
Don't know percent of sales from crops	-.10	-.01
Tenancy relative to part owners:		
Full owners	.08	.02
Renters	.05	.14
Neither owners nor renters	.12	.06
Woman's Legal Relation to Land		
Own name on deed or rental contract for land	-.12	-.05
Decision Makers		
Include other than husband and wife	.10	.07
Region		
Relative to South:		
Northeast	-.27	-.32*
Northcentral	-.22	-.18
West	-.38**	-.33*

Table 5.5. *continued*

Independent Variables[a]	Excluding Husband's Work Variables	Including Husband's Work Variables
Labor Structure of Farm		
More than 1 hired hand	-.40**	-.28*
Husband's work relative to husband who regularly does farm work and has no off farm job:		
No husband		.66*
Husband regularly does farm work and has off-farm job		.69**
Husband does not regularly do farm work and has off-farm job		.20
Husband does not regularly do farm work and has no off-farm job		-.22
Number of sons at least 18 who regularly do farm work	-.25**	-.23
Number of children ages 6-17 who regularly do farm work	-.20**	-.20**
Number of other household members who regularly do farm work	.05	-.06
Number of other non-household members who regularly do farm work	-.006	-.002
Farm Woman's Characteristics		
Education relative to high school graduate:		
Less than high school	-.45**	-.35*
Postsecondary vocational or some college	.47**	.44**
College degree or above	1.19**	1.14**
Percent of life spent on farms or ranches	.00	-.00

Table 5.5. *continued*

Independent Variables[a]	Excluding Husband's Work Variables	Including Husband's Work Variables
Farm Woman's Characteristics (cont'd)		
Age relative to over 65:		
less than 31	3.49**	3.22**
31-45	3.12**	2.99**
46-65	2.10**	2.01**
Dependent Children		
Number of children less than age 6	-.77**	-.78**
Number of children 6-17 who do not regularly do farm work	-.20**	-.24**
Constant	-2.11	-2.35
D	.14	.16
Observed probability	.38	.40
N[b]	2349	2031

* $.01 < p < .05$.

** $p < .01$.

[a]For categorical variables, 1 = yes, 0 = no.

[b]N's are less than 2,509 because of missing data.

ment of these farm women. As expected, especially on the largest farms, women were less likely to have off-farm jobs. Having at least two hired hands, which also has a significant negative effect on the log-odds of off-farm employment, might be another indicator of size and profitability of the operation, as well as representing extra domestic responsibilities for the woman. Sales mix, however, has no effect, either as a measure of diversity or of labor needs.

I had speculated that the woman's employment responded to that of her husband and that some of the effects of farm characteristics would be mediated by the husband's work patterns. Adding the husband's work variables as a second step in the analysis allows one to test these speculations. As seen in the second column of Table 5.5, in contrast with women who had full-time farmer husbands, those without husbands and those who had husbands working both on the farm and off were more likely to have had employment. When no husband is present farming full-time, and money is needed, the woman seems to be the one who goes out to get it. But if the husband was farming part-time (in the sense of having an off-farm job and regularly doing farm work), then the woman was also more likely to be employed off the farm. There is no evidence here of the substitution of wife's off-farm employment for the husband's, but rather of a sharing of part-time farming, consistent with Sweet (1972) but contrary to what was hypothesized. Although these effects are statistically significant, the addition of husband's work variables to the model does not significantly improve the overall prediction of the woman's employment status ($\chi^2 = 2.24$ with 4 degrees of freedom, $p < .5$). Addition of the husband's work variables does reduce some of the effect of farm characteristics, although it does not decrease the impact of numbers of children, suggesting that what a husband does determines to some extent what the farm (but not household) then needs in terms of labor.

One might assume that at least some of these effects represent the extent to which a woman provided farm labor. For example, as was seen in chapter 3, the more children who helped with farm work, the greater the range of tasks that a woman did. The negative effect of number of children helping, then, could in part represent the woman's responsibility for supervising them. The inclusion of a measure of farm work is problematic because it is likely that doing work on the farm does not *cause* off-farm employment but is determined simultaneously with it, as discussed in chapter 3. When the percentage of farm tasks that the woman did regularly is also added to the model (not shown), it has a large significant and negative effect on off-farm employment. In general, though, its inclusion leaves the other coefficients much the same with the exception of the regional effects, which are no longer statistically significant. The regional variables, then, probably represent farm rather than off-farm labor market characteristics.

Table 5.6 provides the comparison of farm husbands and wives.[9] As was expected, more of the farm characteristics are significant in predicting whether the husband as compared with the wife had an off-farm job, while child care responsibility inhibited wives' but not husbands' employment. Men on larger farms, those selling a mix of crops and livestock (i.e., more diverse operations), with other decision makers, and with more than one hired hand were less likely to have off-farm employment. On the other hand, the number of children does not affect men's employment chances.

Table 5.6. *Logistic Regression for Whether Farm Wife and Farm Husband Had Off-Farm Jobs 1979–80: FWS Couples (logit coefficients)*

Independent Variables[a]	Wife	Husband
Farm Characteristics		
Total acres in farm relative to less than 50 acres:		
50–299 acres	.34	-1.13**
300–999 acres	-.51	-2.73**
> 1,000 acres	-.92*	-2.74**
Sales relative to mix of crops and livestock:		
Less than 5 percent total sales from crops	-.17	.93**
Greater than 95 percent total sales from crops	-.35	.59*
Tenancy relative to part owners:		
Full owners	-.13	-.34
Renters	-.08	-.14
Neither owners nor renters	.06	.56
Decision Makers		
Include other than husband and wife	.16	-.74*
Region		
Relative to South:		
Northeast	-.97**	.01
Northcentral	-.68*	-.46
West	-.69*	-1.19**
Labor Structure of Farm		
More than 1 hired hand	-.36	-.80**
Number of sons at least 18 who regularly do farm work	-.06	.15
Number of children ages 6–17 who regularly do farm work	-.37**	-.27

Table 5.6. *continued*

Independent Variables[a]	Wife	Husband
Labor Structure of Farm (cont'd)		
Number of other household members who regularly do farm work	.03	-.47
Number of other non-household members who regularly do farm work	.07	-.18
Farm Person's Characteristics		
Education relative to high school graduate:		
Less than high school	-.18	-.12
Postsecondary vocational or some college	.19	.37
College degree or above	1.15**	1.05**
Percent of life spent on farms or ranches	-.003	-.002
Age relative to over 65:		
less than 31	3.29**	2.82**
31-45	3.35**	2.95**
46-65	2.03*	1.91**
Dependent Children		
Number of children less than age 6	-.56*	-.09
Number of children 6-17 who do not regularly do farm work	-.16	.03
Constant	-1.36	-1.49
D	.15	.30
Observed Probability	.39	.47
N[b]	472	470

* $.01 \leq p < .05$.

** $p < .01$.

[a]For categorical variables, 1 = yes, 0 = no.

[b]N's less than 497 because of missing data.

One might be tempted from the size of the logit coefficients to say that the personal characteristics of age and education have a larger effect for women than for men. It is difficult, however, to compare the size of the logit coefficients across groups because the effect of any particular variable will depend on the level of the other independent variables as well as on its own level (Hanushek and Jackson 1977). One way to make such a comparison is to do it at some standard level of the independent variables for each group. A comparison at the observed means for each sex seems reasonable. One can work backwards from the equation for the log-odds to calculate how much the probability will change if all variables except the one of interest remain at their observed means (see Petersen 1985).[10] Doing this confirms that, although for both the men and women off-farm employment is up when the person is younger and when the person has a college education, the effects are somewhat larger for women.

Farm husbands' off-farm employment can be better explained than that of farm wives with a combination of farm and personal characteristics (comparing the *D* statistics). In general, the off-farm employment of farm wives seems to be more a function of the family needs and of the resources they have to find good jobs than of the nature of the operation per se.

JOB CHARACTERISTICS

Given that a person has taken off-farm employment, one might wonder whether certain men and women have an advantage in terms of the types of jobs they get. For example, those from larger farms might be able to wait longer for better jobs than those on smaller farms who need the money more desperately. Those with more education and especially women with fewer children might also find better jobs. As already described, to answer these questions and to compare the answers by sex, OLS regressions were run for hours worked per week, occupational prestige, and 1979 off-farm income for the women and men with some employment, including among the independent variables a selectivity measure. The results for the regressions for hours worked at the 1980 job or last job held between 1979 and 1980 are not shown. The total regressions were significant for neither the husbands nor the wives among the FWS couples.[11]

Table 5.7 shows the results for prestige. As has been found in the general social stratification literature (e.g., Featherman and Hauser

1976; Sewell et al. 1980), educational attainment is an important factor explaining occupational rank. For this group of farm women, education is *the* most important variable. Farm women in general, and farm wives in particular, gain over 18 prestige points when they have finished college as compared with simply finishing high school, whereas some college or vocational schooling after high school increases status by 9 points for the wives and by 6 points for the total group of farm women. For farm wives nothing else in the regression is significant. For the full sample of farm women, being neither owner nor renter has an effect which contrasts with both renting and owning—those in the former situation had somewhat lower status when they take off-farm employment. It is possible that those with no legal control over their land need to take an off-farm job even if it is not the best they could get given their education.[12]

For men, education is less important than farm size. Men on larger farms had higher status jobs when they were employed, even net of their education. Men in the West, controlling for other things, and on operations with more than one hired hand also had a net status gain in their off-farm employment. These variables decreased the chances that a man would be employed. When men on farms with these characteristics were employed, they got better jobs. This could increase socioeconomic class differences among farmers, those on smaller farms being more often employed off-farm, but large-scale farmers with off-farm jobs being in the higher reaches of the occupational structure. There is also an age effect for the men. Men, as compared with women, tend to gain in status over their work lives, and the age effect probably indicates such a career stage effect (see Rosenfeld 1980). In general, similar to the findings on employment, the operation characteristics have more impact on occupational prestige for men than they do for the women.[13]

Table 5.8 presents the regressions for 1979 income.[14] This variable, as discussed before, includes both quantity and quality of off-farm employment because it is affected by the amount of time a person was employed off the farm as well as by the wage level of the off-farm job. For the subsample of farm wives the regression as a whole was not significant and is not shown. For the full sample of farm women, education is again the most important determinant of off-farm job rewards. Here, though, the effect is not linear. Those with certificates earned more in a year off the farm than those without a diploma at a given level. Thus those with some college or

Table 5.7. *OLS Regression for Occupational Prestige of Those Employed 1979–80*

	Dependent Variables	
	Farm Women	
Independent Variables[a]	Unstandard-ized Coefficient	Standardized Coefficient
Farm Characteristics		
Total acres in farm relative to less than 50 acres:		
50–299 acres	.36	.01
300–999 acres	1.11	.03
> 1,000 acres	2.04	.05
Sales relative to mixed crops and livestock:		
Less than 5 percent total sales from crops	.27	.01
Greater than 95 percent total sales from crops	.38	.01
Don't know percent of sales from crops	1.15	.02
Tenancy relative to part owners:		
Full owners	.26	.01
Renters	-1.84	-.04
Neither owners nor renters	-5.36	-.07*
Woman's Legal Relation to Land		
Own name on deed or rental contract for land	-.74	-.02
Decision Makers		
Include other than husband and wife	.30	.01
Region		
Relative to South:		
Northeast	.42	.01
Northcentral	1.02	.03
West	.56	.02

Dependent Variables			
Farm Wives		Farm Husbands	
Unstandard-ized Coefficient	Standardized Coefficient	Unstandard-ized Coefficient	Standardized Coefficient
.76	.03	8.87	.33*
2.30	.07	25.42	.69**
2.77	.07	22.64	.42*
2.66	.09	-.13	-.005
3.50	.11	.88	.03
--	--	--	--
-1.37	-.05	-1.99	-.07
-5.86	-.12	-2.94	-.06
-.66	-.007	-8.14	-.08
--	--	--	--
4.36	.13	-1.28	-.03
-1.80	-.06	1.43	.05
3.21	.10	-2.40	-.07
1.09	.03	8.59	.25**

Table 5.7. *continued*

Independent Variables[a]	Dependent Variables: Farm Women — Unstandardized Coefficient	Standardized Coefficient
Labor Structure of Farm		
More than 1 hired hand	1.43	.05
Number of sons at least 18 who regularly do farm work	-.48	-.01
Number of children ages 6-17 who regularly do farm work	-.48	-.03
Number of other household members who regularly do farm work	-.09	-.002
Number of other non-household members who regularly do farm work	.12	.01
Farm Woman's (Husband's) Characteristics		
Education relative to high school graduate:		
Less than high school	-5.70	-.13**
Postsecondary vocational or some college	6.35	.21**
College degree or above	18.44	.53**
Percent of life spent on farms or ranches	-.01	-.03
Age relative to over 65:		
less than 31	-2.83	-.07
31-45	.003	.00
46-65	-.81	-.03

Dependent Variables			
Farm Wives		Farm Husbands	
Unstandard-ized Coefficient	Standardized Coefficient	Unstandard-ized Coefficient	Standardized Coefficient
1.98	.06	8.84	.27**
-1.57	-.05	.23	.006
.11	.008	-.31	-.02
-4.06	-.08	1.78	.04
-.19	-.01	1.30	.07
-5.57	-.15	-.007	-.00
9.05	.28**	-.13	-.004
18.88	.46**	12.07	.36**
-.04	-.10	-.007	-.02
-18.65	-.46	-17.49	-.32*
-15.68	-.58	-8.86	-.33
-15.80	-.56	-1.90	-.07

Table 5.7. *continued*

Independent Variables[a]	Dependent Variables: Farm Women — Unstandardized Coefficient	Standardized Coefficient
Dependent Children		
Number of children less than age 6	.92	.03
Number of children 6-17 who do not regularly do farm work	-.46	-.03
Selectivity Coefficient	4.79	.06
Constant	36.34	
R^2	.39	
N	785	

* .01 < p < .05.

** p < .01.

[a]For categorical variables, 1 = yes, 0 = no.

postsecondary vocational education earned less than those with only a high school degree, and those with a college degree earned more. For this group of women there is some tendency for those from farms with less diversity (dependence on crops for most of their sales) to have earned more off the farm, either because of a greater need when sales are concentrated in one type of product or because selling less livestock made fewer demands on a woman's time. There is also an effect of being on an operation with two or more hired hands, again perhaps an indicator of women's lower involvement in such operations. These operation characteristic effects, however, disappear when one includes cases where husband's off-farm income was not reported. Number of children has no significant effect, although one might have expected women with more children to spend less time working off the farm.[15] Adding the percent of types of farm tasks the woman did regularly did not increase the percent of variance explained.

Although for employment itself and for prestige there were no

Dependent Variables			
Farm Wives		Farm Husbands	
Unstandardized Coefficient	Standardized Coefficient	Unstandardized Coefficient	Standardized Coefficient
.16	.007	-2.11	-.09
-1.96	-.12	-.81	-.05
.99	.01	48.81	.88**
61.71		3.43	
.44		.44	
173		212	

effects of the family variables for the men, here every indicator of family size is significant. Men with more children, especially very young children or adult sons, earned more off the farm in a year. There are probably two different effects here. Having younger children may indicate a greater need for money. The general literature on men's earning suggests that children spur men to earn, but their presence keeps women out of the labor forces (Duncan, Featherman, and Duncan 1972). At the same time, having more people help with the farm work might free the man to spend more time on off-farm work. The extent of the wife's farm work, when added, however, had no significant effect. For men, too, there is some indication that those on less diversified farms earned more off the farm when they were employed.

In summary, then, women's off-farm employment depends more than men's on their educational credentials and on their family responsibilities, whereas men's off-farm employment is influenced more by the nature of the operation. Once in the labor force, how-

Table 5.8. *OLS Regression for 1979 Off-Farm Income (in 1,000s) for Those Employed with Some Off-Farm Income*

Independent Variables[b]	Farm Women[a] Unstandardized Coefficient	Farm Women[a] Standardized Coefficient	Farm Husbands Unstandardized Coefficient	Farm Husbands Standardized Coefficient
Farm Characteristics				
Total acres in farm relative to less than 50 acres:				
50-299 acres	-.05	-.003	-1.76	-.06
300-999 acres	.78	.04	3.03	.07
> 1,000 acres	1.38	.05	4.59	.08
Sales relative to mixed crops and livestock:				
Less than 5 percent total sales from crops	-.81	-.05	5.50	.19*
Greater than 95 percent total sales from crops	1.57	.09*	4.65	.14
Don't know percent of sales from crops	.67	.02	--	--
Tenancy relative to part owners:				
Full owners	.74	.05	2.14	.07
Renters	.05	.002	-2.57	-.05
Neither owners nor renters	-1.17	-.03	-4.53	-.04
Woman's Legal Relation to Land				
Own name on deed or rental contract for land	.30	.02	--	--
Decision Makers				
Include other than husband and wife	-1.14	-.06	-2.18	-.05
Region				
Relative to South:				
Northeast	1.20	.07	-3.14	-.10
Northcentral	1.51	.09	-1.21	-.03
West	1.25	.07	4.42	.12

Table 5.8. *continued*

Independent Variables[b]	Farm Women		Farm Husbands	
	Unstandard-ized Coefficient	Standardized Coefficient	Unstandard-ized Coefficient	Standardized Coefficient
Labor Structure of Farm				
More than 1 hired hand	1.50	.09*	5.27	.15
Number of sons at least 18 who regularly do farm work	-.78	-.04	6.00	.16*
Number of children ages 6-17 who regularly do farm work	-.09	-.01	2.83	.17*
Number of other household members who regularly do farm work	.50	.02	14.47	.24**
Number of non-household members who regularly do farm work	-.21	-.04	-.22	-.01
Farm Woman's (Husband's) Characteristics				
Education relative to high school graduate:				
Less than high school	-.05	-.002	.75	.02
Postsecondary vocational or some college	-1.64	-.10*	-1.61	-.04
College degree or above	2.55	.13**	2.87	.08
Percent of life spent on farms or ranches	-.01	-.04	-.06	-.14
Age relative to over 65:				
less than 31	-4.41	-.19	7.60	.13
31-45	.12	.008	7.54	.26
46-65	1.85	.12	9.93	.33
Dependent Children				
Number of children less than age 6	.66	.04	4.12	.17*
Number of children 6-17 who do not regularly do farm work	-.57	-.06	2.67	.15*

Table 5.8. *continued*

Independent Variables[b]	Farm Women Unstandardized Coefficient	Farm Women Standardized Coefficient	Farm Husbands Unstandardized Coefficient	Farm Husbands Standardized Coefficient
Selectivity Coefficient	15.39	.36**	1.03	.02
Constant	-2.69		-1.83	
R^2	.18		.32	
N	642		191	

* .01 < p < .05.

** p < .01.

[a]Regression for farm wives is not significant at the .05 level and not shown.

[b]For categorical variables, 1 = yes, 0 = no.

ever, women's earnings and status are determined almost entirely by their education—family responsibilities play no part in the type of jobs they get. For men the nature of the operation continues to have an influence on the kind of job they take in terms of its status. But family structure seems to be both a prod and a facilitator for a farm husband earning more off the farm.

Patterns of Couples' Off-Farm Employment

Up to this point, women's and men's off-farm employment statuses have been examined separately for the most part. We now turn to examining the outcomes and correlates of different combinations of husbands' and wives' employment off the farm.

The top row in Table 5.9 shows the distribution in the FWS couples' subsample of joint husband and wife employment.

Although the employment of husbands is not statistically independent of their wives' employment, all four possible combinations of wives' and husbands' employment exist in some numbers. In over a third of the families neither the husband nor the wife had been employed outside the operation at all in 1979–80; in almost a quarter of the couples, both spouses had been employed off the

Table 5.9. *Characteristics of Off-Farm Employment by Wife's and Husband's Employment Status*

A[a]	Both Husband and Wife Employed Off-Farm	Only Husband Employed Off-Farm	Only Wife Employed Off-Farm	Neither Husband Nor Wife Employed Off-Farm
**Percent	24	25	14	37
Average occupational prestige - wife	42.0	--	42.2	--
(s.d.)	(14.1)	--	(14.1)	--
Average occupational prestige - husband	40.8	42.7	--	--
(s.d.)	(13.6)	(13.2)	--	--
Average weekly hours on off-farm job - wife	32.8	--	33.3	--
(s.d.)	(12.3)	--	(12.5)	--
Average weekly hours on off-farm job - husband	40.4	39.4	--	--
(s.d.)	(12.7)	(13.3)	--	--
B	**Both Husband and Wife Had Off-Farm Income 1979**	**Only Husband Had Off-Farm Income 1979**	**Only Wife Had Off-Farm Income 1979**	**Neither Husband Nor Wife Had Off-Farm Income 1979**
1979 average off-farm earnings - wife	7,380	--	7,673	--
(s.d.)	(5,638)	--	(5,135)	--
*1979 average off-farm earnings - husband	15,702	22,535	--	--
(s.d.)	(10,348)	(19,003)	--	--
*Wife's average percentage contribution to family income[b]	.28	--	.54	--
(s.d.)	(.18)	--	(.35)	--
*Husband's average percentage contribution to family income[b]	.56	.79	--	--
(s.d.)	(.22)	(.26)	--	--
Average family income 1979[b]	29,359	28,265	28,339	26,139
(s.d.)	(24,907)	(21,685)	(50,314)	(38,605)
Median family income 1979[b]	24,000	24,000	15,000	15,000

*Test for difference between means significant at .05 level.

**χ^2 = 24.2, df = 1, p <.001, N = 485.

[a] Those employed off-farm 1979-80.

[b] Family income here includes only husband's 1979 off-farm earnings, wife's off-farm earnings and 1979 net farm income.

farm. When one or the other was employed, it was somewhat more likely to be the husband (25 versus 14 percent of the 485 couples for whom employment status was known).

Which combination of husband and wife is engaged in off-farm employment might have implications for the nature of off-farm work. The evidence in chapter 3 and other accounts of farm women's work suggest that women substitute on the farm for men who have employment off the farm. I will examine this issue further in this section. It is also possible that with respect to off-farm employment husbands and wives trade off intensity of employment, with perhaps a greater likelihood of part-time or lower paid or lower prestige employment when the other member of the couple is also employed than when that person is not. Table 5.9 suggests that on average this is not so. Earnings of the wife and the hours worked are about the same by category of the spouses' off-farm employment. However, husbands who were the only member of the couple working off the farm earned over $6,000 more on average than if their wives were also employed off the farm.[16] At the same time, when only one member of a couple was employed off the farm, that person made a relatively greater contribution to family income than when the other member of the couple also had a job. When only the husband was employed off the farm, he provided almost 80 percent of the family income (as calculated from the total of spouse's income and net farm income); when his wife was employed, he contributed just under 60 percent. When a wife was the only member of the couple with off-farm income, she brought in over half of the family's income, although the level of her earnings was lower than a man's, on average. One of the results of this is that families who depended on the wife's off-farm earnings had lower median family incomes than those where the husband or both the husband and the wife were employed.

Average occupational prestige is also the same regardless of whether the other spouse was also employed off the farm. Behind these averages, though, are some differences in the distributions across occupational and industrial categories. As shown in Table 5.10, when only the wife was employed off the farm, she was more likely than when her husband was also employed to be either a professional or an operative. When the husband alone was employed off the farm, he was much more likely to have a crafts occupation and much less likely to have an operative position.[17] When only the wife has an off-farm job, it may indicate her greater commitment to a profession (consistent with the somewhat greater percent of responses "to keep up or use skills" to the question about why the woman had an off-farm job among these women) or the greater availability of typically female operative jobs in the rural area. A man may be somewhat more likely to go off the farm alone when he has skills and can get a higher wage. The overall distributions for the wives and for the husbands, however, do not significantly differ by spouse's employment.[18]

One would expect, too, that who is employed off the farm would be related to the psychic satisfaction that people feel from farming, though perhaps not to their feelings about their community. As Kada (1980:98) shows, many people who enter part-time farming from another occupation do so because of enjoyment of country life. A large proportion say a preference for farm work is a major reason as well (see also Coughenour and Gabbard 1977). Continued involvement with farming when either husband or wife or both have off-farm jobs could in general indicate the attraction of farming for a family. When combining the two jobs, however, a person or a family might feel extra pressure. Kada reports that almost 50 percent of the dual job-holding Wisconsin farm operators he interviewed felt at least some conflict between the off-farm job and farming. Thus one might expect less satisfaction with farming among families with some off-farm employment. If one agrees with Coughenour and Swanson that going from only the wife to only the husband to both members of the couple employed off the farm represents "successively greater disruptions of the farm labor process," then one should expect to see greater dissatisfaction as one goes across these types. Also, both members of the couple may get off-farm jobs when the farm income is particularly precarious, and thus the couple may be especially dissatisfied in this situation.

The FWS contains data relevant to these issues. It asked men and women about their satisfaction with their community, with farming as a way of life, and with farming as a way of making a living. Because the responses of the wives and husbands were very similar, only the wives' are shown in Table 5.11.[19] There is no significant difference by employment pattern in satisfaction with community. Over 75 percent of the women in each group said they were very satisfied. In all employment groups, the wives and the husbands were more likely to be satisfied with farming as a way of life than with farming as a way to make a living, which is not surprising given the financial pressures on farmers. Those in couples with off-farm earners were in general less satisfied than those where both the husband and the wife worked only on the farm and in the

Table 5.10. *Occupations of Farm Wives and Farm Husbands Employed off the Farm 1979–80 by Spouse's Employment: FWS Couples (percentages)*

	Wife's Occupation[a]		Husband's Occupation[b]	
	Husband also Employed Off-Farm	Only Wife	Wife also Employed Off-Farm	Only Husband
Professional, technical	20	28	17	15
Managerial, administrative	10	6	18	22
Sales	6	9	5	5
Clerical	37	21	4	4
Crafts	1	0	22	32
Operative, except transportation	7	16	18	9
Transport, operative	3	1	5	5
Laborer, except farm	0	3	6	5
Farm laborer	0	1	1	2
Service	16	14	4	2
Total[c]	100	99	100	101
(N)	(114)	(64)	(114)	(118)

[a] χ^2 test of independence not significant at .05 level but significant at .10 level.

[b] χ^2 test of independence significant at neither .05 nor .10 level.

[c] Totals differ from 100 due to rounding.

home. There is not, however, the progression across types of couples that Coughenour and Swanson suggested. With respect to satisfaction with farming as a way of life, the most dramatic split is between those with neither member of the couple employed off the farm as compared with those in the other categories: 82 percent of those in the former group, as compared with 63–65 percent in other groups, said that they were "very satisfied." Dissatisfaction was no higher when only the husband was employed off the farm than when only the wife was. There was only a very slightly higher rate of dissatisfaction or ambivalence for the group with both spouses employed.

With respect to farming as a way to make a living, the big distinction is between the women whose husbands were and those whose husbands were not employed off the farm (whether the women were themselves). As seen before, husbands' off-farm income makes a larger contribution to family income than wives'. Thus off-farm employment is associated with lower satisfaction with farming as a way of life, regardless of which member of the couple was employed off the farm, and the husband's off-farm employment is especially associated with less satisfaction with farming as a way to make a living.

To this point, I have looked primarily at outcomes of couples' off-farm employment. I have speculated about what these outcomes might imply about the effects of farm, family, and individual characteristics on whether either a husband or a wife had off-farm employment. Such effects were analyzed separately for husbands and wives in an earlier section of this chapter. But the decisions and implications of off-farm employment are probably not independent for the husband and wife. I now turn to looking at how farm, family, and individual characteristics are associated with the joint distribution of farm husbands' and wives' off-farm employment.

To do this I use discriminant analysis, a way of understanding major differences among a priori distinct groups. It finds the linear combination of variables describing groups that form discriminant functions that maximally discriminate among the groups. (See Nunnally 1967 and Klecka 1980 for good introductions to discriminant analysis.) It derives the first, most powerful, canonical discriminant function (linear combination), then a second canonical discriminant function uncorrelated with the first, and so on, up to a number of discriminant functions equal to one less than the number of groups or the number of discriminating variables, whichever is smaller. Here, three canonical discriminant functions can be derived (four groups − 1), but only the coefficients for the first are shown, because they are of the most substantive interest.

One can imagine each canonical discriminant function as taking

Table 5.11. *Satisfaction with Farming and Community by Couples' Off-Farm Employment: Wives' Responses (percentages)*

	Both Husband and Wife Employed Off-Farm (N=115)	Only Husband Employed Off-Farm (N=123)	Only Wife Employed Off-Farm (N=66)	Neither Husband Nor Wife Employed Off-Farm (N=180)
Satisfaction with community of residence:				
Very satisfied	75	80	78	80
Somewhat satisfied	19	16	21	19
Dissatisfied or don't know	6	4	1	2
Total[a]	100	100	100	101
**Satisfaction with farming (ranching) as a way of life:				
Very satisfied	65	63	65	82
Somewhat satisfied	24	29	27	12
Dissatisfied or don't know	10	8	9	6
Total[a]	99	100	101	100[b]
**Satisfaction with farming (ranching) as a way to make a living:				
Very satisfied	20	19	31	49
Somewhat satisfied	25	23	36	26
Somewhat dissatisfied	30	42	14	18
Very dissatisfied	18	10	12	5
Don't know	8	6	6	2
Total[a]	101	100	99	100

**χ^2 test of independence significant at .01 level.

[a]Totals differ from 100 due to rounding.

[b]N = 181.

the information on the discriminating variables and using it to create a new dimension, along which the groups are as far apart as possible. The average values of the groups along this dimension help interpret the substantive meaning of the function. These average values (group centroids) are given at the bottom of Table 5.12. The first discriminant function seems to distinguish among groups by whether the husband was employed off the farm. The "most" off-farm employment is where only the husband was employed off the farm, followed by the case where both the husband and wife had jobs off the farm, although these two cases are close. The "least" off-farm employment is where neither the husband nor wife had work off the farm. When only the wife was off-farm employed, the group falls halfway between the 0 point and neither husband nor wife employed off the farm. Again this is not the order predicted by Coughenour and Swanson (1983). (Notice that signs change in the second column, where farm work variables are added. This does not affect the interpretation.) One might almost imagine that this dimension measures the unobserved variable "total hours worked on the farm." When the husband alone is employed off the farm, he spends the least time on farm work, and the total time for on the farm labor is not made up by the wife's farm work; when both husband and wife are employed, it might mean that the husband is employed less intensely so that he is able to put in more time than when he alone is employed (although this did not show up in average hours per week employed off the farm). When only the wife is employed, the loss in hours on the farm on her part might be more than compensated for by the hours the husband puts in, whereas when both are on the farm, the total hours invested there is maximal.[20]

The relative magnitude of the standardized coefficients indicates the relative contribution of the corresponding variables to the canonical discriminant function.[21] What come across as the most important variables differentiating along the first dimensions are operation size and age. Those on larger farms, especially those in the 300–999-acre range as compared with operations of under 50 acres, are the furthest along the first dimension in the direction of "less" off-farm employment. Age has a curvilinear effect. Those couples with "more" employment are relatively more likely to be the ones where the wife was in her early thirties to mid forties, less than thirty, or between forty-six and sixty-five, in that order. (Because husband's age is very highly correlated with wife's age, it was dropped from the analysis.) Sumner (1978) reported that farmers' participation off the farm increased with age up to about forty-five and then declined. Being over sixty-five (the reference category) has an implicit coefficient of 0, so that those with "more" employment on the first function are relatively less likely to be over the usual retirement age.

These results and examination of mean farm characteristics by couple's off-farm employment (not shown) suggest that the situation in which only the husband goes off the farm for income may be

Table 5.12. *Discriminant Analysis of Farm Couples' Joint Off-Farm Employment Patterns (standardized discriminant function coefficients)*

	First Function	
Independent Variables[a]	Without Husband, Wife Farm Work Variables	With Husband, Wife Farm Work Variables
Farm Characteristics		
Total acres in farm relative to less than 50 acres:		
50-299 acres	.30	-.28
300-999 acres	.69	-.66
> 1,000 acres	.60	-.57
Sales relative to mixed crops and livestock:		
Less than 5 percent total sales from crops	-.21	.23
Greater than 95 percent total sales from crops	-.10	.10
Tenancy relative to part owners:		
Full owners	.03	-.04
Renters	.01	-.006
Neither owners nor renters	-.09	.07
Decision Makers		
Include other than husband and wife	-.16	.16
Region		
Relative to South:		
Northeast	.05	-.06
Northcentral	.17	-.17
West	.28	-.31

Table 5.12. *continued*

Independent Variables[a]	First Function: Without Husband, Wife Farm Work Variables	First Function: With Husband, Wife Farm Work Variables
Labor Structure of Farm		
More than 1 hired hand	.19	-.18
Husband regularly does farm work	—	-.13
Percent of farm tasks wife does regularly	—	.11
Number of sons at least 18 who regularly do farm work	-.05	.06
Number of children ages 6-17 who regularly do farm work	.12	-.11
Number of other household members who regularly do farm work	.17	-.17
Number of other non-household members who regularly do farm work	.05	-.04
Farm Wife's Characteristics		
Education relative to high school graduate:		
Less than high school	.08	-.07
Postsecondary vocational or some college	-.01	-.01
College degree or above	-.004	-.004
Percent of life spent on farms or ranches	.08	-.11
Age relative to over 65:		
less than 31	-.46	.41
31-45	-.60	.53
46-65	-.35	.28

Table 5.12. *continued*

Independent Variables[a]	First Function: Without Husband, Wife Farm Work Variables	First Function: With Husband, Wife Farm Work Variables
Farm Husband's Characteristics		
Education relative to high school graduate:		
Less than high school	.09	-.09
Postsecondary vocational or some college	-.04	.05
College degree or above	-.19	.19
Percent of life spent on farms or ranches	.04	-.007
Dependent Children		
Number of children less than age 6	.03	-.02
Number of children 6-17 who do not regularly do farm work	.02	-.02
Relative percent of discriminating power:	69.5	69.0
Canonical correlation	.60	.61
Group Centroids:		
(1) Both husband and wife employed off-farm	-.50	.50
(2) Only husband	-.69	.71
(3) Only wife	.31	-.35
(4) Neither husband nor wife	.67	-.67

[a]For categorical variables, 1 = yes, 0 = no.

the one in which the farm is the most shaky. It was not the farms with both members of the couple employed off the farm that were the smallest, of lowest value, and least diverse, but the farms on which only the husband was employed off the farm. Because the husband working full-time can earn more than the wife, he may do so, even though this cuts down on the time he can farm, in which case the wife fills in. There is some support for this interpretation in both the discriminate analysis coefficients and the means by off-farm employment patterns. When the husband alone was employed off the farm, he was the least likely to do farm work regularly (although the proportion of husbands in this category who regularly farmed is still high, 87 percent). Wives, on the other hand, did the widest range of types of farm work when only their husbands were employed off the farm, although they did more when both they and their husbands worked off the farm than when their husbands did not have off-farm jobs. When the wife alone was employed, she, on average, did the smallest range of types of farm tasks. The wife does seem to take over for the man employed off the farm, even when she herself is also employed.

Conclusions

Thirty-seven percent of the FWS women and 47 percent of the men reported that they had held an off-farm job at the time of the survey or in the preceding year. Women were somewhat more likely than the men to be less than full-time when they were employed off the farm, and they earned less in a year. At the same time, they made important contributions to family incomes, especially among those with lower farm incomes. The types of occupations and industries differed by sex, too, in ways similar to that for the U.S. occupational structure as a whole. Women were concentrated in white-collar occupations and professional and retail trade industries, but men were more dispersed among occupations and industries. Women on larger farms were less likely to be employed than other women, but the effects of farm characteristics were less for them than for men and mediated by what a husband was doing, although effects of home responsibilities and credentials were larger. When a husband was not present or was both employed off the farm and farming, women were more likely to be employed off the farm. Both the other kinds of work the women were doing, especially child care, and the work of a husband here, as in chapter 3, affected women's participation in work in a particular domain. Personal characteristics were the ones with the greatest effects on the *kinds* of positions women held off the farm, but farm characteristics and the need to fill the provider role affected men's off-farm work.

In almost 40 percent of the FWS couples neither member had had an off-farm job in the previous year or at the time of the survey, but in almost a quarter both partners had jobs. When one or the other was employed off the farm, it was more likely to be the husband, who generally had higher earnings in such a case. When only the wife was employed off the farm, though, she on average contributed over half of the family income. With respect to hours of employment, prestige, and wife's off-farm earnings, there were no differences by whether the other spouse was also employed. Satisfaction with farming as a way to make a living was associated with who was employed off the farm: the smallest proportion of "very satisfied" were among those with the husband employed off the farm, whereas the highest percentage was among those with neither spouse holding an off-farm job. Other farm characteristics followed this pattern as well, leading to the conclusion, supported by a discriminant analysis, that situations in which only the husband was employed were those in which the farm was least developed and where more of the types of tasks were done by the woman.

Over the past decades, a number of people have pondered the implications of part-time farming and its increasing frequency. Some of these issues were discussed in the introduction to this chapter. Another concern is that increasing off-farm employment represents increasing "proletarianization" among farm people, that is, the transformation of self-employed people into those dependent on wage work. At least some combinations of off-farm and on-farm work might lessen the dependence of wage workers on those wages, however. In addition, as discussed in chapter 1, even those who depend solely on farming for their family's income and who do not sell their own labor are integrated into a number of larger market relationships. A prediction from the proletarianization perspective would be that those who are dependent for some of their income on wages are more alienated. There is some support for this in the questions on satisfaction with farming, but inconvenience and a feeling of being overloaded could be at the heart of this rather than alienation from the work process itself. Another prediction is that part-time farmers, in part because of their integration into the larger wage labor force, would be more progressive in their political attitudes and actions. Buttel and Larson (1982), however, provide arguments and evidence contrary to this hypothesis.

Instead, one might view farm people with off-farm jobs as largely belonging to the "new middle class" in addition to the "old middle class" (Mills 1956), that is, as having middle-class status because of their white-collar jobs as well as from having small property holdings. Further, as was seen in the analysis of men's off-farm occupational prestige, it is those from larger farms who have the higher level jobs when they are employed off the farm, such that occupational differences off the farm may reinforce class differences among farm families based on their operations' characteristics.

At the same time, this chapter has shown that the implications of off-farm work vary according to which member of the couple is employed off the farm. The wife's earnings may be making an important contribution to family income, but it is in families with smaller average farm incomes that only the husband has an off-farm job. When farming pays, men do it; when it does not, they go off the farm for income. The wife seems to substitute more for her husband when he alone is employed off the farm. When both members of the couple are employed off the farm, there may be a more equal division of labor with both members of the couple helping out on the farm as needed, as well as contributing to family income from their wages. With more U.S. families, not to mention farm families, consisting of dual earners, we need more investigation of *family* employment patterns and their implications.

6
Community and Farm Voluntary Organizations and Political Bodies

Through voluntary organizations, such as the PTA or Shriners, people provide unpaid service to the community. They and their families can also receive social support, a chance to socialize, and recreation from belonging to such organizations. Voluntary organization memberships in some cases (e.g., in unions) provide very concrete economic benefits and give the particular group's members more power than if they were unorganized. Further, membership brings with it a chance to develop social communications networks, providing an opportunity to meet with others with similar interests and with whom one can share information and other resources (McPherson and Smith-Lovin 1982). What one learns through participating in a club or other voluntary group, as well as whom one meets, might help one move up in one sphere or into another. Women might tool up for reentry into the labor market by doing volunteer work, for example (see Mueller 1975; Grantham 1982).

Although recent research shows women and men now have about the same likelihood of voluntary organization memberships and political participation (as noted in chapter 1), there are still sex differences in types of voluntary organizational activities. As McPherson and Smith-Lovin (1982:900) summarize their study of sex differences in voluntary organizational size, "The image of the voluntary sector which emerges from our analysis is a system of organizations divided into large, male-dominated, economically oriented organizations and small, female-dominated, domestically oriented organizations . . . there is very substantial sex segregation in the voluntary sector." Men, at least in part but not entirely because of their greater labor force participation, have more organizational memberships that are linked to occupational and economic structures. Women's organizational memberships more often reflect "female" concerns with children and social welfare. In at least some cases, women and men belong to the same organizations, but women take part through auxiliaries, which are not only smaller (and therefore contain fewer potential contacts, McPherson and Smith-Lovin 1982:889), but which also "lack autonomy and executive function" (Glasgow, c. 1978:8). Although women who achieve political office often do so through their voluntary activities, "Key male organizations are important training grounds and pathways into politics" (Glasgow, c. 1978:7; see also Epstein 1981). Of course, women are a very small minority among those who hold higher level political positions or offices (e.g., Lynn 1979; Field 1982).

Farm women are active in voluntary organizations. In her study of Saskatchewan farmers and ranchers, Kohl (1976) reports that the majority of women belonged to at least one organization and that only 23 percent could be classified as having "very low" organizational participation. Only one of the 27 farm and ranch women Boulding (1980) interviewed belonged to no voluntary organization, and the modal number of organizations to which the women belonged was 3 to 4. Kohl sees such memberships as providing not only community but also national linkages through national women's groups. She argues that this gives farm women the same sort of middle-class orientation as other women (Kohl 1976:41). At the same time, agricultural organizations that lobby for measures favorable to farmers and attempt to educate consumers may be those in which farm women show an orientation different from women in other areas, an orientation toward agricultural production as a way of life and of earning a living.

The FWS asked women and men about their memberships in community and farm organizations, as well as about their participation in Extension Service activities. In light of other research on women's, and particularly farm women's, organizational involvements, one would expect to find the FWS women with high levels of memberships in both community and farm organizations, as well as of participation in Extension activities. Although men and women would be predicted to be similar in extent of organizational memberships and Extension participation, the *types* of memberships and participation might vary by sex. Farm women would be expected to be more involved than farm men in organizational activities related to the family and home, and less likely than men to participate in those which are production- and marketing-oriented, just as they participate less in production and market activities and decisions. Hoiberg and Huffman (1978) did find such sex differences among Iowa farm families surveyed in 1977. The women were less likely than the men to have memberships in major farm organizations, in producers' organizations and in cooperatives, and were equally likely to belong to other, nonchurch community organizations. The FWS should show similar patterns.

The FWS also asked women whether they had served on any local governing board and asked both men and women about their participation on agricultural committees and panels. Through such positions people can have a say in policymaking. In light of the general finding that there is underrepresentation of women in elected and appointed positions we would expect the percent of women who have held such positions to be low.

Because the FWS asked both men and women about their organizational and committee activities, it is possible to look at the sexual division of labor. There are two, opposite kinds of patterns one might expect. On the one hand, there could be a specialization, such that one spouse tends to represent the family in a given kind of activity, probably women in community and family activities and men in agricultural ones. On the other hand, one might argue that there is a greater chance of one spouse participating in an activity if the other does so. Some organizations, such as churches and PTA, actively encourage family participation. The husband's membership is often the motivation for the woman's membership in an auxiliary. Duncan and Duncan (1978:175–79), using data on Detroit couples, found association between spouses' organizational memberships, with weaker association for labor unions and professional groups. Although many farm women are also in farming, one might expect to find the same sort of pattern among the couples in the FWS, with weaker association between couples' memberships in agricultural than in community organizations.

One explanation for predicted sex differences in organizational and other public participation could be direct exclusion. In her study of Wisconsin agricultural cooperative managers, Kau (1976: 36) discovered that although 44 percent of the managers said that their cooperative was making a special effort to communicate with women, "a substantial number of managers were discouraging if not outright hostile to the idea of more women in their cooperative." Managers are usually appointed by a board of directors, which is elected from among the members. Their attitudes can both reflect the members' opinions and also have a disproportionate influence in cooperative decision making. When they say, as one manager did, "My feeling is that women's place is in the home" (p. 44), they might act on those feelings to keep women from developing direct market contacts. At the same time, although women farm, they are often reluctant to identify themselves as farmers, as will be seen in the next chapter, and so perhaps less likely to feel they *should* participate in production and marketing activities. Other women might not cross the boundaries between "women's" and "men's" organizational activities because they fear being unaccepted or feeling awkward. When women are in production or economic organizations, they may be more likely to be in auxiliaries. One cannot predict that men will be in the auxiliaries of organizations in which women predominate because rarely are there auxiliaries for men, but men, too, might feel uneasy participating in typically and predominantly female activities. The FWS included two questions that attempted to tap the extent to which external or internalized barriers prevented women (and men) from participating in voluntary organizational and other public activities. Responses to these questions will be presented below.

To the extent that at least some of the deterrents to participation are due to different levels of interest and involvement in farming, one would hypothesize that women who do a greater range of their farms' tasks and who operate farms without husbands would be more likely to participate in various farm organizations and activities, especially those related to marketing and production .In talking about Saskatchewan commodity associations, Taylor (1976: 162) said, "Women in these groups are there only if they own the land and produce the product; otherwise, they make the sandwiches for meetings." One might object that those who are more involved with farming would have less time for organizational work and political participation. Boulding (1980:283), though, found no support for this in her interviews. In the more general literature, too, there is some evidence that employed women who might be thought to have less time for such activities are actually more active in politics (Epstein 1983:291; Jaquette 1975:149). Post hoc, one can argue that, as for men, work ties women into occupational and community networks and interests.

The general literature on volunteer work, voluntary organizational memberships, and political participation suggests other factors that might affect women's and men's participation and help explain sex differences in the nature of their participation. There are strong life cycle and age effects. Looking at life cycle stage as a combination of age, marital status, and presence and ages of children, Knoke and Thomson (1977) found that people with children, but especially older children, or with children when they themselves were older, had the highest levels of voluntary organizational participation. Those in early or the latest stages of family formation had lower levels. Other researchers fail to find an effect of having younger children (e.g., Epstein 1981; Mueller 1975; Schram and Dunsing 1981). One of the reasons that having children would be expected to inhibit especially women's organizational activity was that child care takes away from time available for other activities. But as Knoke and Thomson point out (1977:48), family commitments can include activities outside the home that are family focused. Community and farm organizations for farm men, but perhaps more for farm women, could be considered extensions of family and farm activities. Having children might increase, rather than decrease, participation, especially for women.

A few people have described the age and life cycle patterns of organizational participation for farm women. From her farm women interviews Boulding (1980:282–83) concludes: "For them, the forties are the peak age for involvement in organizations, but there is also substantial involvement in the thirties. Scouts, 4-H, and Sunday School teaching are the child-oriented involvements, more important for the younger women. When they reach their forties, broader community tasks are taken on, with a tapering off in the fifties and sixties. This may be partly a generational phenomenon. Older women may never have been as organization-minded. . . . Interestingly, farm women have a strong sense that they should 'retire' from leadership roles when they reach their sixties, particularly in church affairs."

She thus describes a somewhat curvilinear relationship between organizational activities and age, with a change in type of activity over the life cycle. Kohl (1976:61–65) gives a similar picture. One might expect to see stronger positive effects of age and negative effects of children on participation in public boards and panels, especially for women, because such political participation often involves more time and travel away from the family.

Across the farm life cycle, too, there might be changes in time spent on organizational activities. As the farm gets larger and more capitalized, it might no longer demand as intense a labor input from each family member. As the children mature and begin to help on the farm, the family life cycle intersects with the farm life cycle to further allow the parents the chance to participate in volunteer activities off the farm. In addition, those on the largest operations are those who have the most to gain from lobbying by major agricultural and producer organizations (Kohl 1979). This would be another reason for seeing higher levels of farm memberships and committee participation among women (and men) on larger farms and ranches, as chapter 1 hypothesized. The tendency for women to have less direct contact with farm marketing activities on larger farms, seen in chapters 3 and 4, though, might counterbalance such positive effects of size for organizations and activities related to marketing.

For at least some men, effects of farm size could reflect shifts in interests as the farm becomes successful. "The mature man ideally has assumed control of the enterprise and has, over the years, developed its resources to a point we have called the 'maintaining' stage. . . . economically, if he so desires, he is able to consider alternatives other than the development of the enterprise. [For at least some men] the focus changes to participation within the community, often into fields divorced from agriculture: town lodges, sports, politics" (Kohl 1976:63). One New York State farmer expressed such a change of focus in terms of needing new challenges (Elbert and Colman 1975). Therefore men with larger farms might be more likely to belong to community organizations.

One consistent finding from the general literature is that those with higher socioeconomic status participate more. Whereas family income does not necessarily increase with farm size, as seen in the previous chapter, in a farm community, having a large, successful farm might indeed be a mark of status, in addition to representing more time and money to spend outside the operation. Men might receive status from operation characteristics more than women, if the man is viewed as the "real" operator. Therefore a man from a larger enterprise might be more likely to participate in agricultural activities, and perhaps especially to represent farmers on boards and panels at various levels of government. Just as farm characteristics have more impact in predicting men's as compared with women's off-farm employment, so might they be more important in explaining men's unpaid off-farm work and participation.

More education, an important component of socioeconomic status, has been found to lead to more hours of volunteer work for women (Schram and Dunsing 1981), a higher level of organizational affiliation for men and women for most types of organizations (McPherson 1981; Duncan and Duncan 1978:179), membership in larger organizations for women (McPherson and Smith-Lovin 1982), and a higher level of political participation (see reviews in Lynn 1979; Epstein 1981). Such effects could represent greater interest in outside affairs by those with higher socioeconomic status, as well as a greater ease in such situations and a higher sense of ability to influence events. One would expect similar effects of education in the FWS. Because there is no reason to expect the effects of education to vary greatly by sex, however, such effects would not give insight into sex difference in levels of participation.

In the rest of this chapter, I consider first farm women's and men's association with voluntary organizations and activities, then their participation on advisory and governing bodies. For each set of activities, I will describe the extent of women's and men's participation, the overlap in participation within couples, and how farm, family, and the individual's characteristics and work predict participation.

Community and Farm Voluntary Activities

Results from the FWS do indeed indicate a high level of organizational memberships among farm women and men. As Table 6.1 shows, 74 percent of the women and 79 percent of the men belonged to at least one farm or community organization in the last two or three years. Because the question was about types of organizational memberships, one can only say that farm men and women had about the same extent of memberships, not the same number.[1]

As expected, there are differences by sex in types of memberships. Women are somewhat more likely than men to have belonged to a community organization (61 percent versus 57 percent), but men are more likely to have belonged to some type of agricultural organization (64 percent versus 45 percent). Although the list of farm organizations about which men were asked was shorter than that for women, men had a higher average number of membership types (though the difference by sex is not statistically significant). Both women and men were most likely to have belonged to a general farm organization, such as the Grange, although women were less likely to have belonged than men. Only 7 percent of the women belong to a women's auxiliary of a general agricultural organization. The same sort of pattern holds for commodity associations—women were less likely to belong than men, although here the proportion of women saying they belonged to an auxiliary is

Table 6.1. *Membership in Last 2–3 Years in Community and Farm Organizations*

	Women		Men	
	Percent	N[a]	Percent	N[a]
A. Marketing cooperative	8	2,492	20	568
B. Farm supply cooperative	13	2,486	29	567
C. Any general farm organization, such as the Grange, Farm Bureau, National Farmers Union, or American Agricultural Movement	33	2,496	50	569
D. Any women's auxiliaries of general farm organizations, such as Farm Bureau Women	7	2,499	Not Asked	
E. Any commodity producers' associations, such as the American Dairy Association or National Wheat Producers Association	8	2,500	17	568
F. Any women's auxiliaries of commodity organizations, such as the Cowbelles or the Wheathearts	6	2,502	Not Asked	
G. Any women's farm organizations, such as United Farm Wives, American Agri-Women, or Women involved in Farm Economics	2	2,502	Not Asked	
H. Any community organization, such as a church group, PTA, League of Women Voters	61	2,503	57	566
Belonging to any listed farm organization type	45		64	
Belonging to any farm or community organization type	74		79	
Mean number listed types of farm organizations belonged to	.75		1.16	
(standard deviation)	(1.07)		(1.15)	

[a] N's differ from 2,509 for women and 569 for men because those not responding or responding "don't know" were excluded from the base from which percents were calculated.

about the same as the proportion who said they belonged to a parent organization. Even if women belonged to *either* an organization *or* its auxiliary (which is not the case), their level of association with general farm and commodity producers' organizations would not be quite as high as men's. Very few women reported belonging to politically or economically oriented women's farm organizations, perhaps because these organizations are relatively new. Cooperatives are much more like businesses than the other farm organizations. Men's higher membership could reflect situations where there is only one family membership and that is in the man's name, although in Wisconsin, Kau (1976) found that how memberships were listed varied across cooperatives. The possibility of exclusion here was discussed above.

The Extension Service provides a host of voluntary activities for farm people, as well as other audiences. Some of the participation in Extension activities would show up as organizational memberships, as in membership in a Homemaker Club, whereas others would not, for example, participation in special production-related workshops. Although Extension activities usually provide information directly, participation in these activities can provide a chance for socializing and getting information informally, as well. The FWS asked a series of questions about participation in Extension classes and activities in the last two or three years. The percentage of women and men who participated in at least one of the listed Extension activities was about the same: 42 percent of the women and 43 percent of the men (see Table 6.2).[2] However, there is again a sex difference in type of activity. Men were over twice as likely as women to take part in farm production or management activities. Women were much more likely to say that they had taken part in home- and family-oriented activities.

These last results, though, deserve more comment. Men were not asked about activities on family living or nutrition. It is probable that very few men, if asked, would have said that they participated. On the other hand, men participated to about the same extent as the women in activities for inheritance planning and youth. Especially with respect to 4-H and other youth activities, one might have expected lower involvement of men. It may be, though, that through these activities, men help teach their children about farming, so that it becomes a family activity related to their occupation. Thus, although the difference in participation in home and family programs and activities probably reflects a true difference by sex, in

Table 6.2. *Experiences in Last 2–3 Years with Extension Service Programs and Activities (percentages)*

Activity	Women	Men
A. Classes or other activities on agricultural production	9	26
B. Classes or other activities on farm or ranch management	6	18
C. Homemaker clubs or other activities on family living	18	Not asked
D. Classes or other activities on inheritance laws or estate planning	10	11
E. Any activities on food or nutrition	20	Not asked
F. 4-H or other youth activities	24	22
Participating in any farm production or management activity or program (A or B)	11	28
Participating in any home or family program or activity (C-F)	40	28
Participating in any Extension activity	42	43
(N)	(2,509) (2,505 for F)	(569)

family-focused activities that involve both men and women, men are present in proportions equal to those of women.

Within couples there is evidence of a sexual division of labor by type of organization, as can be seen in Table 6.3. This table (using the household file) shows the distribution of joint membership statuses by type of organization or activity after further collapsing these for easier presentation. When only one member of a couple belonged to a given type of organization or participated in a given type of Extension activity, it tended to be the member whose sex matched the stereotype of the organization or activity. For example, when only one member of a couple belonged to a farm supply or market cooperative, in 84 percent of the cases (26/[26 + 5]) it was the man. When only one member of a couple took part in Extension domestic and family activities, it was much more likely to be the woman. For community organizations the difference is not as great, although the particular organizations to which members of a couple belonged could be sex-segregated.

There is also some evidence of how auxiliary memberships work. It is more likely that the husband belonged to some general farm organization or commodity producers' association and that his wife did *not* belong to the corresponding auxiliary than that she did. Not all of the specific farm organizations, of course, will have auxiliary branches. When the husband belonged to a type of organization, though, his wife was more likely to belong to an auxiliary than when the husband did not belong, especially for general farm organizations. There are, however, a few cases (and more for commodity producers' associations) where the wife reported belonging to an auxiliary of a given type and the husband did *not* report belonging to the parent organization. There are proportionately fewer couples where the woman's membership was in an auxiliary than where both belonged to the main organization, indicating that women do not necessarily substitute auxiliary membership for regular membership or fail to join the main organization if an auxiliary is not available.

Table 6.3 also shows association within couples of organizational participation (or, conversely, nonparticipation). This is demonstrated in the odds ratios. If F_{yy} is the number of couples where both members take part in some activity; $F_{yn'}$ is the number where the husband takes part, but not the wife; $F_{ny'}$ is the number of couples where the wife takes part but not the husband; and $F_{nn'}$ is the number where neither husband nor wife participates, then

$$\frac{F_{yy'}/F_{ny'}}{F_{yn'}/F_{nn'}}$$

is the odds ratio, which says how much more likely the wife is to take part in the activity or organization if the husband also does than if he does not. As can be seen by rearranging the terms, this measure is symmetric: it does not matter which term is "husband" versus "wife." Odds ratios greater than 1 show a positive association between couples' participation in types of activities.

For an example of calculating odds ratios, note from Table 6.3 that of the 496 couples where both members responded to the relevant questions, in 26 cases (5 percent) the husband belonged to a general farm organization and the wife to an auxiliary; in 219 cases (44 percent), the husband had a membership but the wife did not belong to an auxiliary; in 3 cases (1 percent), the wife belonged

Table 6.3. *Association between Members of FWS Couples in Types of Organizational Memberships and Involvement in Extension Activities*

	Members of Couple Belonging[b] (percent)						
Type of Organization or Activity[a]	Both	Husband Only	Wife Only	Neither	Total[c]	Odds Ratio	N[d]
Farm supply or marketing cooperative	9	26	5	60	100	4.62	495
General farm or commodity producers' association	30	25	6	39	100	7.85	496
Husband, commodity producers' association/ wife, commodity producers' association auxiliary	4	15	4	77	100	4.59	495
Husband, general farm organization/ wife, general farm organization auxiliary	5	44	1	50	100	9.77	496
Community organization	45	13	17	25	100	4.89	494
Agricultural Extension farm activities[e]	7	23	6	65	101	3.50	497
Agricultural Extension home and family activities[e]	20	9	20	51	100	5.94	497

[a] Refers to memberships or participation in the last 2-3 years.

[b] All tests for association between husbands' and wives' memberships and activities are significant at the .05 level or below.

[c] Totals differ from 100 due to rounding.

[d] N less than 497 because of missing data.

[e] See Table 6.2.

to an auxiliary but the husband did not have a membership; and in 247 (50 percent) neither member of the couple belonged. The odds ratio is thus

$$\frac{26/219}{3/247} = 9.77$$

The odds ratio gives in compact form the same conclusion reached earlier by comparing percentages: when the husband belongs to a given type of farm organization, his wife is then more likely to belong to a corresponding type of auxiliary, in fact almost 10 times as likely, as when the husband does not belong to the parent organization type.

In Table 6.3, all the odds ratios are greater than one. Contrary to extrapolation from Duncan and Duncan's (1978:175–79) results, the association between couples for farm organizations is not consistently lower than for nonfarm activities and memberships.

The results in this section confirm the expectations that women are less likely than men to take part in Extension activities related to running an agricultural enterprise, less likely to belong to production oriented organizations, and more likely to take part in traditionally female programs and organizations, although there is sharing of organizational participation within couples. Given the high level of organizational membership and participation of these women, obviously more is going on than simply a lack of time to take part in off-farm agricultural activities.[3]

As discussed above, there could be active exclusion of people from "inappropriate" organizations and programs. To begin to see whether this was a problem, the FWS asked respondents whether they had tried to participate in any of the listed Extension activities, but had been discouraged from doing so by Extension personnel. Only 1 percent of the women and 2 percent of the men reported any such experience. One problem with a question such as this is that some exclusion occurs without an individual's knowing it, as when he/she is *not* told about a meeting or class. Direct channeling, however, is not always necessary. People usually have a good sense of who the "appropriate" participants are in a given situation and hesitate to show up if they are not in that category. Further, spouses and other family members, as well as activity personnel, can discourage people of the "wrong" sex from being active. Unfortunately, the FWS does not provide any further information on this topic.

PREDICTING INVOLVEMENT IN FARM AND COMMUNITY ORGANIZATIONS AND PROGRAMS

To see how individual, farm, and family characteristics relate to different types of memberships and Extension involvements I estimated logistic regressions for memberships in the main types of organizations and for participation in farm and domestic Extension activities for the FWS women and for the wives and husbands in FWS couples. I included in these models the off-farm and on-farm work variables for both the women and their husbands, if they were married. In general, one would expect organizational memberships and participation to follow from or fit around other work activities. It is possible, of course, that a woman did more farm tasks because of what she learned in Extension classes or a farm organization. A more likely scenario is that a woman already interested in and performing farm tasks participated in the other activities. Because questions on organizational memberships and Extension involvement asked about membership or involvement in the last few years, however, the direction of causality is more problematic. Most farm, family, and individual characteristics were measured as of 1979–80. Thus, a person might be employed in 1980 because of contacts made or experience gained earlier in community organizations. A farm might be larger in 1980 because of knowledge the husband or wife acquired through Extension activities or farm organization memberships. As usual, there is no clear way to disentangle these relationships; one can only make reasonable substantive assumptions. Even though the strength of effects could be attenuated because of the disjunction between the time frame for the independent and the dependent variables, it seems reasonable to assume that farm, family, individual, and work characteristics affect organizational memberships and activities rather than vice versa.

Greater involvement on the farm appears to increase women's organizational participation, as expected (see Table 6.4). Having one's name on the land deed or rental contract increases the chances that a woman belonged to a cooperative, a general farm or commodity producers' organization, and a community organization (although the last effect is no longer significant when those with missing data on husbands' income are brought in). With respect to cooperatives, legal ownership of land may be a correlate of membership. Further, women with their names on deeds and rental contracts may be those who were more likely to see that they did belong to organizations associated with their farm. Having had an off-farm job does not decrease the chances of belonging to any type of organization—and even increases the chances that a woman belonged to a cooperative, perhaps because of her financial contribution to the farm. Doing a greater range of farm tasks seems to lead to a greater interest in farm organizational activities: percent of farm tasks done regularly has no significant effect on having belonged to a community organization but significantly increases the chances of having belonged to each of the three types of farm organizations. Those who spent a greater percent of their lives on farms and ranches, net of everything else, however, were more likely to belong to community organizations, but not to farm organizations.

Contrary to what was expected, however, having a husband did not seem to inhibit a woman from participating in farm organizations in her own right. Married women (not surprisingly) were more likely to take part in auxiliaries and community activities that were perhaps couple oriented. When a woman had a husband who was a part-time farmer, that is, holding an off-farm job as well as doing farm work regularly, she was less likely to belong to women's farm auxiliaries and organizations than when he did full-time farm work. The effect of a husband's combining farm and off-farm work is significant and negative on belonging to a general farm or commodity producers' association when those who did not know their husbands' off-farm income are included. One can speculate that the wives of part-time farmers had husbands who were less likely to belong to general farm and commodity organizations, and so the women themselves were less likely to belong, whereas those women whose husbands did not do farm work might have belonged on their own.

There are some life cycle effects, but not those that traditional thinking about women's home roles might lead one to expect. Consistent with other results discussed in the introduction to this chapter, having children did not decrease the chances that a woman belonged to an organization. In fact, having children ages six to seventeen increased the log-odds of having belonged to a community organization. In families whose children helped with farm work the women were slightly more likely to belong to an organization, perhaps because of somewhat more free time. In addition, for all types of organizations, women's chances of membership increased with age, but the contrasts were significant only for membership in community organizations.

As expected, those from larger farms and from operations with more than one hired hand were more likely to belong to community organizations, general farm and commodity organizations, and women's farm auxiliaries and organizations. The negative effect of full ownership (as compared with both owning and renting land) on membership in general farm and commodity associations might be an additional indicator that those from larger operations were more likely to be organization members: even within size categories, full owners may have had smaller operations than those both owning and renting. However, the effect of farm size, when significant, is not always monotonic: those in the second category (300–999 acres) were the most likely to have belonged to community and general farm and commodity associations. The results are weaker for cooperatives, where acreage has no significant effect, and the effect of hired hands is no longer significant when those who did not know their husband's off-farm income are included.

Finally, even controlling for all the other variables, for each type of organization, women with more education were more likely to belong, a finding consistent with most of the other literature on organizational membership and participation.

Among couples, as can be seen in Table 6.5,[4] children do not significantly affect either sex's community memberships. Age patterns differ by sex, however. For women, membership did not significantly vary by age category; for men, community organizational membership was least likely when they were under thirty-one, a stage in the life cycle when one might have expected pressure on women's time as well from farm and family demands. Although experience with farm living here has the same positive effect for wives that it did for all the women, there is no effect of this variable for men. There are no significant effects of farm characteristics on having belonged to community organizations unless the regional effects represent variation among types of operations across parts of the country. These regional contrasts are significant only for the husbands. There is no support here for the picture of men with larger farms or later in the farm life cycle turning to community organizations. Education, however, increases chances for community memberships, and somewhat more so for husbands.

Farm characteristics do affect the odds of membership in cooperatives and farm associations and more so for husbands than for wives, as expected. For example, the effect of having a very large operation of over 1,000 acres, in contrast with having an operation of less than 50 acres, is only marginally significant in predicting whether a wife was a cooperative member, and the magnitude of the coefficients at the observed means is larger for husbands than for wives: being in the largest operation size category increases the probability of membership in a cooperative by .19 for women and .22 for men. With respect to general farm and producers' organizations, having spent more of one's life on a farm increases the proba-

Table 6.4. *Logistic Regression for Membership in Community and Farm Organizations in Last 2–3 Years: FWS Women (logit coefficients)*

Independent Variables[a]	Organization Type: Community Organizations	Organization Type: Farm Supply or Marketing Cooperative
Farm Characteristics		
Total acres in farm relative to less than 50 acres:		
50-299 acres	.53**	.28
300-999 acres	.70**	.32
> 1,000 acres	.58**	.22
Sales relative to mixed crops and livestock:		
Less than 5 percent total sales from crops	-.13	-.14
Greater than 95 percent total sales from crops	-.06	-.17
Don't know percent of sales from crops	-.36	-.65*
Tenancy relative to part owners:		
Full owners	-.04	-.11
Renters	.05	.41
Neither owners nor renters	-.30	.15
Woman's Legal Relation to Land		
Own name on deed or rental contract for land	.30*	.74**
Decision Makers		
Include other than husband and wife	.09	.26
Region		
Relative to South:		
Northeast	-.18	-.13
Northcentral	.18	.35
West	.003	.28

Organization Type	
General Farm Organization or Commodity Producers' Associations	Women's Auxiliary of General Farm or Commodity Producers' Association or Women's Farm Organization
.58**	1.03**
.76**	1.12**
.66**	1.76**
-.26*	-.21
-.12	-.35
-.69**	-.18
-.27*	.16
-.23	-.10
-.33	.25
.42*	.19
.04	.12
.36*	.48
.20	.30
.10	1.03**

Table 6.4. *continued*

	Organization Type	
Independent Variables[a]	Community Organizations	Farm Supply or Marketing Cooperative
Labor Structure of Farm		
More than 1 hired hand	.24*	.27*
Husband's work relative to husband who regularly does farm work and has no off-farm job:		
No husband	-.69**	-.10
Husband regularly does farm work and has off-farm job	.09	-.20
Husband does not regularly do farm work and has off-farm job	-.03	-.14
Husband does not regularly do farm work and has no off-farm job	-.16	-.31
Number of sons at least 18 who regularly do farm work	-.02	.11
Number of children ages 6-17 who regularly do farm work	.29**	-.04
Number of other household members who regularly do farm work	-.07	-.19
Number of other non-household members who regularly do farm work	.01	.03
Farm Woman's Characteristics		
Education relative to high school graduate:		
Less than high school	-.79**	-.52*
Postsecondary vocational or some college	.25	.21
College degree or above	.73**	.30
Percent of life spent on farms or ranches	.005**	-.002

Organization Type	
General Farm Organization or Commodity Producers' Associations	Women's Auxiliary of General Farm or Commodity Producers' Association or Women's Farm Organization
.45**	.53**
-.33	-1.37**
-.19	-.62**
-.09	-.39
.06	.18
.23*	.02
-.10	-.05
.04	-.07
.05	-.01
-.46**	-.73**
.24	.17
.29	.49**
.005**	.004

Table 6.4. *continued*

Independent Variables[a]	Organization Type: Community Organizations	Organization Type: Farm Supply or Marketing Cooperative
Farm Women's Characteristics (cont'd)		
Age relative to over 65:		
less than 31	-.96**	-.41
31-45	-.47*	-.19
46-65	-.18	.06
Dependent Children		
Number of children less than age 6	.08	.05
Number of children 6-17 who do not regularly do farm work	.16*	.08
Woman's Work		
Woman currently employed off-farm	.17	.32*
Percent of types of farm tasks done regularly	.004	.02**
Constant	-.02	-1.83
D	.10	.06
N[b]	2,026	2,024
Observed probability	.63	.17

* $.01 \leq p < .05$.

** $p < .01$.

[a]For categorical variables, 1 = yes, 0 = no.

[b]N's less than 2,509 because of missing data.

Organization Type	
General Farm Organization or Commodity Producers' Associations	Women's Auxiliary of General Farm or Commodity Producers' Association or Women's Farm Organization
-.47	-.28
-.33	-.16
-.20	-.09
.00	.08
.02	-.19
.16	-.07
.009**	.01**
-1.26	-3.86
.10	.09
2,027	2,027
.40	.13

Table 6.5. *Logistic Regression for Membership in Community and Farm Organizations in Last 2–3 Years: FWS Couples (logit coefficients)*

	Organization Type	
	Community Organization	
Independent Variables[a]	Wife	Husband
Farm Characteristics		
Total acres in farm relative to less than 50 acres:		
50-299 acres	.32	.13
300-999 acres	.30	.55
> 1,000 acres	.03	.23
Sales relative to mixed crops and livestock:		
Less than 5 percent total sales from crops	.04	-.21
Greater than 95 percent total sales from crops	.38	-.05
Tenancy relative to part owners:		
Full owners	.12	-.19
Renters	-.41	-.34
Neither owners nor renters	.95	.29
Decision Makers		
Include other than husband and wife	.26	.88
Region		
Relative to South:		
Northeast	-.23	-.75*
Northcentral	.36	.01
West	-.14	-.81*

Organization Type			
Farm Supply Or Marketing Cooperative		General Farm Or Commodity Associations	
Wife	Husband	Wife	Husband
.45	.46	.47	.30
.10	1.06**	.71	1.31**
1.07	.91*	1.14*	1.63**
-.26	-.12	-.45	-.24
-.23	.19	-.12	.39
-.04	-.04	-.23	.22
-.02	-.50	-.86	-.72
.09	-.69	-.86	-1.11
.51	.71**	.04	.39
.33	-.33	.19	-.42
.87	.51	.48	-.63
.46	.20	.21	-.47

Table 6.5. *continued*

Independent Variables[a]	Organization Type: Community Organization	
	Wife	Husband
Labor Structure of Farm		
More than 1 hired hand	.02	.24
Number of sons at least 18 who regularly do farm work	.43	.34
Number of children ages 6-17 who regularly do farm work	.18	.22
Number of other household members who regularly do farm work	-.32	.13
Number of other, nonhousehold members who regularly do farm work	-.10	-.13
Farm Wife's (or Husband's) Characteristics		
Education relative to high school graduate:		
Less than high school	-.75*	-.28
Postsecondary vocational or some college	.13	.46
College degree or above	1.29**	1.68**
Percent of life spent on farms or ranches	.01**	.006
Age relative to over 65:		
less than 31	-.24	-1.61*
31-45	-.007	-.85
46-65	-.20	-.37
Dependent Children		
Number of children less than age 6	-.28	.27
Number of children 6-17 who do not regularly do farm work	.09	.26

Organization Type			
Farm Supply Or Marketing Cooperative		General Farm Or Commodity Associations	
Wife	Husband	Wife	Husband
.06	.11	.52*	.54*
-.08	.02[b,c]	.24	.48
		-.18	.16
		.12	.18
		.006	-.08
-.72	-.17	-.12	-.70*
-.23	.48	.10	.47
.55	.78*	.86*	.77*
-.000	-.001	.009*	.01**
.01	-.006[d]	.07	1.69*
		-.18	.67
		-.12	.87*
		-.16	-.01
.12	.04[c]		
		-.12	-.19

Table 6.5. *continued*

	Organization Type	
	Community Organization	
Independent Variables[a]	Wife	Husband
Wife's Work		
Woman currently employed off-farm	.20	.03
Percent of types of farm tasks done regularly	.003	-.004
Husband's Work		
Husband currently has off-farm job	-.07	.41
Husband regularly does farm work	.14	-.05
Constant	-.01	2.75
D	.12	.14
N[e]	471	468
Observed probability	.63	.58

* $.01 \leq p < .05$.

** $p < .01$.

[a]For categorical variables, 1 = yes, 0 = no.

[b]In this model number of sons over 17, of other family helpers, and of other nonfamily helpers were combined in order to estimate the model for wives.

[c]The variable here is number of children under 18 years of age.

[d]Age was used as a continuous variable in this model.

[e]N's less than 497 because of missing data.

Organization Type			
Farm Supply Or Marketing Cooperative		General Farm Or Commodity Associations	
Wife	Husband	Wife	Husband
.39	.22	.34	.24
.01	-.005	.02**	-.000
.12	-.23	.39	-.64*
1.22	.58	.56	-.46
-2.81	-.24	-1.26	-1.25
.07	.15	.15	.23
470	468	471	469
.15	.39	.39	.58

bility of membership about equally for women and men. Age has no significant effect for either husbands or wives on membership in cooperatives but does have significant variation for men with respect to farm organizations. Men under thirty-one and middle-aged were *more* likely than men in other age categories to belong to these organizations. Although for women other work and family responsibilities do not depress their odds of having been a member of a given type of organization (and farm work even increases the log-odds for farm organizations), for general farm organizations and commodity producers associations, men with off-farm jobs were less likely to have belonged. Education again affects membership in cooperatives and farm organizations more for husbands than for wives.

Results for participation in Extension Service activities show many of the same patterns seen in the analysis of farm and community organization memberships. For all women farm size again has effects. Women from larger farms are more likely to have taken part in Extension activities related to farm production and management, but women from farms with more than one hired hand are more likely to have participated in domestic and family activities, as can be seen in Table 6.6. Again contrary to what was predicted, unmarried women were less likely to take part in Extension farm-related activities, significantly so when women lacking data on husbands' off-farm income are included. The presence of other decision makers facilitated taking part in these activities (and for domestic and family activities, the effect was significant when the missing-data cases were also analyzed). These last results seem counterintuitive unless it is the case that families tend to participate in Extension activities together, as Table 6.3 suggested. Keep in mind, too, that members of a family may be participating in the same *types* of activities, but not in exactly the same activities. Here, doing a greater range of farm tasks increased the probability that a woman would be involved in both types of Extension work. In a way resembling the difference between community and farm organizations, having spent more of one's life on a farm or ranch increased the chances of having been involved in Extension domestic and family activities, but not in farm production and management activities. Again, having more children did not prevent a woman from taking part in Extension activities, but actually encouraged it, especially when the children helped with the farm work. There are, however, no age effects. There are education effects for both types of activities, with less educated women less likely to have participated.

From the results for the couples in Table 6.7, one finds again that the effects of farm size are stronger for the men than for their wives. There are no significant age effects here. Higher education, though, again has significant effects for both husbands and wives, effects that are, as before, larger for husbands. Although women who had off-farm jobs did not have significantly different probabilities of participating in Extension activities, men with off-farm jobs were less likely to have taken part in farm management and production activities—and so, to a lesser extent, were their wives. This effect is like the one on organizational memberships. One could speculate that some of this effect for wives is due to the greater responsibilities they then had on the farm. Doing a greater range of tasks, though, net of other things, increased women's chances of participation in both home- and farm-focused Extension activities. Although having children active on the farm increased wives' chances of having taken part in Extension management and production activities, children under six actually inhibited men from taking part in home-directed activities, even controlling for the presence of older children who might be eligible for 4-H. There is certainly no evidence that responsibility for children inhibits *women's* participation in Extension classes and activities. Although there are some life cycle effects, there are no age effects here.

Involvement in Committees, Panels, and Governing Boards

The previous section looked at sex differences in organizational memberships and Extension Service activities. This section looks at sex differences in participation in bodies that advise, plan, or govern at various levels. In the wider society, women are especially underrepresented in political and administrative positions, although some progress has been made. One would expect the same to be true in rural communities and on agricultural bodies.

The FWS asked women whether they had been elected or appointed to any local governing body, and asked both men and women whether they had ever served on an Extension program committee, a local, county, or state committee or board concerned with agricultural matters, or a USDA panel or committee. A summary of responses to these questions is shown in Table 6.8. Almost 30 percent of the women and almost a quarter of the men said

Table 6.6. *Logistic Regression for Involvement in Extension Service Activities in Last 2–3 Years: FWS Women (logit coefficients)*

	Type of Activity[b]	
Independent Variables[a]	Farm Production and Management	Domestic and Family
__Farm Characteristics__		
Total acres in farm relative to less than 50 acres:		
50–299 acres	.15	-.08
300–999 acres	.58*	.29
> 1,000 acres	.81**	.38
Sales relative to mixed crops and livestock:		
Less than 5 percent total sales from crops	-.04	-.35**
Greater than 95 percent total sales from crops	.04	-.54**
Don't know percent of sales from crops	-.13	-.20
Tenancy relative to part owners:		
Full owners	.17	.02
Renters	-.15	.007
Neither owners nor renters	-.69	-.09
__Woman's Legal Relation to Land__		
Own name on deed or rental contract for land	.14	.07
__Decision Makers__		
Include other than husband and wife	.37*	.18
__Region__		
Relative to South:		
Northeast	.28	.20
Northcentral	-.04	.40**
West	-.14	.51**

Table 6.6. *continued*

	Type of Activity[b]	
Independent Variables[a]	Farm Production and Management	Domestic and Family
Labor Structure of Farm		
More than 1 hired hand	.09	.34**
Husband's work relative to husband who regularly does farm work and has no off-farm job:		
No husband	-.72	-.10
Husband regularly does farm work and has off-farm job	-.15	.19
Husband does not regularly do farm work and has off-farm job	.006	.35
Husband does not regularly do farm work and has no off-farm job	-.39	-.19
Number of sons at least 18 who regularly do farm work	-.009	.02
Number of children ages 6-17 who regularly do farm work	.23**	.27**
Number of other household members who regularly do farm work	-.11	-.05
Number of other non-household members who regularly do farm work	.06	.01
Farm Woman's Characteristics		
Education relative to high school graduate:		
Less than high school	-.35	-.68**
Postsecondary vocational or some college	.63**	.38**
College degree or above	.76**	.46**
Percent of life spent on farms or ranches	-.001	.004*

Table 6.6. *continued*

Independent Variables[a]	Type of Activity[b]	
	Farm Production and Management	Domestic and Family
Farm Woman's Characteristics (cont'd)		
Age relative to over 65:		
less than 31	.10	-.16
31-45	-.17	.12
46-65	-.11	.09
Dependent Children		
Number of children less than age 6	-.14	.11
Number of children 6-17 who do not regularly do farm work	.003	.20**
Woman's Work		
Woman currently employed off-farm	.26	-.01
Percent of types of farm tasks done regularly	.03**	.009**
Constant	-2.59	-1.31
D	.07	.11
N[c]	2,031	2,031
Observed probability	.12	.42

*.01 ≤ p < .05.

**p < .01.

[a]For categorical variables, 1 = yes, 0 = no.

[b]See Table 6.2.

[c]N's less than 2,509 because of missing data.

Table 6.7. *Logistic Regression for Involvement in Extension Service Activities in Last 2–3 Years: FWS Couples (logit coefficients)*

	Type of Activity[b]			
	Farm production and management		Domestic and family	
Independent Variables[a]	Wife	Husband	Wife	Husband
Farm Characteristics				
Total acres in farm relative to less than 50 acres:				
50-299 acres	.39	.09	-.22	.23
300-999 acres	.28	.96*	.34	.99*
> 1,000 acres	.79	.81	.69	1.17*
Sales relative to mixed crops and livestock:				
Less than 5 percent total sales from crops	.16	-.55	-.61*	.16
Greater than 95 percent total sales from crops	.82*	-.02	-.47	-.20
Tenancy relative to part owners:				
Full owners	-.005	-.25	.17	-.25
Renters	-.67	-.58	.26	-1.07
Neither owners nor renters	.56	.03	.37	-.75
Decision Makers				
Include other than husband and wife	.19	.10	.46	.73*
Region				
Relative to South:				
Northeast	.22	-.11	.34	.76
Northcentral	.52	.04	.61	1.02*
West	.14	-.13	.38	.70

Table 6.7. *continued*

	Type of Activity[b]			
	Farm production and management		Domestic and family	
Independent Variables[a]	Wife	Husband	Wife	Husband
Labor Structure of Farm				
More than 1 hired hand	.11	.20	.08	.30
Number of sons at least 18 who regularly do farm work	-.20	.21	.17	-.26
Number of children ages 6-17 who regularly do farm work	.37*	-.16	.19	.17
Number of other household members who regularly do farm work	-.32	.04	.03	.41
Number of other, nonhousehold members who regularly do farm work	-.05	-.03	-.01	-.14
Farm Wife's and Husband's Characteristics				
Education relative to high school graduate:				
Less than high school	-.71	-1.05**	-.84*	.01
Postsecondary vocational or some college	.25	.67*	.33	.83*
College degree or above	.86*	2.07**	.71*	2.00**
Percent of life spent on farms or ranches	-.003	.000	.006	.01**
Age relative to over 65:				
less than 31	-.98	-.07	-.01	.23
31-45	-1.19	.45	-.18	.99
46-65	-1.16	.29	-.64	.58

Table 6.7. *continued*

	Type of Activity[b]			
	Farm production and management		Domestic and family	
Independent Variables[a]	Wife	Husband	Wife	Husband
Dependent Children				
Number of children less than age 6	-.29	.21	-.15	-.53*
Number of children 6-17 who do not regularly do farm work	.09	-.11	.25	-.04
Wife's Work				
Woman currently employed off-farm	.34	-.29	-.44	.04
Percent of types of farm tasks done regularly	.04**	.009	.01*	.008
Husband's Work				
Husband currently has off-farm job	-.92*	-.79**	.20	.58
Husband regularly does farm work	1.21	.35	.68	.23
Constant	-4.79	-3.65	-1.58	-2.27
D	.12	.23	.17	.20
N[c]	471	469	471	469
Observed probability	.13	.32	.41	.29

* $.01 \leq p < .05$.

** $p < .01$.

[a]For categorical variables, 1 = yes, 0 = no.

[b]See Table 6.2.

[c]N's less than 497 because of missing data.

Table 6.8. *Involvement in Agricultural and Community Panels, Committees, or Boards*

Official Body on Which Have Served	Women		Men	
	Percent	N[a]	Percent	N[a]
Local extension program committee	29	2,504	23	569
State, county, or local level committee, board, or panel	6	2,501	17	567
USDA committee, board, or panel	6	2,502	16	567
Election or appointment to local governing board, such as school board	8	2,501	Not asked	

[a] N's differ from 2,509 for women and 569 for men because those not responding or responding "don't know" were excluded from the base from which percents were calculated.

that they had at some time served on a committee to develop or carry out Extension Service activities. One would suspect that this more than equal representation for women results from their leadership in typically female Extension programs. Participation in other policymaking and advisory positions is much lower, and the sex difference greater. Almost a fifth of the men had served on local and state agricultural bodies, but only 6 percent of the women had. Eight percent of the women reported having served on some local governing board.

Although there are sex differences in service on boards and committees, it is again true that within couples, one spouse having served on some committee increased the likelihood that the other had as well, as can be seen in Table 6.9. This could reflect farm, family, and attitudinal variables common to a couple that increase the participation of both in such bodies or could indicate a sharing of networks and contacts. At the same time, when only one member of the couple had served on some agricultural board, panel, or committee, it was more likely to have been the husband. For example, in 14 percent of the couples, the husband was the only one who said that he had served on a USDA body; in 4 percent the wife said she had served but the husband had not.[5]

There are a number of explanations for women's lower representation on official agricultural committees. Women may not be selected for such positions, or they may choose not to take part. Sex

Table 6.9. *Association between Members of FWS Couples in Participation in Extension Program Committees and Agricultural Committees, Panels, and Boards*

	Members of Couple Who Have Ever Served (percentages)[a]						
Type of Committee or Board	Both members	Husband only	Wife only	Neither	Total[b]	Odds Ratio	N
Extension program committee	13	11	17	59	100	4.09	496
Local, county, state agricultural committee panel or advisory board	3	14	3	80	100	7.06	494
USDA committee, panel or advisory board	3	14	4	80	101	3.78	496

[a] All tests for association between husbands' and wives' participation are significant at the .05 level or below.

[b] Totals differ from 100 due to rounding.

differences in effects of farm, family, and individual characteristics on participation on various kinds of committees and boards will be shown below. The FWS did try to assess whether self-selection was a reason for nonparticipation by asking whether the respondent would be willing to serve on or run for election to these bodies in the future. As Table 6.10 shows, a much higher percentage of women than men gave negative responses. In the pretest of the survey, reasons for such refusal included not wanting to travel, not having the time, and not feeling comfortable in such situations.

Studies of attitudes toward job promotions have found similar differences by sex in willingness to take on managerial responsibilities (e.g., Hoffmann and Reed 1981; Kanter 1977a). Some people (e.g., Hoffmann and Reed) conclude that women do not want to serve (or be promoted) and should not be forced to do so. Kanter (1977a), on the other hand, found that women who were nudged upward found they could perform at the higher levels. Their unwillingness to be promoted was, in part, an acceptance of their past lack of opportunity as well as uncertainty about taking on an atypical position (see also Jacquette's 1976 discussion of effects of blocked

Table 6.10. *Willingness to Serve on Official Groups in the Future (percentages)*

Would Agree to Serve?	Women	Men
Definitely yes	4	11
Probably yes	27	43
Probably no	38	28
Definitely no	27	14
Don't know	4	4
Total	100	100
(N[a])	(2,503)	(568)

[a] N's differ from 2,509 for women and 569 for men because of missing data.

opportunity on political activity and attitudes). Further, looking at the figures another way, one sees that 35 percent of the women said definitely yes, probably yes, or don't know that they would serve or run for election. These women might be persuaded to take part. This is a sizable proportion, although lower than the 58 percent for men. Even in the absence of external barriers to women's participation on these committees, special efforts might be necessary to seek out those who are willing to serve and to interest those who otherwise might not consider this an opportunity for themselves.

Experience in atypical positions does not always lead to willingness to continue in such positions, however. In a study of women in traditionally male nonprofessional jobs, McIlwee (1982) reported that at least some of the women were dissatisfied with their jobs because they did not like the type of work or the pressure on them from being a minority. In the FWS, people who had served on some committee or board in the past were more willing to do so in the future, but men were more willing to consider further service than women. Of the women who had served in the past, 45 percent said that they would be willing to be on such a committee later, in contrast with 25 percent of the women who had not been on one of the three types of committees and boards. For men, almost two-thirds of those who had served and nearly half of those who had not said they would probably or definitely serve in the future if asked (see Jones and Rosenfeld 1981:122–24). The FWS did not ask why people who had served would rather not again. But the results suggest that experiences for women in such situations differ from those for men.

PREDICTING MEMBERSHIP ON POLICYMAKING AND ADVISORY BODIES

To predict membership on policymaking and advisory bodies, local, county, and state boards were collapsed with USDA boards to decrease the skew on the dependent variable. Appropriate organizational memberships and Extension activity participation were included as one step in the analysis. As mentioned in the introduction to this chapter, participation in voluntary organizations and volunteer work has been a path to political appointment and office, especially for women. For example, in May 1983 the California Women for Agriculture newsletter, *Compass*, announced the appointment of its charter president, who was also a member of a number of other organizations, to the state board of food and agriculture. Therefore, these variables might affect women more than men. On the other hand, if men hold more central or critical memberships, then they might benefit from these memberships to a greater extent than women. Again, there is a problem of the direction of causality. The questions about committee, board, and panel participation have no time referent. They begin, "Have you ever . . . ?" Farm, family, and individual characteristics, and organizational and Extension involvement may have changed because the person served. These results, then, are only suggestive of the forces behind doing committee work.

The results for the full sample of women are shown in Table 6.11. There is no evidence here that other work and family responsibilities prevented a woman from serving on local governing boards, Extension program committees, or agricultural bodies. For local governing boards, women with off-farm jobs were more likely to have served, and the range of farm tasks has no effect. This is consistent with research finding employment and political activity to be complements rather than substitutes. On the other hand, the women who served on governing boards could be women who ordinarily had off-farm employment and served on such a board (perhaps with some nominal salary) rather than take other employment. Without data on the timing of office holding, it is not possible to test these hypotheses against each other. Having children

Table 6.11. *Logistic Regression for Having Served on Community and Agricultural Committees, Panels, and Boards: FWS Women (logit coefficients)*

	Type of Body	
	Local Governing Board	
Independent Variables[a]	without organization memberships, activities	with organization memberships, activities
Farm Characteristics		
Total acres in farm relative to less than 50 acres:		
50-299 acres	.13	.01
300-999 acres	-.006	-.16
> 1,000 acres	.21	.07
Sales relative to mixed crops and livestock:		
Less than 5 percent total sales from crops	.01	.02
Greater than 95 percent total sales from crops	-.10	-.11
Don't know percent of sales from crops	-.34	-.26
Tenancy relative to part owners:		
Full owners	-.05	-.07
Renters	.04	.02
Neither owners nor renters	-.34	-.34
Woman's Legal Relation to Land		
Own name on deed or rental contract for land	.52	.45

Type of Body			
Extension Program Committee		Local, County, State, or USDA Agricultural Committee, Panel, or Advisory Board	
without organization memberships, activities	with organization memberships, activities	without organization memberships, activities	with organization memberships, activities
.25	.28	.51	.32
.52**	.41*	.79**	.56
.62**	.44	1.10**	.87**
-.19	-.11	-.16	-.15
-.49**	-.38*	-.51*	-.47*
-.20	-.14	-.30	-.02
.11	.09	.09	.18
.11	.15	-.18	-.20
-.45	-.35	.23	.31
.27	.29	.36	.09

Table 6.11. *continued*

Independent Variables[a]	Type of Body: Local Governing Board — without organization memberships, activities	Type of Body: Local Governing Board — with organization memberships, activities
Decision Makers		
Include other than husband and wife	-.03	-.03
Region		
Relative to South:		
Northeast	.17	.21
Northcentral	.21	.21
West	.18	.21
Labor Structure of Farm		
More than 1 hired hand	.57**	.52**
Husband's work relative to husband who regularly does farm work and has no off-farm job:		
No husband	-.71	-.56
Husband regularly does farm work and has off-farm job	-.33	-.35
Husband does not regularly do farm work and has off-farm job	-.49	-.52
Husband does not regularly do farm work and has no off-farm job	-.13	-.09
Number of sons at least 18 who regularly do farm work	-.08	-.09

Type of Body			
Extension Program Committee		Local, County, State, or USDA Agricultural Committee, Panel, or Advisory Board	
without organization memberships, activities	with organization memberships, activities	without organization memberships, activities	with organization memberships, activities
.42**	.39**	.14	.07
.33*	.28	.10	-.05
.29	.19	-.24	-.52*
.41*	.28	.14	-.07
.25*	.12	.40*	.14
.15	.30	-.45	-.17
.06	.009	.18	.44*
.13	-.02	-.41	-.23
.13	.29	.30	.34
-.11	-.16	-.07	-.17

Table 6.11. *continued*

	Type of Body	
	Local Governing Board	
Independent Variables[a]	without organization memberships, activities	with organization memberships, activities
Labor Structure of Farm (cont'd)		
Number of children ages 6-17 who regularly do farm work	.29**	.26**
Number of other household members who regularly do farm work	-.50	-.52
Number of other nonhousehold members who regularly do farm work	.03	.03
Farm Woman's Characteristics		
Education relative to high school graduate:		
Less than high school	-.65*	-.47
Postsecondary vocational or some college	.19	.14
College degree or above	.71**	.62**
Percent of life spent on farms or ranches	.005	.004
Age relative to over 65:		
less than 31	-.47	-.35
31-45	.76	.80
46-65	1.03	1.04
Dependent Children		
Number of children less than age 6	.11	.09
Number of children 6-17 who do not regularly do farm work	.31**	.28**

Type of Body			
Extension Program Committee		Local, County, State, or USDA Agricultural Committee, Panel, or Advisory Board	
without organization memberships, activities	with organization memberships, activities	without organization memberships, activities	with organization memberships, activities
.19**	.09	.03	.05
-.19	-.24	.39*	.44*
.008	-.004	.05	.04
-.82**	-.66**	-.65*	-.45
.37**	.20	.43*	.36
.57**	.40*	.83**	.68**
.008**	.008**	.006	.005
-.91**	-1.05**	-.64	-.66
-.59*	-.75**	-.74*	-.80*
-.29	-.35	-.38	-.44
-.15	-.20	-.15	-.19
.06	-.005	-.11	-.08

Table 6.11. *continued*

	Type of Body	
	Local Governing Board	
Independent Variables[a]	without organization memberships, activities	with organization memberships, activities
Woman's Work		
Woman currently employed off-farm	.50**	.47*
Percent of types of farm tasks done regularly	.007	.007
Organizational Memberships, Activities[b]		
	--	1.03**
Constant	-3.92	-4.50
D	.05	.06
N[c]	2,023	2,020
Observed probability	.09	.09

*.01 ≤ p < .05.

**p < .01.

[a]For categorical variables, 1 = yes, 0 = no.

[b]For local governing board, this is whether the woman belonged to any community organization; for Extension program activity, it is whether the woman took part in Extension production or family focused activities; for agricultural committees, panels and boards, it is number of types of farm organization memberships.

[c]N's are less than 2,509 because of missing data.

Type of Body			
Extension Program Committee		Local, County, State, or USDA Agricultural Committee, Panel, or Advisory Board	
without organization memberships, activities	with organization memberships, activities	without organization memberships, activities	with organization memberships, activities
.20	.22	-.06	-.15
.005	-.002	.01**	.01*
—	.83** (production)		
—	1.75** (family)	--	.66**
-.92	-1.41	-3.47	-3.84
.09	.21	.06	.11
2,025		2,028	
.30		.10	

ages six to seventeen actually increased the likelihood that the woman held office. If the office was one held in the past, then it was more likely that the woman held office even when she had very young children. For involvement in Extension program committees, before considering whether the woman recently participated in Extension activities, the number of children ages six to seventeen who did farm work has a positive effect. When women who did not know their husbands' off-farm income were included, the positive effects of off-farm employment and of range of farm tasks (before controlling for recent Extension activity participation) were statistically significant. The presence of children has no effect on serving on agricultural boards at various governmental levels, and having done a wider range of farm tasks only increased the probability of having served. The positive effect of having other household members who did farm tasks on serving on agricultural committees, panels, and boards suggests some substitution for a woman's labor by other family members when she was gone, but it is an effect that is not statistically significant when those missing data on husband's off-farm income are included.

There are farm effects as well. Those from larger farms were more likely to be on Extension program committees and official agricultural bodies. Having more than one hired hand increased the odds that a woman served on a local governing board, even controlling for organizational memberships, and on agricultural panels in equations without other measures of organizational participation. This could represent a labor substitution effect, but might also represent the prosperity of the farm. Coming from a farm that concentrated its sales on crops had a depressing effect on serving on Extension or other agricultural committees, perhaps because such programs involve livestock production.

As was true for organizational memberships and Extension activities, those with more education were more likely to have played a part in planning, advising, and policymaking off the farm. In contrast with results for memberships and Extension activities, older women were more likely to have served. Experience with farm living, measured by percent of life spent on farms and ranches, also increased the probability of serving on Extension program committees, though only marginally on agricultural panels, boards, and committees. Rather than reflect the effects of age or experience, however, such measures might simply indicate a longer time over which to have had the chance to have been placed on these boards and committees.

Organizational memberships and Extension involvement have large effects on serving in some planning, advisory, or policymaking capacity. With respect to Extension program committees, the effect of participating in home and family activities is much greater than that of taking part in farm production and management activities, perhaps because women were more likely to be on program committees for activities dealing with more traditionally female domestic concerns.

From Table 6.12 one can compare the results for husbands and wives. There is no clear evidence here that family and work responsibilities inhibit women more than men from serving on various kinds of committees and boards. In fact, the only significant effect of children's presence is a negative effect of the number of children under six on *husbands* having served on agricultural committees, panels, and advisory boards. In magnitude, too, the effect of children under six is larger for men than for women, when comparisons are made at the observed probabilities for the two groups. Some evidence of substitution of other family members facilitating the participation of both men and women on agricultural boards is seen in the positive effects of number of other household members who do farm work (for women) and of other nonhousehold members (for men). At their observed probabilities, having one more household member who does farm work increases by .1 the probability that a woman had served on some agricultural board; for men, having another nonhousehold member who helped out increases the probability of his having served on an agricultural committee or board by .06, before controlling for number of farm organizational memberships. These life cycles and labor effects, then, are similar by sex.

However, age has effects on the involvement of both women and men, although there is some suggestion that women's committee participation reaches its low at an earlier age than men's: at thirty-one to forty-five for women and at forty-six to sixty-five for men. These differences, although not strong, may represent different life cycle pressure for women and men at the different ages. Despite the lack of significant effects of number of children, women in their early thirties to mid-forties may have had more family responsibilities than those in other age groups, whereas men in their mid-forties to sixties may have been at a stage when they were continuing to build up their operations. However, the main conclusion from the pattern of age effect is that, among both men and women, those over retirement age were somewhat more likely to have

Table 6.12. *Logistic Regression for Having Served on Agricultural Committees, Panels, and Boards: FWS Couples (logit coefficients)*

	Type of Body			
	Extension Program Committee			
	Wife		Husband	
Independent Variables[a]	without organization memberships, activities	with organization memberships, activities	without organization memberships, activities	with organization memberships activities
Farm Characteristics				
Total acres in farm relative to less than 50 acres:				
50-299 acres	-.06	-.05	.41	.45
300-999 acres	.44	.28	.30	.003
> 1,000 acres	.68	.35	.72	.46
Sales relative to mixed crops and livestock:				
Less than 5 percent total sales from crops	-.05	.18	-.32	-.31
Greater than 95 percent total sales from crops	-.44	-.41	-.19	-.14
Tenancy relative to part owners:				
Full owners	-.15	-.30	.49	.63*
Renters	-.45	-.56	-.09	.23
Neither owners nor renters	.11	-.14	1.23	1.51
Decision Makers				
Include other than husband and wife	.46	.36	.39	.21
Region				
Relative to South:				
Northeast	.61	.59	.56	.50
Northcentral	.53	.37	.46	.29
West	.82*	.89*	.85*	.83*

Type of Body			
Local, County, State, or USDA Agricultural Committee, Panel, or Advisory Board			
Wife		Husband	
without organization memberships, activities	with organization memberships, activities	without organization memberships, activities	with organization memberships, activities
1.33	1.34	1.15*	1.09*
1.71*	1.80*	1.41**	1.17*
1.98*	1.82*	1.78**	1.53**
.16	.18	-.48	-.48
-.22	-.07	-.15	-.24
-.06	.11	.31	.35
-1.17	-.80	-.60	-.59
.55	.87	-.30	-.03
.49	.48	.22	.12
-.17	-.44	-.22	-.18
.22	-.32	-.05	-.16
.12	-.14	.18	.18

Table 6.12. *continued*

	Type of Body			
	Extension Program Committee			
	Wife		Husband	
Independent Variables[a]	without organization memberships, activities	with organization memberships, activities	without organization memberships, activities	with organization memberships, activities
Labor Structure of Farm				
More than 1 hired hand	.46	.57*	.39	.31
Number of sons at least 18 who regularly do farm work	-.03	-.17	.21	.26
Number of children ages 6-17 who regularly do farm work	.16	.07	-.06	-.06
Number of other household members who regularly do farm work	.03	-.12	.02	-.11
Number of other, nonhousehold members who regularly do farm work	.00	.01	.007	.06
Farm Wife's (Husband's) Characteristics				
Education relative to high school graduate:				
Less than high school	-.55	-.16	-.53	-.40
Postsecondary vocational or some college	.23	.13	.00	-.33
College degree or above	.90**	.65	1.00**	.16
Percent of life spent on farms or ranches	.01**	.01**	.008	.005
Age relative to over 65:				
less than 31	-1.30	-1.48	-.67	-.83
31-45	-1.16*	-1.27	-.53	-.93
46-65	-.89	-.62	-.74	-.97*
Dependent Children				
Number of children less than age 6	-.34	-.32	-.14	-.03
Number of children 6-17 who do not regularly do farm work	.03	-.08	-.21	-.21

Type of Body			
Local, County, State, or USDA Agricultural Committee, Panel, or Advisory Board			
Wife		Husband	
without organization memberships, activities	with organization memberships, activities	without organization memberships, activities	with organization memberships, activities
.67	.44	.16	.04
.16	.31	.46	.37
.07	.15	.06	.03
.85*	.92*	.62	.51
-.08	-.06	.31*	.35**
-.95	-.99	-.44	-.35
.36	.29	.25	.12
1.43**	1.02*	.92*	.74
.006	.004	.009	.008
-1.25	-1.80	-1.00	-1.37
-1.74*	-2.28**	-.88	-1.13*
-1.59*	-1.99**	-.87*	-1.15**
-.57	-.47	-.78**	-.82**
.11	.19	-.14	-.14

Table 6.12. *continued*

Independent Variables[a]	Type of Body: Extension Program Committee — Wife: without organization memberships, activities	Wife: with organization memberships, activities	Husband: without organization memberships, activities	Husband: with organization memberships, activities
Wife's Work				
Woman currently employed off-farm	.14	.40	-.44	-.47
Percent of types of farm tasks done regularly	.003	-.006	-.005	-.008
Husband's Work				
Husband currently has off-farm job	.69*	.82*	.40	.47
Husband regularly does farm work	-.12	-.61	.63	.53
Wife's (Husband's) Organizational Memberships and Activities[b]				
	--	.76*	--	.88** (production)
	--	2.33**	--	1.34** (family)
Constant	.62	.59	-2.15	-2.32
D	.12	.26	.10	.17
N[c]	471		469	
Observed probability	.29		.23	

*.01 ≤ p < .05.

**p < .01.

[a]For categorical variables, 1 = yes, 0 = no.

[b]See Table 6.12. For local governing board, this is whether the person belonged to any community organization; for Extension program activity, it is whether the person took part in Extension production or family focused activities; for agricultural committees, panels and boards, it is number of types of farm organization memberships.

[c]N's are less than 497 because of missing data.

Type of Body			
Local, County, State, or USDA Agricultural Committee, Panel, or Advisory Board			
Wife		Husband	
without organization memberships, activities	with organization memberships, activities	without organization memberships, activities	with organization memberships, activities
.05	-.11	-.17	-.29
.02*	.02	-.005	-.004
.51	.76	-.19	-.04
.38	.45	.02	.09
--	.65**	--	.46**
-2.08	-2.00	-2.39	-2.68
.11	.15	.17	.20
471		469	
.10		.26	

served on various committees, either because current participation was facilitated by having less work responsibility or because those who are older have had a longer time over which to have served.

Also, it is not clear whether women gained more from their organizational memberships and activities than men in terms of their chances to serve various bodies. At the observed probabilities, the effect on having been on an Extension program committee of taking part in domestic and family activities is close to twice as large for women as for men: having taken part in such activities increased the chances that they had served on a program committee by .52, in contrast with .30 for men. However, the effect of participation in farm production and management activities is about the same for husbands and wives: .19 and .18. Again, this may represent the greater participation of women in planning youth and home related programs. With respect to other agricultural bodies, each additional farm organizational membership increased the probability of women having served by .08, at the observed probability; for men, each additional membership increased the chances of serving by .10. The difference is very small, but consistent with the idea that men have memberships that are more likely to lead to policymaking and advising positions than those of women. As shown earlier in this chapter, at least some of the women's farm organizational memberships were in auxiliary organizations.

Farm size affects whether husbands as well as wives served on agricultural boards and committees, and the effects are slightly larger for men. Education also affects both husbands' and wives' chances of having been on Extension program committees and agricultural boards in roughly the same way: those with a college education were those who were more likely to serve.

Conclusions

Farm women and farm men are involved in a wide range of community and farm organizational activities, and their overall involvement is about the same. There are striking differences, though, in the types of activities followed by women and men. In the FWS women were less likely than men to belong to farm organizations and to take part in Extension farm management and production activities. Couples showed some tendency to take part in broad types of organizational activities together. However, sex typing appeared whenever only one spouse reported involvement. For example, if only one member of a couple belonged to a cooperative, it was most likely the husband. Sex differences in levels of participation showed up with respect to serving on committees, panels, and boards at various governmental levels: men were much more likely to have served (and to be willing to serve) than women.

Women's other work responsibilities, including child care, do not seem to cause the sex differences in types of organizational and political participation. In fact, for women, having an off-farm job, doing a greater range of farm tasks, and having school-age children actually increased the likelihood of their participation in various types of organizational activities and in political and advisory positions. It was for men that some negative effects showed up. In general, though, life cycle effects were less than expected from the general literature on voluntary activities. In contrast with the analysis of other types of work, married women were not less likely to take part in community and agricultural affairs than unmarried women. In fact, perhaps because many community and Extension activities are oriented toward traditional families, unmarried women in some cases were less likely to participate. Women's memberships in farm and community organizations, as well as their participation in Extension activities, increased their chances of serving in policymaking and advisory positions to an extent about the same as for men.

A consistent finding is that those with larger farms were more likely to participate in most types of activities. These effects of farm size were usually stronger for husbands than wives. It is the person from a large farm who has the time, money, or inclination to take part in nonwage activities off the farm and who may reap the benefits from this involvement. At the same time, husbands did not seem to turn to community organizations after they had met the challenge of developing the farm.

Thus farm families are tied in with the wider community. There is sex segregation in the formation of these ties, however, that is not explicable by women's other work roles. Women's answers to questions about serving on boards, panels, and committees suggested some self-selection, but this could be based on anticipation of difficulties in filling a "male" role in terms of pressures from other participants. Further, there are what might be called "class effects," as there were with respect to off-farm employment, that could contribute to intensifying stratification in rural communities.

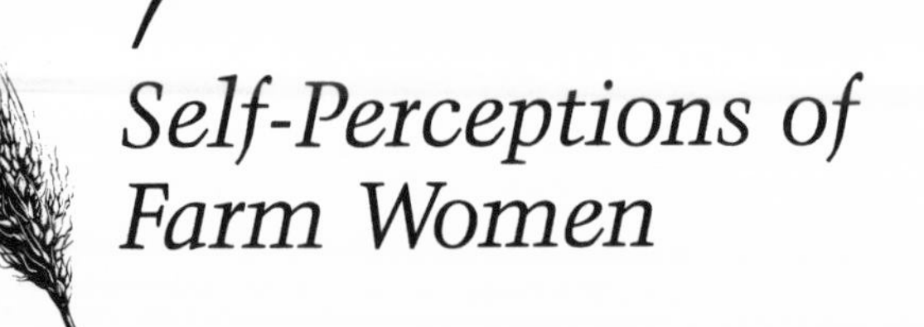

7
Self-Perceptions of Farm Women

The previous chapters have shown the large extent to which farm women take part in farm and other work. Although other research suggests that farm husbands underestimate their wives' farm roles, there was no such evidence in this survey. In discussing data sources and results of earlier analyses, however, I pointed to situations in which data gatherers, the farm family, the community, and the women themselves might see even active farm women as other than "farmers." In this chapter, I will look at responses to four questions from the FWS that provide evidence as to how the farm women saw themselves: (1) which occupation a woman listed on her income tax form; (2) whether the woman considered herself one of the farm's main operators; (3) whether the woman thought that she could farm if something happened to her husband; and (4) what the woman thought the USDA could do to help farm women. Comparisons among responses to these different questions provide additional insight into the ways in which farm women see themselves and their roles on their operations. I will first describe the responses to these questions and show their interrelationships. Then I will look at the effects of farm, family, and the woman's characteristics on her answers to the four questions.

Ideally we would have data from other family members and from those in the community as well, and would compare the women's self-perceptions with the perceptions of others around them. These additional data, unfortunately, are not available in the FWS.

Occupations, Roles, Ability, and Opinions

One way in which the FWS attempted to explore the women's occupational self-identifications was by asking what occupations they put on their income tax forms. The majority (60 percent) said "wife, mother, housewife, or homemaker" (see Table 7.1). Only 5 percent said farm wife, but less than 4 percent said farmer, rancher, or producer. Those who held an off-farm job at the time of the FWS were those most likely to put down another occupation on their tax forms (usually the one associated with their off-farm job, e.g., nurse, teacher).

If these results are interpreted in terms of self-identification, then we can conclude that the majority of farm women identify with traditional women's roles within the family. The term "farm wife," which some women say they have begun using to emphasize their roles both within the family and on the operation (see also ads for T-shirts in *Farm Wife News*), does not seem to have caught on widely in this context. Identification seems greater with occupations held off the farm than with work women do on the farm.

This theme of *not* identifying as "farmers" came out in our focus group interviews, as well as in Boulding's (1980). Some of those interviewed said explicitly that only men can be farmers—and that they are not like men. "Farmer" is an occupational label. In our language it does not have an explicit gender, as do, for example, "waiter" and "waitress." But like "airline pilot," "lawyer," or even "professor," in general it calls to mind the image of a man doing the work. Of course, women who are lawyers will give that as their occupation. Farming, though, is a less well defined occupation, especially for women, because it often takes place in the context of a family operation. Taking on this title, then, is not automatic for women even when they do the work of farming. In the next section I examine the effects of doing farm work on using this label.

There are, however, other plausible explanations for these results, aside from a lack of identification as a producer. The structure of the tax and Federal Insurance Contributions Act (FICA) laws could make it advantageous to some women to describe themselves as neither operators nor even employees on their own farms in order to avoid compulsory FICA withholdings (see Salamon and Markan 1984). Moreover, women who must report even the smallest amount of income earned from off-farm jobs may feel constrained to identify the occupation that produced the reportable

Table 7.1. *Self-Identification of Farm Women*

	Percent
1. Occupation on income tax form:	
Wife, mother, housewife	60
Farm/ranch wife	5
Farmer, rancher, producer	3
Other	30
Don't know	2
Total	100
(N[a])	(2,494)
2. One of main operators:	
Yes	55
No	44
Don't know	1
Total	100
(N[a])	(2,499)
3. Ability to run farm without husband:[b]	
Definitely yes	25
Probably yes	35
Probably no	18
Definitely no	20
Don't know	2
Total	100
(N[a])	(2,395)

[a]N's differ from 2,509 because of missing data.

[b]Asked only if husband in household.

income.[1] Tax forms do not routinely provide enough room for filers to enter multiple occupations.

Although the results for income tax form occupation are consistent with Boulding's and the focus groups', they are quite different from what Hill (1981b:70) found in her interviews with 103 Wisconsin farm women: "My research shows that well over half of the women interviewed and surveyed identified themselves as either 'farmers' or farmwives, but rarely as simply 'housewives.' These women report that this is a change in self-perception during their own lives and is also a change from the self-identities of the women in their mother's generations. Farm women in other generations also worked. The change is that women seem to be deriving more personal gratification from this work."

It is possible that Hill was catching the first wave of a trend toward farm women seeing themselves as farmers and that this did not show up in our more general sample. At the same time, the FWS also provides evidence that women recognize their contributions to their operations. Very early in the interview, before asking anything about the women's work, the FWS asked each female respondent whether she considered herself to be one of the main operators of the farm or ranch. If a respondent had trouble with the term "main operator," the interviewer defined it as "a person who makes day-to-day decisions about running the whole operation." We had hoped with this question to identify those women Pearson (1979:190) called "independent agricultural producers," women who "manage farms or ranches largely by themselves." What we found was that 55 percent of the women responded in the affirmative (Table 7.1). This is more than the 17 percent of Michigan farm women whom Lodwick and Fassinger (1979) classified as either independent producers or agricultural partners, and considerably more than the 8 percent who said that they put "farmer" or "farm wife" on their tax forms. Indeed, as can be seen in Table 7.2, almost 60 percent of the FWS women who said they were one of the main operators listed themselves as homemakers on their income tax forms.

Differences between the responses to this and to the previous question could result either because of the change in context (from a term put on a legal form to the woman's own self-identification) or because of use of a less sex-typed term than "farmer."

The percent of those who said both that they were one of the main operators and also put an "other" occupation on their tax forms suggests that seeing oneself as a farm operator is not incon-

Table 7.2. *Occupation Listed on Income Tax Form by Whether Woman Reports Herself as Main Operator (percentages)*

Occupation Listed on Income Tax Form	One of Main Operators	
	Yes	No
Wife, mother, homemaker	59	63**
Farm/ranch wife	7	3
Farmer, rancher, producer	5	2
Other	29	32
Total	100	100
(N)	(1,350)	(1,083)

**$\chi 2 = 45.5$, df = 3, $p < .01$.

sistent with having another occupational identity. Looking directly at off-farm employment reveals that half of those who had an off-farm job at the time of the FWS interview also considered themselves to be one of the main operators of their farm or ranch, although this was lower than the 57 percent of those without such employment (results not shown). As mentioned, this dual occupational identification is not possible in response to the first question. The next section will see whether off-farm employment has an effect on responses to the main operator question when other variables are controlled.

A third question asked of women who were currently married was whether they could run their farms on their own if something should happen to their husbands. Altogether just under 60 percent said "yes" or "probably yes." This is about the same percentage who identified themselves as main operators, and it is reasonable to suppose that those currently running their farms would feel more capable of doing so in the future, even without a husband. As Table 7.3 shows, 69 percent of the women who considered themselves to be one of the main operators said either definitely or probably that they could run the operations by themselves. In contrast, 47 percent of those who rejected the "main operator" label felt capable of farming alone, although in absolute terms this percentage seems high. Those who described themselves as farmers, ranchers, or producers on tax forms were most likely to feel they could run their

Table 7.3. *Ability to Run Operation without Husband by Whether Woman Reports Herself as Main Operator (percentages)*

Could Run Operation Without Husband[a]	One of Main Operators	
	Yes	No
Definitely yes	31	16**
Probably yes	38	31
Probably no	15	21
Definitely no	13	29
Don't know	2	2
Total[b]	99	99
(N)	(1,294)	(1,085)

**χ^2 = 149.24, df = 4, p < .01

[a]Asked only if husband in household.

[b]Totals differ from 100 due to rounding.

operations without a husband, with nearly three-fourths making this response (see Table 7.4).

Joyce and Leadley (1977:7) report the results from a 1976 International Harvester survey in which a similar question was asked of farm men and women. Fifty-six percent of the men, but 81 percent of the women, said that if something happened to the husband, the wife could successfully manage the operation alone or with help. They point out that the husbands were not asked if they could run their operations without their wives, who may contribute to the farm in a multitude of ways. Although men were not asked about income tax occupations and roles as main operators, the married men were asked whether they could run their operations if something happened to their wives. Male respondents were more optimistic about running their operations without a spouse than were the women—92 percent said they could definitely or probably run their operations without their wives (see Table 7.5). Perhaps men assume that they can hire labor to replace the work their wives do or that they could intensify their own work if their wives could not work. Or perhaps they underestimate the amount of time their

Table 7.4. *Ability to Run Operation without a Husband by Woman's Occupation Listed on Income Tax Form*[a] *(percentages)*

Could Run Operation Without a Husband	Wife, Mother, Housewife, Homemaker	Farm, Ranch Wife	Farmer, Rancher, Producer	Other
Definitely yes	22	20	49	29**
Probably yes	37	40	24	32
Probably no	18	24	10	16
Definitely no	21	12	12	22
Don't know	2	4	5	1
Total	100	100	100	100
(N)	(1,458)	(127)	(65)	(690)

**χ^2 = 55.47, df = 12, $p < .01$

[a]Asked only of women with husband present.

wives contribute directly or indirectly to the operations, even though they do not underestimate the extent of their wives' involvement.

Still a fourth set of questions provides some evidence on the extent to which farm women perceive themselves as a distinct group within agriculture. In closing the interviews, the interviewers asked both men and women for the most important thing that the USDA could do for farm and ranch people. Then they asked the women for the most important thing that the USDA could do for farm and ranch *women*. The answers to these questions were recorded verbatim and later assigned to one of about 50 coding categories. These categories have been collapsed here for a more manageable presentation. (Complete categories are available in the FWS codebook.)

In response to the general question, the largest group of both men and women wanted help in defending farmers' abilities to make a living. Forty-one percent of the women and 34 percent of the men mentioned things that would increase prices, cut costs, or otherwise allow farmers to have a higher net income. Marketing issues were mentioned by another sizable group. Combining these responses, almost 50 percent of the women and men mentioned

Table 7.5. *Men's Perceived Ability to Farm without a Wife*[a] *(percentages)*

Definitely yes	63
Probably yes	29
Probably no	4
Definitely no	2
Don't know	2
Total	100
(N)	(529)

[a]Asked only if wife in household.

economic issues in response to a question about the most important thing the USDA could do for farmers and ranchers. This is consistent with expressions of dissatisfaction with farming as a way to make a living shown in chapter 5. The next largest group (10 percent of the women and 18 percent of the men) wanted the government to reduce or eliminate intervention in the agricultural economy. Although some people mentioned specific programs or policies that they wanted curtailed, a typical response from this group was "get the government out of it and let supply and demand take care of themselves." Such concern about too much government intervention, of course, was being expressed by the wider public as well at this time. Only 18 percent of the women and 7 percent of the men were unable to give a response. (See Jones and Rosenfeld 1981, for table and a more detailed discussion of these responses.)

Although these responses are interesting in their own right—and demonstrate the concern of both farm women and men with the economic issues associated with their way of making a living—this question was actually included to strengthen the response to the last question in the women's survey. Originally the women's questionnaire finished with an open-ended question about what the USDA could do for farm women. We had expected women to answer from a clearly female perspective, though not necessarily from a "women's liberation" point of view. This question was also to detect any concern with unfair or discriminatory treatment from the USDA that might have been missed by the more narrowly focused items earlier in the interview. However, no matter how much the question was worded to indicate an interest in the problems and views of farm *women*, most pretest respondents answered the question from the broader perspective of the agricultural producer. When interviewers probed, reemphasizing the focus on the USDA and farm women, many respondents still could give no answer, explaining that they had never considered farm policy issues in gender terms. As a result of the pretest experience, we included a general question about the USDA before the one about farm women, hoping to filter out the general responses in this way.

As can be seen in Table 7.6, in the actual survey, even with the more general question asked first, women still had trouble defining actions that the USDA could take for them as farm women. Over a third of the women were unable to give a response. In some cases, the interviewers probed but got responses of "I just don't know. Let me think. No, I'm sorry, I just don't know."

One needs to keep in mind the nature of the question in interpreting the high proportion of "don't know's." The question is about action the USDA could take. Some women may not have known what the USDA could do in a certain situation, or they may have had concerns, such as credit access, that they considered beyond the USDA's jurisdiction. In another question about *satisfaction* with USDA programs and services to farmers and ranchers, just over a quarter of the women (26 percent) and 16 percent of the men could not give an opinion. In response to a question about satisfaction with USDA programs and policies for farm *women*, 56 percent of the women could not answer. One reason for the difference in responses to questions about general versus women-focused actions by the USDA could be that women simply did not know what the USDA was doing for them (which was not a great deal specifically for women). Thus, one cannot unambiguously interpret "don't know" responses to the last survey question as an absence of concern for or awareness of women's issues.

At the same time, many women said explicitly that they had never considered the question of what could be done for them as women. In addition, other sorts of answers suggest that this question is indicating that farm women do not see themselves as a group apart. Eight percent said that the USDA could help women by helping their husbands, and another 8 percent gave answers similar to the ones they had just given to the question about help for farmers and ranchers in general. Four percent said that there was nothing the USDA could do for them in particular. Thus another 20

Table 7.6. *What USDA Can Do to Help Farm and Ranch Women: FWS Women's Responses*

	Percent
Help change inheritance laws and estate taxes; help women keep farms if widowed; help with estate planning	14
Provide/improve education and information programs for women	10
Promote wider recognition of farm women's roles; recognize economic contribution of farm women	6
Provide other (non-educational) programs for farm women	4
Help women obtain access to loans or credit in their own names	1
Help women maintain roles on farm rather than in off-farm jobs	1
Keep USDA/government out of women's lives	1
All equity-related comments: eliminate discrimination against women; treat men and women equally	4
Satisfied with USDA as it is	4
Help women by helping their husbands	8
Answer duplicating response to previous question on USDA help for farm and ranch people (no focus on women as a group)	8
Nothing	4
Don't know	35
Total	100
(N)	(2,495)

percent gave answers that did not distinguish farm women as a separate group.

These results suggest that the majority of farm women do not consider themselves a unified, separate constituency of the USDA. This is not to say that these women have no sense of common feminine identification or that these women are generally without common political interests or concerns. As seen in chapter 6, many of these women do take part in both community and agricultural programs and organizations. The point is rather that these women may not see their needs as separate from those of their operations.

To help the operations of which they are a part is to help the women themselves. Even in the agricultural organizations that are run by and for farm women (and to which a relatively small number of the FWS women belong), major themes are increasing sales, influencing legislation, and otherwise helping maintain the economic health of agriculture.

Among those who gave responses, three-fourths of the answers focused on one of three issues. The first was a concern that the USDA act to improve the situations of women who attempt to continue the operations after the death of their husbands. A large proportion of those giving this sort of response mentioned the USDA's help in changing inheritance laws and taxes to make it possible for women to retain the family farm intact. A large percentage of the women felt that they were capable of running the operations without their husbands, but at least some were upset that the legal process treated farm property as "inheritance," for them, rather than as something that belonged to them after years of cooperative involvement. (Recent changes in inheritance laws have eased the situation considerably for farm families in this respect.) A second concern was the need for more and better education and information programs for farm women. At least some of these women wanted information on what programs were available through the USDA. Although the USDA has newsletters and so on that give overviews of various programs and services, at least some women were not getting access to distribution channels. In this group, too, were women who wanted additional information and training in business and farm management practices and also special information on inheritance laws and estate taxes.

A third group (6 percent of all respondents) wanted more recognition for the part they played. At least some of these women wanted not just public awareness of their roles, but also legal and economic rights. As one woman put it, "Women should be recognized as copartners with their husbands. When we do business with the government, all papers and forms should have spaces for both men and women to sign. That way, if I'm on my own, I can support my position as a farmer." Very few women (4 percent) explicitly mentioned ending sex discrimination or a need for equal treatment by sex.

In general, 40 percent of the women offered some response that suggested the USDA do more for them as producers. (Again, see Jones and Rosenfeld 1981, chapter 5, for a more extensive discussion of these responses.) The nature of the responses leads to the

Table 7.7. *Woman's Having Opinion on What USDA Can Do for Women by Other Role Variables (percentages)*

Woman Has Opinion:	Farmer or Farm Wife as Income Tax Occupation	One of Main Operators	Definitely or Probably Could Run Farm without Husband
Yes	10**	62**	63**
No	8	50	57

**χ^2 for complete cross-tabulation significant at .01 level.

speculation that the women who identify themselves as producers are those who have ideas about what the USDA can do for them as women. Table 7.7 supports this speculation. Those who gave some opinion as to what the USDA could do for farm women (as compared with giving a "don't know" answer, an answer similar to the previous one, or the response that the USDA could help their husbands or do nothing specific for farm women) were significantly more likely to put "farmer" or "farm wife" as their occupation on income tax forms, to identify as one of the main operators, and to say they could run the operation if something happened to their husbands.

EXPLAINING ROLE IDENTIFICATION

The previous sections showed women's identifications with the producer role and as part of a separate USDA constituency as measured by the questions on income tax occupation, main operator status, ability to farm without a husband, and opinions on USDA actions for farm women. One would expect the responses to these questions to be related to women's work on the farm, their membership in agricultural organizations, and to some extent to their holding off-farm jobs. It is possible that even net of variables measuring women's work and organizational involvement, farm, family, and individual characteristics would affect the type of answers to each of the four questions.

If one assumes that listing oneself as a "farmer" or "farm wife," considering oneself an operator, believing that one can farm even if something happens to one's husband, and having an opinion about what the USDA can do for farm women represent less traditional attitudes toward farm women's roles, then one can use the literature on sex role attitudes and political opinions in general to suggest some of the ways in which the farm, family, and individual characteristics may affect the responses under consideration here.

Younger and more highly educated women tend to be less traditional with respect to sex roles in the general population (Huber and Spitze 1983; Huber et al. 1978; Waite 1978; Mason et al. 1976; Mason and Bumpass 1975; Thornton et al. 1983). One thinks of the young as more open to new ideas and less set in traditional ways. As Thornton et al. put it (1983:220), "Education can also be a liberalizing factor, because it provides both opportunities for economically and psychologically rewarding jobs and access to news, ideas and aspirations." In at least some studies, the tendency of the young to be less traditional is not apparent when education and work experience are controlled (e.g., Mason et al. 1976; Mason and Bumpass 1975; Huber et al. 1978), with the implication that age differences may reflect cohort differences in educational and work histories. On the other hand, Thornton et al. (1983), in their very complete model, report effects of age even after controlling for education and work variables, and report that, again controlling for other factors, younger women were more likely to have changed their sex role attitudes toward more egalitarian ones between 1962 and 1977. One might thus expect to see that, controlling for other things, younger and more educated farm women are the ones who are more likely to give less traditional answers to the four questions.

Women farming on their own, as compared with having a husband present, might also be those who identify more strongly as "farmers" and "farm operators," and who see themselves as part of a USDA constituency. In the general literature, the effect of being married has usually been insignificant or inconsistent (Huber et al. 1978; Mason et al. 1976; Thornton et al. 1983). At the same time, marital status influences the extent to which farm women are involved in their operations. The general literature has found clear evidence that employed women have more liberal sex role attitudes, even after controlling for other characteristics (e.g., Thornton et al. 1983; Huber and Spitze 1983; Mason et al. 1976; Mason and Bumpass 1975). Therefore, we would expect to find that both work variables lead to less traditional responses and also marital status's effect is stronger for the FWS women than in the general population because marital status also represents work participation for farm women. Using the same reasoning, to the extent that women are excluded from running the operation of larger farms and ranches in ways not captured by the work variables, one might expect to see effects of farm size, with women from larger farms less likely to see themselves as separate operators.

One might reason that, other things being equal, women who are more involved with child care are those who are involved in more traditional women's roles, perhaps less involved in atypical female roles, and therefore those with less liberal sex role attitudes. In the general literature, numbers and ages of children have not been found to affect sex role attitudes (e.g., Mason and Bumpass 1975; Huber and Spitze 1983; Mason et al. 1976; Thornton et al. 1983). Given the limited impact of the presence of children on various aspects of farm women's work, we would expect here also to find that the number of children at home does not affect responses to questions about being a farmer or operator and about women as a group for which the USDA can provide help. The presence of children who help on the farm, as well as of other helpers, might, however, lead a woman to be more likely to say that she could run the farm without her husband, because she would have other family and household labor available.

Region is another factor found to be associated with sex role attitudes. Women from the South are often described as more traditional. The same could be true for farm women.

To test these hypotheses, I did logistic regression for each of the four attitude questions on farm, family, and individual characteristics. Although work involvement and organizational membership are associated with responses to the role identity questions (as will be seen), it is not clear whether women identify as producers because they are involved in agriculture or take part in a greater range of agricultural activities because they identify as producers. It seems likely, though, that work and organizational involvement lay the foundation for the way in which a woman views herself. Because it makes sense to consider women's work and organizational activities as independent variables affecting their work and political identities although at the same time the causation is possibly reciprocal, the work variables will be entered into the logistic regressions only in the second step after other farm, family, and individual characteristics are in. Table 7.8 shows the results of this analysis.

Contrary to what is found in the general literature on sex role attitudes, farm women with higher education are not those who

Table 7.8. *Logistic Regression for Farm Woman's Role Identification (logit coefficients)*

	Dependent Variables			
	Occupation on Tax Form = Farm Wife or Farmer		Is One of Main Operators	
Independent Variables[a]	Without Woman's Work Variables	With Woman's Work Variables	Without Woman's Work Variables	With Woman's Work Variables
Farm Characteristics				
Total acres in farm relative to less than 50 acres:				
50-299 acres	.59	.81*	-.60**	-.46**
300-999 acres	.91**	1.05**	-.62**	-.53**
≥ 1000 acres	.71	.97*	-.81**	-.60**
Sales relative to mixed crops and livestock:				
Less than 5 percent total sales from crops	-.07	-.25	.32*	.20
Greater than 95 percent total sales from crops	-.24	-.10	-.42**	-.28*
Don't know percent of sales from crops	-.09	.14	-.54**	-.35
Tenancy relative to part owners:				
Full owners	-.11	-.001	-.15	-.08
Renters	.07	.05	.01	-.14
Neither owners nor renters	.22	.35	-.38	-.59
Woman's Legal Relation to Land				
Own name on deed or rental contract for land	.51	.25	.51**	.27
Decision Makers				
Include other than husband and wife	-.30	-.24	-.28*	-.09
Region				
Relative to South:				
Northeast	.35	.12	.47**	.09
Northcentral	.38	.18	.49**	.27
West	.12	-.13	.47**	.10

Dependent Variables			
Could Definitely or Probably Run Operation without Husband		Has Opinion about What USDA Can Do for Farm Women	
Without Woman's Work Variables	With Woman's Work Variables	Without Woman's Work Variables	With Woman's Work Variables
-.34*	-.28	-.02	.05
-.21	-.11	.19	.27
-.21	-.03	.30	.44*
.10	.06	-.22	-.27*
-.12	.01	-.38**	-.30*
-.08	.13	-.73**	-.61**
-.09	-.03	.24*	.31**
-.50*	-.62**	.27	.26
-.81**	-.89**	.37	.38
.007	-.20	.39**	.27
-.15	-.06	.19	.26*
-.22	-.47**	.28	.14
-.27	-.47**	.56**	.46**
-.18	-.45**	.39**	.24

Table 7.8. *continued*

	Dependent Variables			
	Occupation on Tax Form = Farm Wife or Farmer		Is One of Main Operators	
Independent Variables[a]	Without Woman's Work Variables	With Woman's Work Variables	Without Woman's Work Variables	With Woman's Work Variables
Labor Structure of Farm				
More than 1 hired hand	-.15	-.24	.07	.10
Husband's work relative to husband who regularly does farm work and has no off-farm job:				
No husband	.97**	.65*	.94**	.33
Husband regularly does farm work and has off-farm job	-.88**	-.80**	.06	.05
Husband does not regularly do farm work and has off-farm job	-.48	-.79	.51*	.16
Husband does not regularly do farm work and has no off-farm job	.60	.44	.09	-.19
Number of sons at least 18 who regularly do farm work	-.14	-.09	.002	.06
Number of children ages 6-17 who regularly do farm work	-.002	-.03	.07	.01
Number of other household members who regularly do farm work	-.09	-.13	.14	.05
Number of other non-household members who regularly do farm work	.04	.07	.01	.06
Farm Woman's Characteristics				
Education relative to high school graduate:				
Less than high school	.51*	.58**	.05	.08
Postsecondary vocational or some college	-.07	-.10	.17	.08
College degree or above	-.14	-.09	.21	.23
Percent of life spent on farms or ranches	.004	.003	.006**	.004

Dependent Variables			
Could Definitely or Probably Run Operation without Husband		Has Opinion about What USDA Can Do for Farm Women	
Without Woman's Work Variables	With Woman's Work Variables	Without Woman's Work Variables	With Woman's Work Variables
.03	.02	.14	.11
N.A.	N.A.	-.02	-.34
.28*	.24*	.06	.06
1.08**	.90**	.06	-.09
1.13**	1.07**	-.37	-.48
.29*	.33**	-.09	-.07
.18**	.17**	-.008	-.02
.31	.29	-.001	-.03
-.00	.02	.03	.04
-.21	-.18	-.12	-.09
.15	.05	.27*	.20
.11	-.04	.69**	.64**
.008**	.006**	-.001	-.002

Table 7.8. *continued*

	Dependent Variables			
	Occupation on Tax Form = Farm Wife or Farmer		Is One of Main Operators	
Independent Variables[a]	Without Woman's Work Variables	With Woman's Work Variables	Without Woman's Work Variables	With Woman's Work Variables
Age relative to over 65:				
Less than 31	-.59	-.70	.22	-.03
31-45	-.64*	-.79*	.13	-.19
46-65	-.68**	-.75**	.03	-.19
Dependent Children				
Number of children less than age 6	-.17	-.17	-.14	-.14
Number of children 6-17 who do not regularly do farm work	-.07	-.02	-.16*	-.13
Woman's Work				
Woman currently employed off farm	—	-.82**	—	-.41**
Percent farm task types woman does regularly	—	.02**	—	.04**
Percent of types of farm decisions in which woman participates	—	.01**	—	.01**
Number of types of farm organization memberships	—	.20**	—	.14**
Constant	-3.45	-5.87	-.91	-2.49
N[b]	1,997	1,995	2,023	2,021
D	.06	.09	.08	.24
Observed probability	.10	.10	.57	.57

* $.01 < p < .05$.
** $p < .01$.

[a]For categorical variables, 1 = yes, 0 = no.

[b]N's less than 2,509 because of missing data.

Dependent Variables			
Could Definitely or Probably Run Operation without Husband		Has Opinion about What USDA Can Do for Farm Women	
Without Woman's Work Variables	With Woman's Work Variables	Without Woman's Work Variables	With Woman's Work Variables
.86**	.59*	.41	.32
.84**	.54*	.45*	.34
.73**	.56*	.39*	.31
-.10	-.03	-.06	-.05
.005	.06	.05	.07
--	.24*	--	-.05
--	.02**	--	.008**
--	.006**	--	.006**
--	.20**	--	.15**
-.86	-.80	-.94	-1.30
1,935	1,934	1,950	1,948
.07	.13	.06	.09
.61	.61	.48	.48

were more likely to list themselves as "farmer" or "farm wife" on their tax returns, to consider themselves to be one of the main operators of their farm or ranch, or to feel they could farm if something happened to their husbands. In fact, with respect to tax form occupation, women with less than a high school degree, in contrast with those having a higher educational level, were most likely to put down farmer or farm wife. Of course, the effects of responses to this question are complicated by the fact that many of those with off-farm employment list these occupations on their tax forms. If those with more education have better jobs (as was the case according to chapter 5), and thus jobs with which they identify more strongly, then this could account for the unexpected effect of education on this variable. Only in the case of giving an opinion about what the USDA can do for women does education act as it has in other studies. Here, those with postsecondary education were more likely to give an opinion. This sort of effect is consistent with findings that those with more education have more coherent political attitudes generally (Bishop 1976).

The effects of age are not what would be predicted from the literature on sex role attitudes. Age has no significant net effect on whether a woman considered herself one of the main operators of her farm or ranch, and its effects on holding an opinion about what the USDA could do for farm women disappear when the work variables are added. Younger women were more likely to say that they could farm even if something happened to their husbands, although the effects of age are not monotonic: when work variables are included, the biggest contrast is between those under and over age sixty-five. Age could again represent physical energy rather than age- and cohort-varying attitudes. For tax form occupation, it is actually those who were over sixty-five who were more likely to report that they put down "farmer" or "farm wife." Thus, there is no support here for the idea that younger women were "less traditional" in their responses to these questions.

The effect of a husband's presence is similar to that found in the literature: there is no effect (with work variables included) for any of the responses except for tax form occupation, in which cases those without husbands were more likely to say that they were "farmers." Those whose husbands did both farm work and off-farm work were less likely to put down farming as an occupation. As discussed before, because a tax form is a legal document, there may be reasons in the tax codes for listing occupations one way or another in various family circumstances.

It was suggested that one reason for expecting marital status to have an effect here, even though it does not always have an effect in the more general literature, is because it represents additional dimensions of women's involvement on the operation. Including the direct measures of women's work does reduce the effects of a husband's presence and work. More extensive involvement in agriculture on and off the farm significantly increases a woman's tendency to give what might be considered less traditional responses. Off-farm employment has a negative effect on whether a woman put farm wife or farmer on her income tax form and whether she considered herself one of the main operators. As discussed earlier in this chapter, those with off-farm employment were unlikely to say they were farmers or farm wives, perhaps because they linked tax forms with the occupations from which they directly earned their taxable income. Those with off-farm work might also have spent fewer hours farming, even net of the range of their involvement, and thus be less likely to have seen themselves as one of the operators. On the other hand, holding an off-farm job increases the probability that a woman said she could run her farm without a husband and has no significant effect on her offering an opinion as to what the USDA could do for farm women. Post hoc, one could interpret these findings as indicating that off-farm employment gives women a sense of being able to accomplish things, perhaps counterbalancing curtailed hours on the farm. Those with a job off the farm might be less worried about getting credit than other women, with this especially affecting whether they feel they could continue the farm without a husband.

Variables that could be considered indirect indicators of participation on the farm in some cases affect the odds of what might be considered an untraditional response. Those from larger operations were less likely to report themselves to be one of the main operators. This, however, is the only dependent variable where one sees such a pattern of farm size effects. With respect to tax form occupation, it is actually on the larger farms that women were more likely to report that they farmed, though again this may reflect less about the woman's personal identity than efforts to get more favorable tax rates. For the question about the USDA and farm women, when work variables are included, it is also the women on the largest operations who were more likely to give an opinion. A greater proportion of sales from crops (which may reflect less involvement in farm work with animals) or not knowing the percentage of crops has a negative effect on whether a woman considered herself one of the main operators and on whether she had an opinion about what the USDA could do for farm women. (However, in a model with the work variables and including respondents who did not know their husbands' off-farm income, this effect is not statistically significant.) But being on an operation that depended mainly on livestock sales also decreases the chances that a woman had an opinion about the USDA and women. The presence of other decision makers actually has a positive effect on a woman having had an opinion about farm women as a USDA constituency, in contradiction to what one would expect if this variable represented additional information about women's involvement on their operations. Having more experience with farm life increases the chances that a woman said she could continue the operation if something happened to her husband.

In general, the presence of dependent children did not influence women's responses, as predicted. And, also as predicted, having children (including sons over eighteen) who helped with the farm work increased the likelihood that a woman said that she could continue farming if something happened to her husband. Further, the less involved her husband was in farm work at the time of the FWS, the more likely she was to say that she could continue running the operation, perhaps because she was already doing so to some extent.

Farm women from the South, in contrast with other regions (especially the North Central region), were less likely to have an opinion about what the USDA could do for women, but they were more likely to say that they could continue farming. For the other two variables, region has no significant effect in the full model. Southern women's expectations about farming alone may reflect what they see around them: about half of all farms designated as female-operated in the 1978 Census of Agriculture are in the South (Kalbacher 1983).

There are no predictions in the sex roles attitude literature about the effects of tenancy on farm women's attitudes. That nonowners were less likely to have said that they thought they could continue farming if something happened to their husbands could reflect a recognition by these farm women that they would face prejudice on the part of landowners with whom they would have to deal.

In general, the results from the sex roles attitude literature provided only inconsistent guidance to what was found in the farm women's responses to questions about their tax form occupations, their identity as one of the main operators, their ability to run their operations without a husband, and their sense of being part of a separate USDA constituency. In the general sex roles literature itself, what one finds seems to depend on the particular dimension of sex role attitudes that one is examining (e.g., Mason et al. 1976; Mason and Bumpass 1975; Huber and Spitze 1983). But a further problem could be that the variables to be explained here reflect less women's sex role attitudes than their actual and potential work conditions. For example, thinking of oneself as one of the farm or ranch operators may reflect a heightened consciousness of one's contribution to the operation, but this is facilitated by being on an operation where one does have a greater involvement. Saying that one could continue farming if something happened to one's husband might reflect a less traditional attitude for farm women, but it would be more likely when a woman knew she had adult sons who could help her.

Conclusions

On their tax forms very few of the farm women identified themselves as farmers. Yet at the same time, over half of the women did consider themselves to be operators of their farms or ranches, and over half of the married women thought that they could continue farming if something happened to their husbands. Thus there seems to be a relatively high sense among these women of their roles as current or potential farmers. Responses to a question about what the USDA could do for farm women suggested that many farm women do not see themselves as a separate group for which the USDA is responsible but see themselves as helped by whatever the USDA does for farm people in general. The areas mentioned by the women who did have opinions on what the USDA could do for women indicated that they wanted help that would enable them to participate more and in the future in farming.

Variation among women in their responses was related to the range of work and decision making they did on their operations, to their membership in a range of farm organizations, and to their off-farm employment. Those who were more involved in agriculture on and off their farms were more likely to identify themselves as farmers or operators now and to have an opinion about what the USDA could do for them. Various farm, family, and personal characteristics also influenced their responses but often in ways that could be interpreted as reflecting the nature of their work conditions.

These results and their interpretations are consistent with what one finds in talking with farm women. They usually do not like the rhetoric of women's liberation and do not identify with the movement. They know that *they* work hard and at tasks that other women might consider unusual for women (e.g., driving tractors and inseminating cows), even while not taking on the title of "farmer." Therefore, some of the farm women find the emphasis of the movement on women's employment and access to traditionally male jobs irrelevant (despite their own concentration off the farm in traditionally women's jobs, as seen in chapter 5). One farm woman commented, "I'd like to see those women libbers come out here and muck out the barn. *That's* work." At the same time, they (along with many nonfarm women) dislike what they see as the women's movement's disparagement of the traditional family and of women's roles in it. They see themselves as part of the family enterprise, rather than as having a separate identity as a worker. Not only do at least some women want help in doing more for the operation, but also some women have sought additional knowledge about farming and farm management through existing Extension programs, as shown in chapter 6. But this activity is often undertaken to help the farm, rather than to accumulate human capital for themselves. This configuration of attitudes—with the acknowledgement of their work contributions and identification with the enterprise and family rather than as necessarily a "farmer"—has confounded those who try to place farm women in simple categories of traditional versus liberated.

8 The Study of Farm Women

Farming in the United States has changed dramatically over this century. Only a small minority of the population lives and works on farms. Increasingly, there has been a division into a sector of very large, full-time farms and another of small, part-time farms. Although corporations control a disproportionate part of the market, it is still true that most agricultural enterprises are owned and operated by families. It is likely that this will continue to be the case. Farming, a high risk endeavor, requires a very flexible labor force. Family units can essentially exploit themselves when crops are poor or prices low, cutting down on family consumption or seeking other sources of cash, and can provide extra labor by calling in additional family members for times when labor demands are high.

Women are part of family farms. But because farming has been defined as a male occupation, their roles on and for the farm have often been overlooked or undervalued. This book has used data from the 1980 Farm Women Survey, the first national survey of farm women, to examine the nature and determinates of women's work for their farms and families.

Farm Women's Work

I defined work broadly as efforts producing goods and services with and without pay on and off the farm. The results of the FWS documented the wide range of work that these women did. Some of this work was done in the home or on the farm. In the FWS almost all the women said they regularly did household tasks, and almost all in families with children under eighteen responded that they looked after children. Although in some cases this work simply involves direct care of the family, in other cases it is more difficult to separate home from farm tasks. Over 80 percent of the FWS women reported raising some food for the family, for example, something that was classified as farm work but could also be viewed as part of the "extra" family work farm women do. On the farm a majority of the FWS women said they did the traditional farm women tasks of running errands and bookkeeping. When there were farm animals, the majority of the women at least occasionally helped care for them. About half said they helped with harvesting, on operations where crops were harvested. And at least some women did more traditionally male tasks such as field work with machinery, marketing, and getting information from Extension agents. Additionally, over one-fifth said they worked in a family or in-home business other than the farm. As discussed in the first chapter, raising family food and working in in-home businesses may have increased in importance recently, as women seek ways to support the family even without leaving the home domain.

Women took part, too, in decisions about how to do the work and allocate resources. Almost all the women made decisions about household purchases and repairs, often with a husband. Although only a small minority usually made farm management decisions alone, at least half usually took part in decisions about major farm expenditures, when they were made. Fewer participated in production decisions, although almost 40 percent of the women said they took some part in specific types of decisions such as trying new crops and when to market.

These women also belonged to voluntary organizations where they could provide additional unpaid work off the farm. Almost two-thirds of the women said they belonged to some type of community organization; almost half reported membership in some sort of farm organization about which the FWS asked. Men, however, were more likely to belong to agricultural organizations and they belonged to more kinds of them. Close to half of the women also took part in Extension activities. Proportionately more women said they had been involved in home- and family-oriented activities than in activities related to production; men were more likely than women to report the latter sort of activity. Eight percent of the women had served on some local governing board and somewhat smaller percents had served on various agricultural panels and boards. Here again, though, relatively more men were likely to say they had served on agricultural boards and committees.

In addition, these women (and men) worked for pay off the farm; almost two-fifths of the women (and almost half of the men) reported having some sort of off-farm job in the past year (1979–80). The types of off-farm jobs the women held were similar to those held by nonfarm women and different from the sorts of jobs held by men. For example, almost a third of the employed farm women had clerical jobs in contrast with less than 4 percent of the farm men. Women with off-farm jobs earned on average less than half of what the men did, but, especially on poorer farms, women's earnings made a significant contribution to family income.

In general, these women were most likely to be found doing what is often characterized as women's work in the home and in the community. Often this was work without pay. When the FWS made it possible to look at the sexual division of labor, it showed men more likely than women to control and participate in farm and off-farm production and market-related activities. At least some women, though, took part even in traditionally male work. With respect to farming, over half the women recognized their involvement and capability: 55 percent considered themselves to be one of the main farm operators, and 60 percent of the married women felt they could run the farm without a husband.

Farm and Family Effects on Women's Work

There is considerable variation among these women in the nature of their home, farm, and community involvement. What is behind this variation? Speaking of cross-cultural differences, Blumberg (1978) argued that women will be more involved in their societies' main productive activities (1) the more these activities are compatible with child care responsibilities and (2) the scarcer male labor relative to demand. Here these principles were extended to find an explanation for cross-sectional variation among farm women in the types of work they do, hypothesizing that both the needs of the farm and the needs of the family help determine what a woman does, although her tastes for certain kinds of work and her ability to perform them also play a part.

Just as it is difficult to separate home from farm tasks, it is difficult to completely separate family from farm characteristics, because the family may also be a large part of the farm management and labor force. Children, for example, both help with the farm work and require parental care. The presence of a husband as part of the farm labor force is especially important (Sachs 1983). Thus the analysis in this book categorized family members according to their work roles as well as their relationship to the woman.

Given the changes that have occurred in the organization of agriculture, an attempt was also made to see how the relationship of the woman and of her family to factors of production and management would affect the nature of the work she did. When a woman owned land (or helped control it through having her name on a rental agreement), it was expected that she would have a greater part in the operation. When the couple controlled both the land and the management of it, it was also expected that women would play a bigger part, especially in decision making.

In analysis of the FWS data, I used characteristics of the farm, its labor force, the family, and the farm woman to explain variation in women's farm work; farm and home decision making; off-farm employment; and organizational memberships, Extension activities, and office-serving. I will review these results with emphasis on the effects of variables indicating farm and family needs (e.g., farm size, sales mix, labor structure, and the number of children not involved in farm work), and those indicating management and ownership arrangements (family tenancy, women's names on deeds and rental agreements, and the presence of other decision makers). In addition, I will review how one type of work affects another.

FARM TASKS

Researchers have shown that larger farms have less need for women's labor, especially in nontraditional areas, whether because of greater capitalization, greater ability to hire labor, or greater chances for forms of work organization that leave out the woman (Colman and Elbert 1983). Farms depending on livestock, net of other factors, have more constant labor needs and have been described as more likely to demand the woman's labor. The FWS gave additional support to these ideas. Women in the FWS sample on larger farms did a smaller range of tasks, as did women on farms where almost all sales were from crops. FWS women were also less likely to do field work, marketing and purchasing, and labor supervision on larger farms, whereas there was no net difference by farm size in whether they did the female task of bookkeeping.

Having other people doing farm work might reduce the relative need for the woman's labor, although it could also indicate that a particular farm was at a labor intensive stage. There was little evidence in the FWS that others substituted for the farm woman. In fact, the more children six to seventeen who helped with the farm work, the wider the range of tasks she did and, in particular, the more likely she was to supervise farm labor and do field work without machines. A husband's presence and activities were exceptions. Women without husbands did a much larger range of tasks than other women and were more likely to do specific kinds of tasks, with the exception of the farm women's traditional task of bookkeeping. Women whose husbands were employed off the farm, especially if the husbands did not regularly do farm work, were somewhat more extensively involved on their operations and somewhat more likely to do specific tasks (again with the exception of bookkeeping).

Children who were not part of the farm labor force, especially very young children, were expected to constrain women's farm work, especially work physically incompatible with keeping an eye on children. The more nonfarming children, the smaller the range of tasks an FWS woman did, other things being equal; the more children under age six, the smaller the likelihood that the woman did marketing and purchasing and field work without machinery.

As was expected, women whose names were on documents concerning the land did a wider range of farm tasks and were more likely than other women to do field work, marketing, and other tasks. The exception once more was the task of bookkeeping, for which it did not matter if a woman was named on deeds or rental agreements. It seems that whether a woman does a task stereotyped as the farm woman's (bookkeeping, for example) varies little by the nature of the farm. It was not clear *a priori* that women would be less involved with farm work (in contrast to farm decision making) when families did not own all their land or when people in addition to the couple made decisions. The results showed that tenancy status did not have consistent or strong effects. FWS women on farms with other decision makers, however, did a smaller range of tasks and in general were less likely to do any particular task. Contrary to the expectations of chapter 1, though, they were not less likely to do marketing and purchasing or information gathering.

As expected, women with off-farm employment did a smaller range of tasks and were less likely to do particular tasks, net of other factors. There is, then, at least some evidence here that women trade off between off-farm employment and farm work.

FARM AND HOME DECISION MAKING

Arguments about farm size and presence of a husband farming were made with even more force with respect to taking part in farm decision making, and the FWS provided support for this prediction. FWS women on larger farms made a smaller range of types of farm decisions alone or with another person. They made considerably more types of decisions alone when they did not have a husband and somewhat more when they had a husband who did not regularly do farm work. Because decision making is not incompatible with looking after children, it is not surprising that the number of children did not affect the extent of women's part in decision making.

Here, too, the ownership and management arrangements for the operation were expected to exert an influence. Tenancy status, though, did not influence a woman's decision-making role, although women with their own names on deeds or rental contracts did make a larger range of farm decisions alone or jointly. There was also only weak evidence that women were less likely to help make necessary decisions when decision makers other than the woman, and her husband if she was married, were available.

Doing farm tasks seems to reinforce taking part in farm decisions: the wider the range of tasks, the wider the range of decisions. Further, women on farms selling mainly animals (in whose production women tend to be active) were involved in a somewhat wider range of decisions.

Unmarried women also made a somewhat wider range of household decisions alone. Farm characteristics in general did not have much effect on this type of decision making. There were some hints, though, that on larger farms (as measured by having more than one hired hand) women made a larger range of household decisions autonomously, perhaps because the farm business occupied more of a husband's time and attention. Yet when an adult son was also farming, women took part in a somewhat smaller range of household decisions. One explanation for this is that the allocation of resources between house and farm was being controlled by fathers with their sons or by sons with their wives. Although these influences are not strong, they point to the ways in which the nature of the farm and its family labor force might affect the extent to which women make what seem to be purely household decisions.

OFF-FARM EMPLOYMENT

Smaller farms are often those needing cash from nonfarm sources. Net of other things, higher off-farm employment was expected among women on smaller farms. To the extent that women fill in for husbands employed off the farm, it was expected that a husband's absence and off-farm work would decrease the likelihood of off-farm employment for a woman, while the presence of other farm workers would free her to go off the farm. Child care and employment are often difficult to do simultaneously, so that women with small children were predicted as less likely to be employed.

The FWS provided only some evidence consistent with these expectations. Women from very large farms were less likely to be employed off the farm. Instead of seeing clear evidence of women taking off-farm jobs while their husbands farmed, or staying on the farm while their husbands earned cash, women were part-time farmers when they were unmarried or when their husbands were also farming part-time: those without husbands were *more* likely to have off-farm employment, as were women whose husbands both farmed and had off-farm jobs. Although husbands and wives may complement rather than substitute for each other in their off-farm employment, women doing a wider range of farm tasks were less likely to have an off-farm job.

Tenancy, presence of other decision makers, and whether the woman herself was an owner or renter had no influence, net of other factors, on whether the woman had employment off the farm. There is also little evidence that having other farm workers frees a woman for off-farm employment. In fact, having more than one hired hand, perhaps another indicator of farm prosperity, decreased the probability that the woman would have a job off the farm. The presence of children, including those doing farm work, also constrained off-farm employment.

COMMUNITY AND AGRICULTURAL ACTIVITIES AND ORGANIZATIONAL MEMBERSHIP

Larger farms (and perhaps those with more control over their inputs and management) were discussed as those that benefit most from the activities of various agricultural organizations and on which a woman has more time and other resources to spend on voluntary organizations and activities. There is consistent support for this idea in the prediction of whether FWS women belonged to some community organization or to various agricultural organizations, of whether women took part in Extension activities, and of whether women had served on various community and agricultural advisory and governing bodies.

To the extent that only one member of a couple takes part in agricultural activities off the farm, I expected a farming husband to limit the probability of a wife's involvement. Children were initially thought to decrease the probability of organizational memberships and other such activities. These expectations were not supported, in part at least because such memberships and activities seemed to be family ones. When one member of a couple belonged to an organization or activity, the odds increased that the other member did too. Women without husbands were less likely to belong to any community organization or to a women's auxiliary or women's farm organization. Those women with more children six to seventeen were more likely to say they belonged to a community organization, took part in Extension activities, or had been on a local governing board. The presence of other decision makers and non-owner status also did not seem to inhibit memberships in any way.

Other sorts of work the woman did reinforced her membership in voluntary organizations and office holding. Those doing a larger range of farm tasks were more likely to have some involvement in off-farm agricultural activities, although off-farm employment did not seem to constrain such memberships and activities. Those with off-farm jobs were also more likely to have served on a local governing board, with no inhibiting effect from the range of their farm work. Perhaps because of greater interest in what was going on both on and off the farm, women with their own names on deeds or rental agreements were more likely to belong to community and farm organizations too.

Conclusions and Directions for Future Study

A need to find out how extensively women were part of U.S. agricultural operations was one reason for undertaking the FWS. The results presented in this book show that women take part in a wide range of on- and off-farm activities that contribute directly and indirectly to keeping farms running and producing food. U.S. policies to help farm families that ignore women as producers will be less effective than those that recognize their contributions. As mentioned in chapter 1, evidence of the pervasive presence of U.S. women on their farms and in agricultural organizations can sensitize Westerners who are involved with agricultural programs for developing countries. Especially in Third World countries that were horticultural before contact with industrialized countries, women were often the farmers. When outside experts and administrators came in, they often did not see women as producers of food. They therefore gave technology and other agricultural resources to the men, even in the face of the men's indifference or resentment. In the long run, men gained control of cash crops in some developing countries, although women, still responsible for raising the family's food, lost agricultural and other resources (see Sachs 1983; Ward 1984). Although some of the problems of women in agriculture will vary by country, recognition of the part women play in a very technologically advanced country's food production can alert even the ethnocentric outsider to look for those important in raising food, rather than assuming that men do it. Again, building programs around the actual producers can make them more effective for feeding these populations.

Kohl (1976) has characterized farm families as having a less strict sexual division of labor than other sorts of families. Because of the physical and economic closeness of farm and family, women, while doing the work expected of them, have also stepped over and done "men's" work when necessary. Consistent with this picture, the FWS data show a tendency toward sex role stereotyping, in that women are likely to do typically female work (and men are more likely to do production-related work), but also plenty of exceptions where women do what might be considered men's work. Furthermore, the survey showed a considerable proportion of couples sharing decision making, getting off-farm incomes, and being part of farm and community organizations (although more detailed breakdown of these activities might show more sex segregation, as was true for hours and types of off-farm jobs).

A problem with this survey is that it does not have extensive data on men. A further part of Kohl's description of the farm families' division of labor was that men did not do women's work. Just as without evidence one may overlook some of the work women do or assume that they do only "women's" work, so without data on the men there may be the tendency to *assume* what it is they do and assume that this is only "men's" work. The one question where the FWS asked men about something remotely resembling stereotypic women's work gave answers that revealed, contrary to expectations, that men were about as likely as women to say they had taken part in some child-focused Extension activity. It is unlikely that farm men are doing much typically female housework and child care. Wilkening (1981), though, in his over-time study of farm couples found a slight increase in the men's involvement in housework. Similarly, some evidence suggests that men in general are doing slightly more housework as more of their wives have jobs outside the home (Stafford 1980). In general, the sex segregation of tasks changes slowly. Sex role stereotypes probably change even more slowly. We need to investigate and not merely make assumptions about who does typically male and female work. If we do not go out and see what exists, we may miss indications that changes are underway or that exceptions to "what everyone knows" are pervasive.

The women's participation in the activities studied varies by farm and family characteristics, as well as their other work roles. But the relationships among these factors is not the same for the different domains of work. One needs to be careful, therefore, in generalizing what we know about one type of work to another. For example, if farms continue to grow in size and farm women to seek off-farm employment, then we might see farm women less involved in farm work but more involved with farm organizations in the future, if the relationships found here continue to hold. There is a need to put the roles of farm women in broader theoretical perspective. But we also need to keep in mind that the farm is both a family enterprise and a business concern and to be careful about extending concepts used to explain other types of work to explain farm and home work. Valadez and Clignet (1984) make this point with respect to housework in general. Although we need to look at more than just paid employment in order to understand work, we need to avoid blindly bringing in perspectives and concepts from the labor market (or about "economically productive work") to our investigation of work in other spheres.

Not surprisingly, what influenced doing various sorts of work usually varied by sex. Farm characteristics, for example, seemed to be more important for men than women in predicting whether they would have off-farm employment and take part in various farm and community organizations. Family characteristics affected men's, but not women's, off-farm income. While the first set of findings was expected, the second was not. This emphasizes again that we should not rule out factors that affect and result from doing different sorts of work on the basis of our stereotypes about what affects men and what affects women. Further, it also points out that our understanding of family and farm position can vary by the person within the family we pick out to study. For example, results suggesting that class differences among farms are reinforced by or reflected in types of off-farm employment and organizational activity showed up more for men than for women. To understand farm families, or other groups made up of related individuals, we need to study the positions of the different members.

Although the analyses in this book included a large number of variables representing farm, family, and women's characteristics, the models left much to be explained in the variation among women in the nature of the work they did. One reason for this could be that despite the number of variables, some of them were only poor proxies for what was really going on. The work variables, for example, focused on whether a woman did something, rather than on how much she did of it and in what way she did it. Size and sales mix only roughly measured the operation's degree of capitalization and production activities. One would expect the technology used on a particular farm, as well as the steps necessary to produce a particular crop or animal, to influence what women do, how they do it, and how the work is shared among family members. In some cases changing technology will affect women's traditional work. Because they often do the bookkeeping, for example, they may be the ones buying and using the new microcomputer. In other cases, changes in the need for women's labor may influence how work is done. As discussed in chapter 1, mechanization, while reducing the importance of physical strength, may have excluded women from production. Now, however, at least some manufacturers of farm equipment are forming advisory boards on how to design the equipment for women. A few students of the history of farm women (e.g., Bush 1982; Flora and Stitz 1984; Armitage 1982; Haney and Wilkening 1984) have looked explicitly at what has happened to women's roles on the farm with changes in technology, but there is more research to be done on technology's effects, for both farm and other women.

Further, presence of other decision makers only crudely measured management structure. We know little about how the incursion of contract farming has affected women, and little about what happens to women's involvement when their farm becomes part of a partnership or corporation. Anecdotal evidence suggests that even kin partnerships or corporations may exclude women, because the partners or shareholders are usually the men. Hill (1981b:90) illustrates how such arrangements can affect women: "A Wisconsin woman described how her husband had signed a set of corporate by-laws with his father and brothers that required his wife, should she outlive her husband, to sell his stock in the corporation to his surviving male relatives at the stock's 1976 value. Her husband never told her about this arrangement. She found out only when she came across the by-laws in the desk and read them." Here the interface of family and work arrangements spans more than the nuclear family. Yet we know little of how such situations usually function.

Another reason it is hard to predict what a farm woman does could be that, as one North Carolina farm woman put it, "My job is to take over what needs to be done, whatever comes along" (Moore 1984:6A). As seen in the analysis here, at times women seem to substitute for their husbands, but at other times they complement the work they and other family members do. Especially in times of transition or crisis, women's roles may be fluid. The situation now in agriculture is one worth watching, especially with an eye toward what it is that women are doing. The recent period has been a hard one for farmers. The part of women in saving the farm, or in making a transition out of farming, needs to be documented.

Relatively more women are in agriculture now than ever before in the United States—not just running their own operations, but also as wage labor and as agricultural professionals off the farm (Bentley and Sachs 1984). To understand the roles women play in agriculture and the effects of changes in agriculture on the sexual division of labor, one should consider these other groups of workers as well, and a few people have begun doing so (e.g., Rose 1984; Sachs 1983). The study of women's work on and for their families' farms, however, does demand an approach somewhat different from that used for other work, as illustrated in this book. Family farms are both economic enterprises and family concerns. The work that women do needs to be examined in such a context, while at the same time realizing that the maleness of the term "farmer" and the family nature of the farm can lead to overlooking women's roles. We need to continue documenting the extent of women's (and men's) productive roles in all spheres and to study the forces changing the nature of those roles.

Appendix
Survey of Farm Women: Women's Questionnaire

On the original questionnaire more space was left for verbatim answers. Otherwise the format is the same. Questions that also appear on the Men's Questionnaire are starred. Differences in wording between men's and women's questions are indicated.

____ Husband has been interviewed

FEMALE VERSION--Screening Questions

F-1. Hello, may I speak to __________, please?
WHEN R ANSWERS, GO TO F-3.

R is not now available...(GO TO F-2)......1

Named R not at number reached...(CHECK NUMBER/DISCONTINUE INTERVIEW).............2

R does not exist/No wife in household (SEE INSTRUCTIONS BELOW).......................3

IF NO WIFE IN HOUSEHOLD AND MALE OPERATOR HAS BEEN SELECTED, SKIP TO MALE SCREENER, Q. M-1. CHECK BOX ON MALE SCREENER. OTHERWISE, DISCONTINUE.

F-2. Can you suggest a convenient time when I can reach her? RECORD INFORMATION ON RECORD OF CALLS. THANK R. END THIS CALL.

F-3. This is (YOUR NAME) of the National Opinion Research Center at the University of Chicago. In cooperation with the U.S. Department of Agriculture, we are conducting a survey of farm women all over the country.

We recently sent a letter to your address describing our study which is about the part women play in farm operation and decision making. We are also interested in women's experiences with some of the USDA's program activities, and in their opinions on a number of farm-related topics.

IF HUSBAND HAS NOT BEEN INTERVIEWED (SEE LINE AT TOP OF PAGE):
A. Are (you/you and your husband) operating a farm, ranch, or any other agricultural business this year, even a very small one or part-time operation?

Yes..................(GO TO F-4).........1
No...(THANK R, DISCONTINUE INTERVIEW).....2

F-4. Your response to this survey is voluntary and not required by law. However, we would appreciate your answering our questions. It will take about 30 minutes. The results of the study will be shown only in statistical or summary form, with no identification of the individuals who took part. Any answers you give will be entirely confidential.

F-5. May I start the interview now?

IF YES, START WITH Q. 1, IN THE QUESTIONNAIRE.
IF NOT, MAKE APPOINTMENT FOR CALLBACK AND ENTER ON RECORD OF CALLS.

* Question also asked of men.

FARM WOMEN INTERVIEW

PART I

*1. First, do you usually refer to your operation as a farm or as a ranch?

Farm....................................1
Ranch...................................2
Other (SPECIFY____________________).......3

---

2. Are you currently married, widowed, divorced, or separated?
*(Asked of men only when wife has not been interviewed or there is no wife.)

Married.................................1
Widowed.................................2
Divorced................................3
Separated...............................4
(IF VOLUNTEERED) Never married..........5

A. Do you consider yourself to be the main operator or one of the main operators for your (farm/ranch)?

IF NECESSARY: By "operator" we mean a person who makes day-to-day decisions about running the whole operation.

Yes.....................................1
No......................................2
Don't know..............................8

---

3. While you were growing up, did you live mostly on a farm or ranch, or did you live somewhere else?

Farm or ranch...........................1
Somewhere else..........................2

*A. Altogether, how many years have you lived or worked on a farm or ranch? IF "All my life," PROBE: About how many years would that be?

ENTER NUMBER OF YEARS: _______

---

*4. Altogether, about how many total acres are there in your (farm/ranch)? Please include acres you own or lease or rent from other people.

ENTER NUMBER OF ACRES: _______

5. Do (you/you or your husband) own any of this land?

Yes............(ASK Q. 6)..................1
No...........(SKIP TO Q. 7)...............2
Don't know...(SKIP TO Q. 7)...............8

---

6. Is your own name on a deed or title to any of this land?

Yes..1
No...2
Don't know.................................8

---

7. Do (you/you or your husband) rent or lease any of the land in your (farm/ranch)?

Yes............(ASK Q. 8)..................1
No...........(SKIP TO Q. 9)...............2
Don't know...(SKIP TO Q. 9)...............8

---

8. Is your own name on any lease or rental contract for any of this land?

Yes..1
No...2
Don't know.................................8

---

*9. Altogether, how many cropland acres are you operating this year? Please include all owned and rented land planted to crops.

ENTER NUMBER OF ACRES: _______

IF NO CROPLAND ACRES, CODE "0" AND GO TO Q. 12, NEXT PAGE.

---

*10. What are your main crops? CODE FIRST FIVE CROPS MENTIONED.

Alfalfa (hay or seeds)....01
Barley....................02
Beans (dry)...............03
Citrus fruits.............04
Corn (all types)..........05
Cotton, cotton products...06
Durum wheat...............07
Flaxseed..................08
Fruits (non-citrus).......09
Hay (other)...............10
Hops......................11
Oats......................12
Peanuts...................13
Peas (dry)................14
Pecans....................15
Potatoes..................16

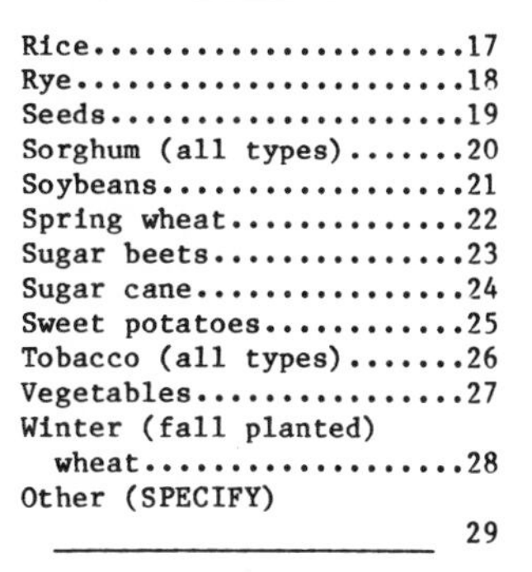

Rice......................17
Rye.......................18
Seeds.....................19
Sorghum (all types).......20
Soybeans..................21
Spring wheat..............22
Sugar beets...............23
Sugar cane................24
Sweet potatoes............25
Tobacco (all types).......26
Vegetables................27
Winter (fall planted)
wheat.....................28
Other (SPECIFY)
______________________ 29

---

*11. If we consider your total gross sales of farm products as adding up to 100%, about what percentage of your total sales would you say comes from crops, as opposed to livestock or animal products?

____
(Percent)

Don't know...........998

IF 100%, SKIP TO Q. 13.

IF LESS THAN 100%, PROBE: So that leaves about (100 MINUS ABOVE) percent of your total gross sales in livestock or animal products--right? IF NO, CORRECT ABOVE FIGURE OR WRITE IN EXPLANATION.

---

*12. What are the main kinds of livestock, poultry, fish, or other animal products you are producing for sale this year? CODE ALL MENTIONED.

*FOR EACH KIND OF LIVESTOCK OR ANIMAL MENTIONED, ASK A:
A. In rough figures, what was the largest number of (KIND OF ANIMAL) you had on hand at any one time last year?

		A.
Beef cattle (include calves, feeder cattle and finished cattle)	01	______
Dairy cattle including calves (milk, cheese, etc.)	02	______
Hogs, pigs	03	______
Horses	04	______
Sheep, lambs	05	______
Broilers (chickens)	06	______
Layers (chickens, eggs)	07	______
All other poultry (turkeys, ducks, geese, etc.)	08	______
Fish or other aquaculture products	09	______
Other (SPECIFY) ______	10	______
None	90	

PART II

13. Now I have some questions about the kinds of work you may do that contribute to the operation of your (farm/ranch). If a particular type of work doesn't apply to your operation, please be sure to tell me and we'll go on to the next one.

First is plowing, disking, cultivating, or planting. Over the last two or three years has this been one of your regular duties, something you help with occasionally, something you never do, or something that's not done on your (farm/ranch)? REPEAT FOR EACH ITEM BELOW.

*(Asked for men only if wife is in household and worded with respect to wife's work.)

	Regular Duty	Occasionally	Never	Not Done
*A. Plowing, disking, cultivating or planting	1	2	3	4
*B. Applying fertilizers, herbicides, or insecticides	1	2	3	4
*C. Doing other field work without machinery	1	2	3	4
*D. Harvesting crops or other products, including running machinery or trucks	1	2	3	4
*E. Taking care of farm animals, including herding or milking dairy cattle	1	2	3	4
*F. Running farm errands, such as picking up repair parts or supplies	1	2	3	4
*G. Making major purchases of farm or ranch supplies and equipment	1	2	3	4
*H. Marketing your products--that is, dealing with wholesale buyers or selling directly to consumers	1	2	3	4
*I. Bookkeeping, maintaining records, paying bills, or preparing tax forms for the operation	1	2	3	4
*J. Doing household tasks like preparing meals, house-cleaning, and so on	1	2	3	4

13. (cont'd)	Regular Duty	Occasionally	Never	Not Done
*K. Supervising the farm work of other family members	1	2	3	4
*L. Supervising the work of hired farm labor	1	2	3	4
*M. Taking care of a vegetable garden or animals for family consumption	1	2	3	4
*N. Looking after children	1	2	3	4
*O. Working on a family or in-home business other than farm or ranch work	1	2	3	4

14. I'd like to ask you about how you make different types of decisions for your (farm/ranch). For each one, please tell me whether you usually make the decision, (your husband/someone else) makes the decision, or you make the decision together with (your husband/someone else).

If I describe a situation that has never come up, please be sure to tell me and we'll go on to the next item.

*(For men, second category is "usually wife/someone else," third is "with your wife/someone else.")

First, who usually makes final decisions about...	Usually respon- dent	Usually husband/ someone else	Both together	Don't Know	NA
*A. Whether to buy or sell land?	1	2	3	8	4
*B. Whether to rent more or less land?	1	2	3	8	4
*C. Whether to buy major household appliances?	1	2	3	8	4
*D. Whether to buy major farm equipment?	1	2	3	8	4

14. (cont'd)

	Usually respon- dent	Usually husband/ someone else	Both together	Don't Know	NA
*E. Whether to produce something new such as a new crop or a new breed or type of livestock?	1	2	3	8	4
*F. When to sell your products?	1	2	3	8	4
*G. When to make household repairs?	1	2	3	8	4
*H. Whether to try a new production practice?	1	2	3	8	4
*I. Whether you take a job off the (farm/ranch)?	1	2	3	8	4

15. Over the last few years, has there been anyone besides (you/you and your husband) who has regularly helped make these kinds of decisions for your (farm/ranch)?
*(For men, question is with respect to self or self and wife.)

Yes............(ASK A)........1
No...........................2

*A. <u>IF YES</u>: Who is that? (CODE ALL THAT APPLY)

Male relative.................1
Female relative...............2
Male non-relative.............3
Female non-relative...........4

16. In general, thinking about the part you have in making decisions for the operation of this (farm/ranch), do you feel that you have too much responsibility for these decisions, or would you like to take a greater part in making these decisions?

Too much responsibility.......1
(IF VOLUNTEERED) About right amount............2
Would like greater part.......3
Don't know....................8

17. ASK ONLY IF HUSBAND IN HOUSEHOLD. IF NO HUSBAND, GO TO Q. 18.

A. If something should happen to your husband, could you continue to run the operation on your own? (PROBE: Would you say definitely yes, probably yes, probably no, or definitely no?)

*(For men, asked only if wife in household and worded, "If something should happen to your wife, could you continue to run the operation on your own?")

Definitely yes................1
Probably yes..................2
Probably no...................3
Definitely no.................4
Don't know....................8

---

*18. We'd like to know something about your feelings toward several aspects of your life today, such as your community, your work, your family, and so on.

First, how satisfied are you with (farming/ranching) as a way of life--are you very satisfied, somewhat satisfied, somewhat dissatisfied, or very dissatisfied? REPEAT FOR EACH ITEM BELOW.

	Very satisfied	Somewhat satisfied	Somewhat dis-satisfied	Very dis-satisfied	Don't Know
*A. Farming/ranching as a way of life?	1	2	3	4	8
*B. The community where where you live?	1	2	3	4	8
*C. Farming/ranching as a way to make a living?	1	2	3	4	8
*D. State or local government programs and services to farmers and ranchers	1	2	3	4	8
*E. USDA programs and services to farmers and ranchers	1	2	3	4	8
F. USDA programs and services for farm women	1	2	3	4	8

PART III

*19. Is your (farm/ranch) on file with the local office of the Agricultural Stabilization and Conservation Service, or ASCS?

Yes..............(ASK A)..................1
No...............(ASK B)..................2
Don't know.......(ASK B)..................8

*A. IF YES: Is your own name listed as an owner, an operator, or a producer in the ASCS file?

Yes...........(GO TO Q. 20)...............1
No...............(ASK B)..................2
Don't know.......(ASK B)..................8

*B. IF NO OR DK TO A: Have you ever tried to get your own name listed in the ASCS file?

Yes.......................................1
No..2

---

20. Next we'd like to find out something about any experiences you or other members of your household may have had with some of the programs run by the U.S. Department of Agriculture.

The first program is usually referred to as the Price Support Program, or Commodity Loan Program. It is administered by the Agricultural Stabilization and Conservation Service or ASCS.

IF NECESSARY:

Under this program, growers of wheat, corn, sorghum, barley, soybeans, rice, or cotton can receive government loans while they decide how to market their products. Program participants may choose to sell their products to the government, keeping the loan amount as payment. They may also receive deficiency payments for their crops if market prices do not reach a specified target price.

*A. Have you ever heard about the Price Support Program before now?

Yes...........(ASK B AND C)...............1
No............(SKIP TO Q. 21).............2
Not sure, don't know.....(SKIP TO Q. 21)..8

*B. How familiar are you personally with this program and the requirements for participating in it? Are you very familiar with it, somewhat familiar, or not familiar with it at all?

Very familiar.............................1
Somewhat familiar.........................2
Not familiar at all.......................3
Not sure, don't know......................8

20. (continued)

*C. In the last two or three years, has your (farm/ranch) tried to participate in this program?

Yes...........(SKIP TO F)................1
No..............(ASK D)..................2
Don't know....(SKIP TO Q. 21)............8

*D. What is the main reason why your (farm/ranch) has not tried to participate in this program in the last two or three years? Is it because your (farm/ranch) is not eligible for the program or because you do not need it, or is there some other reason?

Not eligible...(SKIP TO Q. 21)...........1
No need........(SKIP TO Q. 21)...........2
Other reason......(ASK E).................3
Don't know.....(SKIP TO Q. 21)...........8

*E. Please tell me what that reason is. RECORD VERBATIM.

GO TO Q. 21.

*F. In the past two or three years, did you try to file any of the required forms in your own name and your name only?

Yes...........(SKIP TO I)................1
No..............(ASK G)..................2

*G. In the past two or three years, did your name appear on any required forms along with someone else?

Yes...........(SKIP TO I)................1
No..............(ASK H)..................2

*H. Who filed the most recent forms for this program? (For men, first category is "Brother, son, other male," and second is "Wife, daughter, other female.")

Husband, son, other male.......(GO TO I)..1
Daughter, sister, other female.(GO TO I)..2
Don't know, not sure...........(GO TO I)..3

*I. The last time (you/someone from your operation) tried to participate, did you actually receive the loan or any other payments?

Yes..............(GO TO K)................1
No...............(GO TO J)................2
Still pending....(GO TO K)................3
Don't know.......(GO TO K)................8

20. (cont'd)

*J. IF NO TO I: Was this mainly because you did not meet the program requirements, or because you decided you didn't want the loan, or was there some other reason?

Didn't meet requirements..................1
Didn't want the loan......................2
Some other reason.........................3
Don't know................................8

*K. All in all, do you think your case was treated fairly or unfairly?

Fairly..................(SKIP TO Q. 21)...1
Unfairly...................(ASK L)........2
Not sure, don't know.......(ASK L)........8

*L. IF UNFAIRLY: In what way do you think you (were/might have been) treated unfairly? RECORD VERBATIM.

---

*21. During the last two or three years, have you yourself had any business contacts with ASCS people?

Yes..............(ASK A)..................1
No.............(GO TO Q. 22)..............2

*A. IF YES: In general, were you satisfied or dissatisfied with the way you were treated by ASCS personnel?

Satisfied............(GO TO Q. 22)........1
Dissatisfied............(ASK B)...........2
Don't know...........(GO TO Q. 22)........8

*B. IF DISSATISFIED: In what way were you dissatisfied with the treatment you received? RECORD VERBATIM.

---

22. Next, we'd like to ask about your experiences with a program run by the Soil Conservation Service or SCS through Soil Conservation Districts. The program is called Conservation Operations, and it provides farm and ranch operators with technical advice to deal with a variety of conservation problems. It does not provide either loans, cash grants, or cost-share payments.

IF NECESSARY:

This program provides technical assistance in planning, designing, and laying out conservation practices that deal with erosion control, sediment reduction, water conservation, and so on. Operators who take part in this program are usually asked to become Cooperators with the local Soil Conservation District.

22. (cont'd)

*A. Have you ever heard about this conservation assistance service before now?

Yes...........(ASK B AND C)...............1
No............(SKIP TO Q. 23).............2
Not sure, Don't know....(SKIP TO Q. 23)...8

*B. How familiar are you personally with this service and the procedures for obtaining it? Are you very familiar with it, somewhat familiar, or not familiar with it at all?

Very familiar.............................1
Somewhat familiar.........................2
Not familiar at all.......................3
Not sure, don't know......................8

*C. In the last two or three years, has your (farm/ranch) requested assistance under this program?

Yes...........(SKIP TO F).................1
No..............(ASK D)...................2
Don't know....(SKIP TO Q. 23).............8

*D. What is the <u>main</u> reason why your (farm/ranch) has not requested assistance in the last two or three years? Is it because your (farm/ranch) is not eligible for this program or because you do not need it, or is there some other reason?

Not eligible..(SKIP TO Q. 23).............1
No need..... (SKIP TO Q. 23).............2
Other reason..(ASK E).....................3
Don't know....(SKIP TO Q. 23).............8

*E. Please tell me what that reason is. RECORD VERBATIM.

<u>GO TO Q. 23.</u>

*F. In the past two or three years, did you request these services in <u>your own name</u> and your name only?

Yes.........(SKIP TO I)...................1
No..........(ASK G).......................2

*G. In the past two or three years, did you request these services jointly with someone else?

Yes.........(SKIP TO I)...................1
No............(ASK H).....................2

22. (cont'd)

*H. Who made the most recent request for these services?
(For men, first category is "Brother, son, other male," and second is "wife, daughter, other female.")

Husband, son, other male.........(GO TO I).....1
Daughter, sister, other female...(GO TO I).....2
Don't know, not sure............(GO TO I).....8
(For men, see Q. 20H)

*I. The last time (you/someone from your operation) requested assistance, did you receive the service you wanted?

Yes........................(GO TO J)..........1
No ....(SKIP TO K).........2
Still pending.............(SKIP TO K).........3
Don't know, don't remember.(SKIP TO K).........8

*J. Did the technical assistance help you solve your conservation problem?

Yes...1
No..2
Not sure,
don't know..................................8

*K. All in all, do you think your case was treated fairly or unfairly?

Fairly.......(SKIP TO Q. 23)..................1
Unfairly..........(ASK L).....................2
Not sure,
don't know......(ASK L).....................8

*L. <u>IF UNFAIRLY:</u> In what way do you think you (were/might have been) treated unfairly? RECORD VERBATIM.

---

*23. During the past two or three years, have <u>you yourself</u> had any business contacts with people from the Soil Conservation Office in your area?

Yes............(ASK A).........................1
No..........(GO TO Q. 24).....................2

*A. <u>IF YES:</u> In general, were you satisfied or dissatisfied with the way you were treated by personnel from the Soil Conservation Office?

Satisfied........(GO TO Q. 24)................1
Dissatisfied........(ASK B)....................2
Don't know.......(GO TO Q. 24)................8

*B. <u>IF DISSATISFIED:</u> In what way were you dissatisfied with the treatment you received? RECORD VERBATIM.

---

24. Now a question about the Farmers Home Administration or FmHA. As you may know, FmHA administers many different loan programs for farmers and ranchers. Some examples are farm ownership or farm operating loans, rural housing loans, disaster loans, and small business loans.

<u>IF NECESSARY:</u>

FmHA provides both financing and technical assistance to help operators purchase or enlarge farms or ranches, to buy or improve their housing, to cover operating expenses, organize businesses, set up conservation practices, and to recover from natural disasters or other economic emergencies.

*A. Have you ever heard about any of the FmHA loan programs for farmers and ranchers before now?

Yes...........(ASK B AND C)...............1
No...........(SKIP TO Q. 25)..............2
Not sure,
don't know.(SKIP TO Q. 25).............8

*B. How familiar are you personally with FmHA loan programs and their eligibility requirements? Are you very familiar with them, somewhat familiar, or not familiar with them at all?

Very familiar.............................1
Somewhat familiar.........................2
Not familiar at all.......................3
Don't know................................8

*C. In the last two or three years, has your (farm/ranch) applied for an FmHA loan?

Yes.........(SKIP TO F)...................1
No............(ASK D).....................2
Don't know..(SKIP TO Q. 25)..............8

*D. What is the main reason why your (farm/ranch) has not applied for any FmHA loans in the last two or three years? Is it because your (farm/ranch) is not eligible for these loans, because you did not need them, or is there some other reason?

Not eligible...(SKIP TO Q. 25)............1
Not needed.....(SKIP TO Q. 25)............2
Other reason... (ASK E)...................3
Don't know.....(SKIP TO Q. 25)............8

*E. Please tell me what that reason is. RECORD VERBATIM.

<u>GO TO Q. 25.</u>

24. (cont'd)

*F. In the past two or three years, did you apply for an FmHA loan in <u>your</u> <u>own</u> <u>name</u> and your name only?

Yes.........(SKIP TO I)..............................1
No............(ASK G)................................2

*G. In the past two or three years, have you signed your name as a co-applicant for a loan along with someone else?

Yes.........(SKIP TO I)..............................1
No.......... (ASK H)................................2

*H. Who made the <u>most</u> <u>recent</u> application for an FmHA loan? (For men, the first category is "Brother, son, other male," and the second is "wife, daughter, other female.")

Husband, son, other male..........(GO TO I)...........1
Daughter, sister, other female....(GO TO I)...........2
Don't know, not sure..............(GO TO I)...........8

*I. The last time (you/someone from your operation) applied in this way, were you found to be eligible for the loan or not?

Yes, eligible...... (ASK J).........................1
No, not eligible...(SKIP TO K).......................2
Still pending......(SKIP TO K).......................3
Don't know.........(SKIP RO K).......................8

*J. <u>IF</u> <u>ELIGIBLE</u>: And did you finally receive the loan?

Yes..1
No...2
Still pending..3
Don't know...8

*K. Which of the following types of loans was this? READ CATEGORIES.

A farm ownership loan................................1
A farm operating loan................................2
A disaster loan......................................3
An economic emergency loan...........................4
A housing loan.......................................5
Or some other type of FmHA loan......................6

(IF VOLUNTEERED) Don't know...........................8

*L. All in all, do you think your case was treated fairly or unfairly?

Fairly........(SKIP TO Q. 25)........................1
Unfairly...........(ASK M)...........................2
Not sure, don't know........(ASK M)...................8

24. (cont'd)

*M. IF UNFAIRLY: In what way do you think you (were/might have been) treated unfairly? RECORD VERBATIM.

---

*25. During the last two or three years, have you yourself had any business contact with people from FmHA?

Yes............(ASK A)....................1
No..........(GO TO Q. 26).................2

*A. IF YES: In general, were you satisfied or dissatisfied with the way you were treated by FmHA personnel?

Satisfied........(GO TO Q. 26)............1
Dissatisfied........(ASK B)...............2
Don't know.......(GO TO Q. 26)............8

*B. IF DISSATISFIED: In what way were you dissatisfied with the treatment you received? RECORD VERBATIM.

---

26. We'd also like to know about any experiences you may have had with programs or activities run by the Extension Service in your area. In the last two or three years have you personally been involved with any of the following Extension Service activities:

		Yes	No
*A.	Classes or other activities on agricultural production?	1	2
*B.	Classes or other activities on farm or ranch management?	1	2
C.	Homemaker clubs or other activities on family living?	1	2
*D.	Classes or other activities on inheritance laws or estate planning?	1	2
E.	Any activities on food or nutrition?	1	2
*F.	4-H or other youth activities?	1	2
*G.	Discussing specific problems of your operation with an extension agent or staff member?	1	2
*H.	Getting information about other USDA programs or services?	1	2

*27. Have you ever tried to participate in any of these activities and felt that you were discouraged from doing so by Extension personnel?

Yes....................................1
No.....................................2

---

*28. In the past two or three years, have you yourself had any business contact with Extension personnel?

Yes.........(ASK A).......................1
No......(SKIP TO Q. 29)...................2
Don't recall....(SKIP TO Q. 29)...........8

*A. IF YES: In general, were you satisfied or dissatisfied with the way you were treated by Extension Service personnel?

Satisfied........(GO TO Q. 29)............1
Dissatisfied.........(ASK B)..............2
Don't know.......(GO TO Q. 29)............8

*B. IF DISSATISFIED: In what way were you dissatisfied with the treatment you received? RECORD VERBATIM.

---

*29. Have you ever been involved in any committees or groups that helped to develop or carry out Extension programs in your area? (PROBE: Some examples are education programs, 4-H activities, home economics programs, and so forth.

Yes.....................................1
No......................................2
Don't know, don't recall.................8

---

*30. Have you ever served as a member of any official committee, advisory board, or other group connected with the U.S. Department of Agriculture?

Yes.....................................1
No......................................2

---

*31. Have you ever served on any committee, advisory board, panel, or other group concerned with agricultural matters in your state, county, or local government?

Yes.....................................1
No......................................2

---

*32. In the future, if you were asked to serve on, or run for election to an official committee or group of this kind, do you think you would definitely agree to do it, that you would probably agree, probably not agree or definitely not agree to do it?

Definitely agree	1
Probably agree	2
Probably not agree	3
Definitely not agree	4
Don't know	8

33. Next, we would like to know about your membership in farm organizations. For each of the following organizations, please tell me whether you personally have been a member at any time during the last two or three years.

First, how about marketing cooperatives?

		Yes	No	Don't Know
*A.	Marketing cooperative?	1	2	8
*B.	Farm supply cooperative?	1	2	8
*C.	Any general farm organization, such as the Grange, Farm Bureau, National Farmers Union, or American Agricultural Movement?	1	2	8
D.	Any women's auxiliaries of general farm organizations, such as Farm Bureau Women?	1	2	8
*E.	Any commodity producers' associations, such as the American Dairy Association, or National Wheat Producers Association?	1	2	8
F.	Any women's auxiliaries of commodity organizations, such as the Cowbelles or the Wheathearts?	1	2	8
G.	Any women's farm organizations, such as United Farm Wives, American Agri-Women, or Women Involved in Farm Economics?	1	2	8
*H.	Any community organizations, such as a church group, PTA, League of Women Voters, and so forth? (For men, "League of Women Voters" is replaced with "civic organization.")	1	2	8

34. During the past two or three years, were you appointed or elected to serve on a local governing board, such as a school board, town council, or county board, and so forth?

Yes....................................1
No.....................................2
Don't know.............................8

PART IV

*35. Please tell me, in what year were you born?

_____________ (YEAR)

---

*36. Which one of these categories do you consider yourself. READ CATEGORIES.

American Indian or Alaskan Native.........1
Asian or Pacific Islander.................2
Black............(ASK A)..................3
White............(ASK A)..................4

*A. Do you consider yourself to be of Hispanic origin?

IF NECESSARY:

By Hispanic origin, we mean having ancestors of Mexican, Puerto Rican, Central or South American or other Spanish origins.

Yes.......................................1
No..2

---

37. Please tell me who else usually lives in this household. I don't need their names, but tell me their relationship to you. RECORD RELATIONSHIPS ON LINES BELOW. USE A SEPARATE LINE FOR EACH PERSON. FOR EACH CHILD LISTED ASK: And what is (his/her) age?

---

38. Which of the persons living here are regularly involved in the day-to-day work on this (farm/ranch)? Do not count those who help out only occasionally or for very short periods. CODE YES OR NO FOR EACH PERSON LISTED.

Q. 37 LIVE IN HOUSEHOLD	AGE OF EACH CHILD	Q. 38 INVOLVED IN DAY-TO-DAY WORK	
RELATIONSHIP:			
1) ________	________	Yes... 1	No... 2
2) ________	________	Yes... 1	No... 2
3) ________	________	Yes... 1	No... 2
4) ________	________	Yes... 1	No... 2
5) ________	________	Yes... 1	No... 2
6) ________	________	Yes... 1	No... 2
7) ________	________	Yes... 1	No... 2
8) ________	________	Yes... 1	No... 2
9) ________	________	Yes... 1	No... 2
10) ________	________	Yes... 1	No... 2
11) ________	________	Yes... 1	No... 2

39. Altogether, how many hired hands are employed on this operation? Please include part-time as well as full-time help.
IF NONE, ENTER ZEROS.

____
NO. OF
HIRED HANDS

40. Are there any other people who do not usually live in the household, but who are involved in the day-to-day work on this (farm/ranch)?

Yes ....(ASK A) 1
No 2

A. IF YES: How many are there? PROBE FOR BEST ESTIMATE.

____
Number

---

41. IF EVER MARRIED: Altogether how many children have you had? Please include any stepchildren or adopted children. ENTER NUMBER IN BOX.

IF NONE, CODE "00" AND GO TO Q. 42.

OF CHILDREN: _____________

---

*42. What is the highest grade you finished in school?

1 - 8th grade...........................01
9 - 11th grade..........................02
12th grade or high school equivalent...03
Vocational school beyond high school...04
Some college............................05
Bachelor's degree.......................06
M.A., M.S., other Master's degree......07
Ph.D., M.D., other professional degree.08

---

*43. Have you ever held a job for pay outside the home and farm?

Yes.....................................1
No...........(SKIP TO Q. 45)...........2

---

*44. Do you currently have a job for pay outside home or farm work?

Yes..........(SKIP TO Q. 46)............1
No.............(ASK A)..................2

*A. IF NO: In what year did you leave your last job?

____
(YEAR)

*45. Are you looking for work now or do you intend to start looking for work outside your (farm/ranch) operation during the next 12 months?

Yes.................................1
No..................................2
Don't know..........................8

IF Q. 43 IS "NO" OR IF Q. 44A IS 1977 OR BEFORE, SKIP TO Q. 47.

---

46. IF CURRENTLY EMPLOYED: We'd like to know a bit about this job. (IF MORE THAN ONE: The job at which you spend the most hours.)

IF EMPLOYED '78-'80: We'd like to know a bit about the last job you had.

*A. What kind of work (do/did) you normally do on that job?
PROBE: What is the job called? What (are/were) the main duties?

OFFICE USE ONLY

____

____

*B. What kind of place (do/did) you work for? PROBE: What do they make or do?

OFFICE USE ONLY

____

*C. How many hours a week (do/did) you usually spend on the job?

HOURS: __________

46. (cont'd)

D. What is the main reason you (have/had) an off-(farm/ranch) job? (Is/was) it mainly to keep up and use your career skills, mainly to get out of the house and see other people, or because you need the money? PROBE FOR MAIN REASON.

Keep up, use skills..................1
Get out of house, see people.........2
Need the money...(ASK E).............3
Other (SPECIFY)

_______________________.......4

E. <u>IF NEED THE MONEY:</u> Do you need the money mainly for farm-related expenses, or do you need it mainly for other things?

Farm-related expenses................1
Other things.........................2
(IF VOLUNTEERED) Both equally.........................3
Don't know...........................8

*F. Altogether, how much money did you earn before taxes in 1979 from (off-farm/off-ranch) jobs? PROBE FOR BEST ESTIMATE: ROUND TO NEAREST THOUSAND DOLLARS.

$ __________, 000

---

47. On your income tax forms, what do you put down as <u>your</u> occupation? DO NOT READ CATEGORIES.

Wife, mother, housewife..............1
Farm wife............................2
Farmer, rancher......................3
Other, (SPECIFY)

_______________________.....4

Don't know...........................8

---

48. Does <u>your own name</u> ever appear on checks received in payment for any (farm/ranch) products sold?

Yes..................................1
No...................................2

---

49. We'd like to know if you have any of the following financial arrangements.

A. First, do you have a savings or checking account in <u>your name alone</u>?

Yes................................1
No.................................2

B. Do you have a joint savings or checking account with someone else?

Yes................................1
No.................................2

C. Do you have any credit cards or charge accounts in <u>your own name?</u>

Yes................................1
No.................................2

D. Do you have any joint charge accounts with someone else?

Yes................................1
No.................................2

E. Have you had any loans from banks or other lending institutions in <u>your own name</u>?

Yes................................1
No.................................2

F. Have you had any joint loans with <u>anyone else?</u>

Yes................................1
No.................................2

G. Have you paid enough into Social Security to qualify for benefits in your own name?

Yes................................1
No.................................2
Don't know.........................8

---

50. <u>IF MARRIED</u>: Altogether, about how much money did your husband earn before taxes in 1979 from (off-farm/off-ranch) jobs? PROBE FOR BEST ESTIMATE; ROUND OFF TO NEAREST THOUSAND DOLLARS.

$ ________, 0 0 0

---

51. And how much net farm income did (you/you and your husband) earn in 1979 before taxes, but after production expenses are subtracted? PROBE FOR BEST ESTIMATE, ROUND TO NEAREST THOUSAND DOLLARS.
*(For men, ask about own/own and wife's farm income.)

$ ____________, 0 0 0

---

*52. A. In rough figures, what is the total value of your (farm/ranch) operation today? Please include the value of all land, animals, machinery, and other assets.
(PROBE FOR BEST ESTIMATE. ROUND TO NEAREST THOUSAND DOLLARS.)

$ ____________, 0 0 0

IF "DON'T KNOW," CODE 9898.
IF REFUSED, CODE 9797.

*B. And what is the total debt for your operation today, including all mortgages for farm or ranch property, and other loans for machinery, animals or other things? (PROBE FOR BEST ESTIMATE. ROUND TO NEAREST THOUSAND DOLLARS.)

$ ____________, 0 0 0

IF "DON'T KNOW," CODE 9898.
IF REFUSED, CODE 9797.

---

53. And now just two final questions:
*(For men say, "And now just one final question.")

What do you think is the most important thing the U.S. Department of Agriculture could do to help farm and ranch people? RECORD VERBATIM. PROBE FOR MOST IMPORTANT.

---

54. Finally, what do you think is the most important thing that the U.S. Department of Agriculture could do to help farm and ranch women? RECORD VERBATIM. PROBE FOR RESPONSE FOCUSING ON HELP SPECIFICALLY FOR WOMEN. PROBE FOR MOST IMPORTANT.

TIME AM
ENDED: ________ PM

Notes

Chapter 1

1. All the women in this sample are either operators or married to operators of agricultural enterprises, as described in chapter 2. They are not all "farm" women, though. When asked whether their operation was a farm, ranch, or something else, 82 percent said "farm," 12 percent said "ranch," and 5 percent used another term. Although I recognize this variation, I shall usually use the term "farm women" rather than some more awkward specification to describe these women.

2. Slocum (1974) is unusual because he included discussions of both farms and family retail businesses as work organizations in his book on careers and occupations.

3. Even though unpaid family workers are categorized as employed under some circumstances (as discussed in chapter 2) and people working for pay at home would be included in the labor force participation figures, most of those counted as in the labor force are employed (or looking for paid work) outside the home. For example, in 1981 only 1.2 percent of women in the U.S. labor force were unpaid family workers (U.S. Department of Commerce, 1982: Table 646).

4. See Lipman-Blumen and Tickameyer (1975), Miller and Garrison (1982), and Sokoloff (1980) for reviews of this literature.

5. See, for example, Corcoran, et al. (1984) for a critique and rebuttal of the explanations of occupational choice and the wage gap based on differences between women and men in their labor force participation. However, Coverman (1983), looking directly at the effect of hours of domestic work, found that the more time a woman (or a man) put in on housework and child care, the lower that person's wage.

6. Preliminary results from the 1982 Census of Agriculture (U.S. Department of Commerce 1984) show the same pattern.

7. At times, renting does not involve going outside the family. In a study of one Illinois German-American community, Salamon (1978) found that only 11 percent of the operators who rented some of their land rented exclusively from non-kin. Although this figure may be higher in other sorts of communities, it does emphasize that even when farmers do not own

their land they may be dealing with their relatives or other community members.

1. Some exceptions are Sachs (1983), Janiewski (1979), Jensen (1981), and Jones (1983).

9. See Baker (1964) and Hartmann (1976) for analysis of how men gain or retain control over various kinds of work.

Chapter 2

1. For examples see Kohl (1976) on Saskatchewan women; Hagood (1939) with intensive data on 254 Carolina piedmont, Georgia, and Alabama families; Capener and Berkowitz (1976) with data on 20 New York farm families; Pearson (1979) with data on Colorado farm women; Wilkening (1981) using samples of Wisconsin farm couples; Hepner (1979) with an ad hoc sample of almost 200 Illinois farm couples; Hoiberg and Huffman (1978) from information on 933 Iowa farm households; Bokemeir and Coughenour (1980) for a report on a sample of Kentucky adults; Lodwick and Fassinger (1979) with data on 66 farm families in Michigan; Fassinger and Schwarzweller (1982) from a larger study of mid-Michigan farm wives; Salant (1983) using interviews with 1,087 farm families in northern Mississippi and western Tennessee; Boulding (1980) with interviews with 27 Oklahoma, Colorado, and Vermont women; and articles such as Orr (1979).

2. These regions are the same as those defined by the U.S. Census of Agriculture except that Michigan, Indiana, and Ohio were switched from the Northcentral to the Northeast region to increase the sample size for the Northeast.

3. At the same time, women counted by the Census as farmers are older than male farmers "largely due to the relatively high number of widowed female farmers, many of whom are not officially designated as farm operators until their husbands die" (Kalbacher 1982:4).

4. Some of the analyses for chapters 3 and 4 were done including race as a variable (see Rosenfeld 1982b). Race had no significant direct effect on the range of women's farm work and decision making. Because of the small variance in race and its lack of effect in the preliminary results, it will not be included in the analyses presented here. See USDA-OGPA (1980) for a short overview on black farm families and interviews with four such families, and Jensen (1981) for a discussion of differences in farm women's history by ethnicity.

5. Rogers (1982), in an ongoing study of farm families in Illinois, found differences in the work roles, land transfers, and attitudes toward farming among families of different ethnic origins even within the same geographic area. Among the Yankee families (descendants of migrants from the eastern United States), husbands and wives tend to see each other as partners, sometimes establishing this legally. Among the German-Ameri-

can families, the woman tends to be a helpmate and to provide support services, rather than to act as a full partner. Unfortunately, the FWS was not able to ask about the respondents' ethnicity in any more detail than that shown in Table 2.4, nor was it able to ask about religion, another factor that might affect family, and thus work, organization.

Chapter 3

1. One could argue that item M—taking care of a vegetable garden or animals for family consumption—is home production rather than farm work. Ross (1982), who used factor analysis to create scales for various dimensions of farm women's work from the Farm Women's Survey data, found that the placement of home production of food was ambiguous. It fit into a "home work" as well as an "ancillary farm service" dimension. She included it as part of the latter factor. Others, too, have defined tending a garden or raising other food as a farm task (e.g., Fassinger and Schwarzweller 1982; Lodwick and Fassinger 1979).

2. This distribution is remarkably consistent with that of Lodwick and Fassinger (1979) over categories of women's agricultural roles. They found that about 17 percent of their women respondents were either independent producers or agricultural partners; 21 percent were agriculturally active; 17 percent were farm helpers (who did more farm work during the peak season); 35 percent were farm homemakers; and 11 percent were peripheral helpers.

3. This is consistent with what others have found in small scale surveys. Lodwick and Fassinger (1979), for example, listed bookkeeping and bill paying, keeping a garden, and buying/getting machine parts as "core" tasks, performed by at least half the women.

4. We chose to ask about a few agencies rather than participation in any USDA program because this approach would make comparisons among women and between women and men straightforward, with consistent underlying program and agency referents. These agencies offered programs that were widely available and granted important benefits to the farm population in 1980. ASCS operated the Commodity Loan Program that made loans to producers of certain commodities (wheat, corn, sorghum, barley, rice, and cotton) against the value of future sales. The SCS administered Conservation Operations programs that provided technical assistance to operators who wanted to improve their conservation practices. FmHA offered a series of loan programs as well as other assistance. Extension carried out a number of educational programs, such as 4-H, some of which are discussed in chapter 6 with other organizational activities, as well as providing information and advice services. (See Jones, in Jones and Rosenfeld 1981, for a more extensive discussion of these agencies and their programs.)

5. What is known about farm information gathering in general suggests

that whereas women do it, men predominate. Fassinger and Schwarzweller (1982) report that almost 30 percent of farm wives in their sample at least checked market prices. But only the husband got farm information in 39 percent of 1979 Wisconsin farm couples, while the husband did more of the information gathering than the wife in another 29 percent. In only 6 percent of the couples did the wife do more information gathering than the husband or do it alone (Wilkening 1981).

6. Ross (1982) did this using the FWS data, however. She created a home management index combining women's responses to the questions about housework and child care. Using multiple regression she found that the most important determinants of women's scores on this index were the number of children in the home (the more children in various age groups, the higher a woman's score) and age (the older the woman, the lower her score). Identifying oneself as a wife, having a farm background, and having more education also increased scores on this index to some extent. A woman's score on the home management index had rather low, though positive, association with her scores on indexes measuring involvement in other farm tasks and decision-making activities (p. 105), suggesting that home work is something women do on top of everything else on the farm and not in place of other things, although actual hours spent on the different tasks might have to be adjusted. But as reported in chapter 1, other researchers have failed to find range of housework tasks differing by type of farm (Fassinger and Schwarzweller 1982). Huffman and Lange (1982), using data from a 1976 survey of Iowa farms, also found no farm effects on *hours* of housework and child care.

7. The unstandardized coefficient shows how many percentage points a woman's involvement increases or decreases for a unit increase of the independent (explanatory or predicting) variable, net of every other independent variable. The standardized coefficient gives an idea of the relative importance of the independent variable: the larger it is (disregarding whether it is negative or positive), the relatively more important the variable. The stars show the results of tests for whether a given coefficient, controlling for all the other variables, is statistically significantly different from 0. R^2 indicates the proportion of the variance in the dependent variable (the variable to be explained) that is accounted for by the set of independent variables included.

In cases where a set of categories represents a given variable, one category provides redundant information. For example, if a given operation is not 50 to 299 acres, nor 300 to 999 acres, nor at least 1,000 acres, then logically it must be in the smallest size category—less than 50 acres. Because of this redundancy, to estimate the equations at least one category of such sets must be left out. One then interprets the coefficients for the remaining categories as the difference in effect on the outcome from being in that category relative to the omitted category. The excluded category should have a relatively large number of cases as well as be substantively interesting as a basis for comparison.

8. One could argue that this failure to find large effects of the numbers of people other than husbands and children helping on the farm is a statistical artifact. The numbers of sons over 18, of other household members, and of nonhousehold members who regularly did farm work are highly skewed toward 0. Another form of the variable might be expected to give stronger results. One such alternative would be to make the contrast between those operations with anyone in each of these categories and those with none. Using this alternative specification did not the change the results here—nor generally elsewhere in the analysis.

9. The estimated coefficients express how high values of a given independent variable affect these log odds. A variable that has a positive (negative) effect on the log odds has a positive (negative) effect on the probability of doing a given type of task. Thus one can interpret the signs of the coefficients as though they showed effects on the probability of an outcome. One can test whether coefficients are statistically significant in a manner similar to that in multiple regression. The *D* statistic reported in the tables is analogous to R^2 in OLS regression and measures relative improvement in fit from including the independent variables. (For further discussion of logistic regression and of the program used to obtain the results presented here, see Hanushek and Jackson 1977, chapter 7, and Harrell 1980.)

Chapter 4

1. Boulding (1980:275–76), with a sample of only 27, did not find such a relationship. She suggests that her failure to find an association between number of tasks done and decision-making patterns is because "[m]any husbands do not realize how involved their wives are. High task involvement and low decision-making power for women can indicate a denial by the husband of what the wife actually does." As seen in the previous chapter, at least in terms of the range of tasks women do, FWS husbands do not seem to underestimate their wives' involvement.

2. Whereas Wilkening and Bharadwaj (1967, 1968) found two farm decision dimensions and separated decisions about off-farm work from other household decisions, Ross (1982), when she factor analyzed all the FWS decision-making variables, found two factors, one for farm and one for nonfarm decisions (with loadings of .67, .43, and .31 for buying home appliances, making home repairs, and taking an off-farm job). Her two factors fit with an intuitive reaction about a way to categorize these decisions and will be used here.

3. In contrast with these results, Wilkening and Bharadwaj (1967) found that making decisions for the farm did not necessarily entail making decisions for the home and concluded that the two decision-making domains were separate. The differences in results may be because of differences in the samples (especially the inclusion of unmarried women in the FWS), in

the set of decisions, in the measurement of influence on decision making, or in the periods studied.

4. What predicts decision-making patterns may depend on whose perception of decision making is used. Huber and Spitze (1983:74) conclude their comparison of husbands' and wives' reports on housework and decision making by saying, "When the research goal is to relate relative contributions of demographic characteristics of couples, strong relationships will appear no matter who is the informant, and weak relationships are probably not worth the large additional expense involved in detecting them [by getting both spouses' reports]." Yet they did find different patterns of family and demographic variables' effects on wife's versus husband's perceptions of family decision making (pp.158–60).

5. As described here and in the other studies of farm families, there is some tendency toward couples sharing farm decision making. If one were to examine only joint decision making, one would find that being unmarried reduced the percent of types of farm decisions a woman made with someone else.

6. In the data file created for couples where both the husband and the wife were surveyed, measures of farm characteristics were created by (1) averaging the husband's and wife's responses, if both of them answered a given question, or (2) using the response of one spouse if the other did not answer. This should increase the reliability of measurement of farm characteristic while it dramatically reduces the amount of missing data. There was no need here to employ the method of handling missing data used when the larger data set was analyzed. At the same time, because the couples' data set is much smaller than that for the full sample of women, it is harder for effects to reach statistical significance.

To see what happened as a result of the smaller sample size and exclusion of nonmarried women, models such as those in table 4.3 were reestimated using data only on women in the couples' sample. The general conclusions from using the more restricted sample are the same as from using the larger sample. The main differences are: having a legal title to the land did not affect extent of women's single or joint farm decision making, but age did, with women under 65 making about 20 percentage points fewer of the types of farm decisions; for percent of types of farm decisions the wife made alone, the range was 2 percentage points smaller when the couple were full owners as compared with another tenancy status, a statistically significant difference.

7. It is not clear exactly how one should measure the relative resources of spouses. Relative can imply a ratio. Derivation of household utility functions does lead to this specification of relative characteristics (e.g., Becker [1981]; see also Jasso [1980] for another derivation leading to using a ratio). On the other hand, some researchers talk of the *discrepancy* between husbands' and wives' resources (e.g., Hill and Scanzoni 1982), which leads to using a difference measure, as was done here. When ratios

rather than differences were used for the FWS couples, the results for the extent of women's autonomous or joint farm decision making were the same: when the ratio of the wife's experience with farm living to the husband's was greater, so was the range of types of farm decisions in which the woman took part. For autonomous farm decision making, however, none of the measures of relative characteristics had any significant effect. Relative off-farm income was measured by the ratio of the wife's income to the spouse's and was set to 1 when neither spouse had outside income. It is therefore a less sensitive proxy for the husband's off-farm employment per se. Its lack of effect is consistent with the interpretation of the income discrepancy effect as one of work status rather than of relative resources.

Chapter 5

1. Although husbands and wives are probably the most important off-farm wage earners, children and other household members can also earn money off the farm. Wandersee (1981) speculates that the institution and enforcement of child labor laws and the consequent decline of children's earnings in the 1920s and 30s contributed to the increased labor force participation of U.S. women in general. Wilkening (1981:3) reports that 40 percent of Wisconsin farm families surveyed in 1978–79 had children with off-farm jobs, although it is not clear that such children would be adding to family income rather than earning money for their own consumption or future goals. Kada (1980:96) did find among Wisconsin part-time farm families that household members other than the operator and spouse were least likely to say they had such work to finance the farm. The 1980 NORC survey cannot shed further light on this issue, because it did not ask about paid work off the farm for other family members. Although the 1979 Farm Finance Survey did ask about total family off-farm income and about the details of the types of jobs the operator and the spouse had, it did not ask for the earnings of the operator and spouse, something that would have enabled one to determine the residual contribution of other family members (U.S. Department of Commerce 1982a).

2. Labor force participation rates are calculated as the proportion of a given population either working or looking for work. At the time of the 1980 FWS, 5 percent of the women were looking for work, for a rough off-farm labor force participation rate of 36 percent. Among the men 4 percent reported looking for a job, for a summer 1980 off-farm labor force participation rate of 46 percent. Most of the FWS men and women, though, held an off-farm job at some time in their lives: only 15 percent of the women and 19 percent of the men said they had never had an off-farm job.

3. The proportion indicating that they had wage work to help with the farm is lower than that which Kada (1980) reports, perhaps because he had people list more than one reason for their employment.

4. The few outliers on farm and own income (i.e., those reporting incomes far above the average, incomes that could have been coding error) are excluded from these and other analyses.

The FWS survey asked about 1979 before-tax income only from the farm and from husbands' and wives' off-farm employment. Although farm and off-farm employment income are the most important sources of family income (Hoiberg and Huffman 1978:42; Gladwin and Downie 1982: Table 5; Banks and Kalbacher 1981), summing only these components misses family income from transfer payments, rents, investments, other family members, and so on. It may be for this reason that 19 families who had given some response to all the income questions are calculated to have "0" family income for 1979. Furthermore, production for use and the outcome of trading in kind do not appear in the calculated total family income.

Notice that net farm income here has zero as a minimum; no negative net farm incomes are shown. In response to the net farm income question, in the total sample 155 women and 41 men indicated that their operations had sustained net losses in 1979. Only 11 males and 29 females, however, were willing or able to specify the amount of their losses and did so only after interviewers probed for their "best guess." To minimize loss of information and standardize the treatment of these cases, all respondents who indicated a net loss were classified at the zero point on the income measure. The contribution of off-farm income is thus underestimated. Banks and Kalbacher (1981:5) report that "About a fourth of all farm income people were in families that reported a loss from their farming activities during 1975." However, they point out that others have found the amount of such losses to be small—and offset by off-farm income.

5. Average hours were 32.8 for women and 40.2 for men (with standard deviations of 12.6 and 12.8). In the full sample, 6 women and 9 men reported working over 70 hours a week for their 1978–80 jobs. Because it was not possible to tell whether these were accurate reports or coding errors, responses over 70 hours were recoded to 70.

6. This gives only a rough comparison, of course, of how farm and nonfarm people fare in employment. The FWS people, for example, are more likely to be married, less likely to be black, and somewhat older, among other things, than the U.S. population on which the national distributions are based. Further, many farm women and men will already show up in the U.S. distribution in farming, if that is their primary occupation, rather than as in their off-farm occupation. Recalculating the occupational distributions excluding the "farm" category, though, does not change the conclusions reported here. The same sort of considerations apply to the industrial distributions as well.

7. The prediction equation used what seemed to be the strongest influences on off-farm employment, as evidenced in the logistic equations for off-farm employment to be seen in this chapter. For women, it included size of operation, whether the region was the South, whether the opera-

tion had two or more hired hands, age, number of children under 6, number of children 6 to 17, and education. For the full sample, marital status was also included. For men, the prediction equation contained farm size, whether the region was West, whether there were two or more hired hands, age, and education.

8. I created another measure of on-farm diversity by counting the number of kinds of crops and the number of kinds of livestock produced on the operation. Whereas such a measure is conceptually distinct from the percentage of sales from crops and livestock, the correlations between the two kinds of measures were too high to include both sets in the analyses. I therefore use only the sales mix variables here.

9. The differences between the results from the full sample and for the sample of couples are much less for the men (results not shown) than for the women. As mentioned in note 6 of chapter 4, at least some of the differences in significance levels are due to having much smaller sample size for women in the couples as compared with the full sample.

10. Let P = the probability of something, e.g., being employed. Because

$$L = \text{log-odds} = ln\ (P/[1 - P]),$$

$$P = \exp L/(1 + \exp L).$$

With a one-unit change in an independent variable, L changes by the value of the logit coefficient, B.

$$L_1 = L_0 + B.$$

$$\Delta P = (\exp L_1)/(1 + \exp L_1) - (\exp L_0)/(1 + \exp L_0).$$

For women here, the observed probability (which is the probability predicted from the logit coefficient with all independent variables set to their means) is .39. Taking this as a starting point, $L_0 = ln\ (.39/.61) = -.477$. B for college education = 1.15, so $L_1 = -.447 + 1.15 = .703$. ΔP then = .279. For men, $P = .47$, $L_0 = -.120$, $B = 1.05$, $L_1 = .93$ and $\Delta P = .247$.

11. For women in the full sample, those from the Northeast or the West (as compared with the South), who came from farms with a mix of sales (rather than not knowing the percentage of sales), who had some education beyond high school but not a college degree (in contrast with having only a high school education), and who had more dependent children worked significantly fewer hours per week on the job under consideration here.

12. The percentage of farm tasks a woman did regularly had a significant negative effect on prestige for the full sample. Although the direction of causality is shaky, one might be tempted to interpret this as indicating that those who go off the farm even when involved extensively on their farms are those who are forced to do so, and are those who cannot wait to find better off-farm jobs.

13. When the wife's off-farm employment status and extensiveness of

her farm task involvement were added, the percentage of types of tasks done had a significant negative effect. Among those employed, having a wife doing a greater range of the farm chores might indicate the man having a less flexible, lower level job (Kada 1980).

14. The distribution of income is generally highly skewed. For this and for substantive reasons (see Mincer 1974), income (or earnings) is usually logged before being used as a dependent variable. The effects of the independent variables are then interpreted as proportional changes. The distribution of off-farm income for the farm men and women seems less skewed than is the case for the general population. To facilitate comparison between husbands and wives of dollar returns for various characteristics, income was not logged here.

15. Sumner (1978) did find that women with more children had lower off-farm earnings.

16. The conclusion that the off-farm employment status of the spouse has no effect on job rewards was also reached by including spouse's employment in the regressions for husbands' and wives' hours, prestige, and earnings.

17. Coughenour and Swanson (1983:33) find a *smaller* proportion of women in professional occupations when they were the only member of the couple employed, and women with and without employed husbands equally likely to be operatives. However, they do find that when only the husband was employed he was somewhat more likely to be a craftsman. These differences may reflect differences between the United States as a whole and Kentucky in both off-farm employment opportunities and the nature of farming.

18. There are some specific differences in industrial distributions by employment status of the spouse although the overall distributions are not significantly different. These are shown in Rosenfeld 1982a. As might be expected on the basis of the occupational distributions, women who are the only member of the couple employed off the farm are overrepresented in nondurables manufacturing industries, but men whose wives are not also employed off the farm are overrepresented in construction and durables manufacturing.

19. Bokemeier and Coughenour (1980) also found responses of farm husbands and wives on questions tapping life satisfaction to be very similar, in contrast with some differences between the responses of nonfarm spouses. In the table, the "dissatisfied" and "don't know" response categories are less finely reported for the question about satisfaction with farming as a way of life due to the relatively small numbers of people giving a dissatisfied or ambivalent answer.

20. The second discriminant function is positive and contributes an additional 21 percent of the discriminating power of the three possible functions. The centroid values suggest that this function gives precedence to the wife's employment. It is most positive when she alone had an off-farm

job; somewhat positive when she and her spouse were employed; and, when she was not employed off the farm, equally negative whether or not her husband had an off-farm job.

21. The use of dummy variables violates one assumption of discriminant analysis—that each variable is measured at the interval level. A more serious violation is that of the assumption of equal group covariance matrices. The within group covariance matrices here are not equal. Klecka (1980) suggests that discriminant analysis is a robust procedure, however, and the consistency of the results across different specifications and with predictions from the literature suggests these violations are not leading to wild results.

Chapter 6

1. In 1980 the General Social Survey found that 72 percent of the surveyed men in the United States and 61 percent of the women reported belonging to at least one voluntary organization (including churches). Because the FWS question asked about memberships during the two or three years preceding the survey, the results might somewhat overestimate the membership status of these men and women at any particular date. Unless the memberships of the FWS respondents are very unstable, however, one can conclude that farm people are at least as likely to belong to voluntary organizations as the rest of the U.S. population, and perhaps more so.

2. The percentages that reported experience with the specific listed activities may seem rather low, considering the pervasiveness of Extension activity in agricultural areas. The reader should keep in mind that the question was limited to experiences in the last two or three years. Respondents may have participated in some of the listed activities at an earlier time and have had no need to update the experience. Furthermore, not all of the listed activities are available in all areas at all times. The data thus document only recent participation levels and are not suitable for generalizations about long-run, overall rates.

3. It is not clear from results at this point to what extent, within the group of women and within the group of men, individuals tended to specialize in certain types of organizational activity. Were women who belonged to community organizations, for example, less likely than other women to have taken part in agricultural activities? Or are there "organizational people" who tended to belong to and participate in a large range of organizations? The odds ratios for belonging to an organizational type or taking part in a general sort of activity, given that a person belonged to another type of organization or took part in another type of activity, were all greater than one for both women and men. Membership or involvement in one type of organization or activity is associated with membership or involvement in others. For example, women and men who be-

longed to some sort of community organization in the preceding two to three years were over twice as likely to have belonged to some general farm or commodity producers' association in the same period. Women also seemed likely to belong to *both* farm organizations and women's organizations and auxiliaries. Participation in farm organizations and Extension activities, far from precluding participation in Extension home and family activities, increased involvement in the domestically focused activities, although more so for women than for men. Women and men, then, did not seem to specialize in domestic versus farm organizational activities, but to participate in both when they did participate in voluntary organizations and activities.

4. In order to estimate the logistic regression for wives' membership in cooperatives, the model had to be simplified. The model for men, containing the simplified variables, as compared with the complete set of variables, gives the same substantive results.

5. Serving on one type of committee, panel, or board might also lead to serving on another. This seems to be the case for the FWS respondents. Odds ratios for association among Extension program committees, local, county, and state committees, and USDA committees were all above 9 and were larger for women than for men. For women, having been on a local governing board was also somewhat associated with serving on Extension program committees and agricultural panels (odds ratios between 3 and 5).

Chapter 7

1. Of those employed at the time they were surveyed, 74 percent said "other," compared with about one-third of those recently (but not currently) employed, and 8 percent of those not employed off the farm in the last 2 years.

References

Acker, Joan
1973 "Women and Social Stratification: A Case of Intellectual Sexism." *American Journal of Sociology* 78:936–45.

Anderson, Karen
1981 *Wartime Women: Sex Roles, Family Relations, and the Status of Women during World War II.* Westport, Conn.: Greenwood Press.

Armitage, Susan
1982 "Wash on Monday: The Housework of Farm Women in Transition." Paper presented at the Women Historians of the Midwest Conference, St. Paul, Minn., 30 April–2 May.

Aronoff, Joel, and William D. Crano
1975 "A Reexamination of the Cross-Cultural Principles of Task Segregation and Sex Role Differentiation in the Family." *American Sociological Review* 40:12–20.

Baker, Elizabeth Faulkner
1964 *Technology and Women's Work.* New York: Columbia University Press.

Banks, Vera J., and Diana DeArc
1979 "Farm Population of the United States: 1978." *Current Population Reports,* Series P-27, no. 52.
1980 "Farm Population of the United States: 1979." *Current Population Reports,* Series P-27, no. 53.
1981 "Farm Population of the United States: 1980." *Current Population Reports,* Series P-27, no. 54.

Banks, Vera J., and Judith Z. Kalbacher
1981 *Farm Income Recipients and Their Families: A Socioeconomic Profile.* Rural Development Research Report no. 30. Washington, D.C.: Economic Research Service, United States Department of Agriculture.

Beale, Calvin L.
1978 "Making a Living in Rural and Smalltown America." *Rural Develop-*

ment Perspectives (United States Department of Agriculture, Economic Development Division—Economics, Statistics, and Cooperatives Service), 1 (Nov.):1–5.

Becker, Gary S.
1981 *A Treatise on the Family*. Cambridge, Mass: Harvard University Press.

Becker, Gary S., Elisabeth M. Landes, and Robert T. Michael
1977 "An Economic Analysis of Marital Instability." *Journal of Political Economy* 85:1141–87.

Bentley, Susan, and Carolyn Sachs
1984 *Farm Women in the United States: An Updated Literature Review and Annotated Bibliography*. University Park: Department of Agricultural Economics and Rural Sociology, Center for Rural Women, Agricultural Experiment Station, Pennsylvania State University.

Bergland, Bob
1979 "It's Time to Rethink our Farm Policy." *Country Journal* 6 (Nov.):46–49.

Berk, Richard A., and Subhash C. Ray
1982 "Selection Biases in Sociological Data." *Social Science Research* 11:352–98.

Berk, Sarah Fenstermaker, and Anthony Shih
1980 "Contributions to Household Labor: Comparing Wives' and Husbands' Reports." In *Women and Household Labor*, edited by Sarah Fenstermaker Berk, pp. 191–227. Beverly Hills, Calif.: Sage.

Bielby, William T., and James N. Baron
1984 "A Woman's Place Is with Other Women: Sex Segregation in the Workplace." In *Sex Segregation in the Workplace. Trends, Explanations, Remedies*, edited by Barbara Reskin, pp. 27–55. Washington, D.C.: National Academy Press.

Bishop, George F.
1976 "The Effect of Education on Ideological Consistency." *Public Opinion Quarterly* 40:337–48.

Blau, Francine D.
1977 *Equal Pay in the Office*. Lexington, Mass.: Lexington Books.

Bloomquist, Leonard E.
1981 "Social Consequences of Uneven Development: The American South as an Internal Colony." Manuscript. Department of Rural Sociology, University of Wisconsin, Madison.

Blumberg, Rae L.
1978 *Stratification: Socioeconomic and Sexual Inequality*. Dubuque: William Brown.

Bokemeier, Janet L., and C. Milton Coughenour
1980 "Men and Women in Four Types of Farm Families: Work and Attitudes." Paper presented at the annual meeting of the Rural Sociological Society, Ithaca, N.Y., August.

Bokemeier, Janet L., Carolyn Sachs, and Verna Keith
1983 "Labor Force Participation of Metropolitan, Nonmetropolitan, and Farm Women: A Comparative Study." *Rural Sociology* 48:515–39.

Bolsterli, Margaret Jones, ed.
1982 *Vinegar Pie and Chicken Bread: A Woman's Diary of Life in the Rural South, 1890–1891*. Fayetteville: University of Arkansas Press.

Bose, Christine
1984 "Household Resources and U.S. Women's Work: Factors Affecting Gainful Employment at the Turn of the Century." *American Sociological Review* 49:474–90.

Boserup, Ester
1970 *Women's Role in Economic Development*. New York: St. Martin's Press.

Boucher, Sandy
1982 *Heartwomen: An Urban Feminist's Odyssey Home*. San Francisco: Harper and Row.

Boulding, Elise
1979 "Women in Family Farming." Paper presented at the annual meeting of the American Sociological Association, Boston, 27–31 August.
1980 "The Labor of U.S. Farm Women: A Knowledge Gap." *Sociology of Work and Occupations* 7:261–90.

Bourque, Susan C., and Kay Barbara Warren
1981 *Women of the Andes: Patriarchy and Social Change in Two Peruvian Towns*. Ann Arbor: University of Michigan Press.

Brewer, Michael F.
1981 "The Changing U.S. Farmland Scene." *Population Bulletin* 36 (5).

Brown David L., and Jeanne M. O'Leary
1979 *Labor Force Activity of Women in Metropolitan and Nonmetropolitan America*. Rural Development Research Report no. 15. Washington, D.C.: Economics, Statistics, and Cooperatives Service, United States Department of Agriculture.

Brown, Minnie M., and Olaf F. Larson
1979 "Successful Black Farmers: Factors in Their Achievement." *Rural Sociology* 44:153–75.

Burge, Penny L., and Daisy L. Cunningham
1983 "Roles of Appalachian Farm Women." Paper presented at the annual

meeting of the Southern Association of Agricultural Scientists, Atlanta, 7 February.

Bush, Corlann G.
1982 "The Barn Is His, the House Is Mine: Agricultural Technology and Sex Roles." In *Energy and Transport: Historical Perspectives on Policy Issues*, edited by George H. Daniels and Mark H. Rose, pp. 235–59. Beverly Hills, Calif.: Sage.

Buttel, Frederick H., and Oscar W. Larson III
1982 "Political Implications of Multiple Jobholding in U.S. Agriculture: An Exploratory Analysis." *Rural Sociology* 47:272–94.

Capener, Harold R., and Alan D. Berkowitz
1976 "Farm Families, Variation in Attitude, Style and Structure." *New York's Food and Life Sciences Quarterly* 9 (4):9–11.

Carlin, Thomas A., and Linda Ghelfi
1979 "Off-Farm Employment and the Farm Structure." In United States Department of Agriculture, *Structure Issues of American Agriculture*. Washington, D.C.: United States Government Printing Office.

Carroll, Bernice A.
1979 "Political Science, Part 1: American Politics and Political Behavior." *Signs* 5:289–306.

Carter, Harold O., and Warren E. Johnston
1978 "Some Forces Affecting the Changing Structure, Organization, and Control of American Agriculture." *American Journal of Agricultural Economics* 60:738–48.

Chafe, William H.
1977 *Women and Equality: Changing Patterns in American Culture*. New York: Oxford University Press.

Chafetz, Janet Saltzman
1984 *Sex and Advantage: A Comparative Macro-Structural Theory of Sex Stratification*. Totowa, N.J.: Rowman and Allanheld.

Coleman, James Samuel
1973 *The Mathematics of Collective Action*. Chicago: Aldine.

Colman, Gould P., and Sarah Elbert
1983 "Farming Families: 'The Farm Needs Everyone.'" Manuscript. Department of History, Cornell University, Ithaca, N.Y.

Colman, Gould P., Laurie Konigsburg, and Leslie Puryear
1978 "The Nordahls. Family No. 5." *How Farm Families Make Decisions*. Rural Sociology Bulletin 79, Agricultural Economics Research 78–5. Ithaca, N.Y.: Departments of Rural Sociology, Agricultural Economics, and Manuscripts and University Archives, Cornell University.

1979 "The Crockers. Family No. 6." *How Farm Families Make Decisions.* Rural Sociology Bulletin 79, Agricultural Economics Research 79–7. Ithaca, N.Y.: Departments of Rural Sociology, Agricultural Economics, and Manuscripts and University Archives, Cornell University.

Colman, Gould P., and Jean Lowe
1975 "The Brauns. Family No. 1." *How Farm Families Make Decisions.* Rural Sociology Bulletin 79, Agricultural Economics Research 75–30. Ithaca, N.Y.: Departments of Rural Sociology, Agricultural Economics, and Manuscripts and University Archives, Cornell University.

Colman, Gould P., and Leslie Puryear
1978 "The Sawyers. Family No. 4." *How Farm Families Make Decisions.* Rural Sociology Bulletin 79, Agricultural Economics Research 78–3. Ithaca, N.Y.: Departments of Rural Sociology, Agricultural Economics, and Manuscripts and University Archives, Cornell University.

Corcoran, Mary, Greg Duncan, and Michael Ponza
1984 "Work Experience, Job Segregation, and Wages." In *Sex Segregation in the Workplace,* edited by Barbara Reskin, pp. 171–91. Washington, D.C.: National Academy Press.

Coughenour, C. Milton
1980 "The Impact of Off-Farm Occupation and Industry on the Size and Scale of Part-Time Farms." Paper presented at the meeting of the Southern Association of Agricultural Scientists, Hot Springs, Ark., 4–6 February.

Coughenour, C. Milton, and Anne Gabbard
1977 "Part-Time Farmers in Kentucky in the Early 1970's: The Development of Dual Careers." Paper no. RS-54. Lexington, Ky.: Department of Sociology, College of Agriculture, Agriculture Experiment Station, University of Kentucky.

Coughenour, C. Milton, and Louis Swanson
1983 "Work Statuses and Occupations of Men and Women in Farm Families and the Structure of Farms." *Rural Sociology* 48:23–43.

Coughenour, C. Milton, and Ronald C. Wimberley
1982 "Small and Part-Time Farmers." In *Rural Society in the U.S.: Issues for the 1980's,* edited by Don A. Dillman and Daryl J. Hobbs, pp. 347–56. Boulder, Colo.: Westview Press.

Coverman, Shelley
1983 "Gender, Domestic Labor Time, and Wage Inequality." *American Sociological Review* 48:623–37.

Cramer, James C.
1980 "Fertility and Female Employment: Problems of Causal Direction." *American Sociological Review* 45:167–90.

Cunningham, Daisy, Penny L. Burge, and Steven M. Culver
1982 "Examining Community Networks of Rural Farm Women." In *World Development and Women. Vol. 2. Women's Roles in Rural United States. Conference Proceedings*, edited by Mary Hill Rojas. Blacksburg, Va.: The Virginia Tech Title XII Women in International Development Office; Washington, D.C.: South-East Consortium for International Development, Office of Women in Development.

Davis, Harry L.
1976 "Decision-Making within the Household." *Journal of Consumer Research* 2:241–60.

Davis, John Emmeus
1980 "Capitalist Agricultural Development and the Exploitation of the Propertied Laborer." In *The Rural Sociology of the Advanced Societies: Critical Perspective*, edited by Frederick H. Buttel and Howard Newby, pp. 133–53. Montclair, N.J.: Allanheld, Osmun.

de Leal, Magdalena Leon, and Carmen Diana Deere
1979 "Rural Women and the Development of Capitalism in Colombian Agriculture." *Signs* 5:60–77.

Deere, Carmen Diana
1976 "Rural Women's Subsistence Production in the Capitalist Periphery." *Review of Radical Political Economics* 8(1):9–17.

Douglas, Susan P., and Yoram Wind
1978 "Examining Family Role and Authority Patterns: Two Methodological Issues." *Journal of Marriage and the Family* 40:35–47.

Duncan, Beverly, and Otis Dudley Duncan with James A. McRae, Jr.
1978 *Sex Typing and Social Roles: A Research Report*. New York: Academic Press.

Duncan, Otis Dudley, David L. Featherman, and Beverly Duncan
1972 *Socioeconomic Background and Achievement*. New York: Seminar Press.

Dunne, Faith
1980 "Occupational Sex-Stereotyping among Rural Young Women and Men." *Rural Sociology* 45:396–415.

Edwards, Richard C.
1979 *Contested Terrain: The Transformation of the Workplace in the Twentieth Century*. New York: Basic Books.

Elbert, Sarah
1982 "'The Farmer Takes a Wife, the Wife Takes a Child': Women in American Farm Families." Manuscript. Cornell University, Ithaca, N.Y.

Elbert, Sarah, and Gould P. Colman
1975 "The Roots. Family No. 2." *How Farm Families Make Decisions*. Rural Sociology Bulletin 79, Agricultural Economics Research 75–34. Ithaca, N.Y.: Departments of Rural Sociology, Agricultural Economics, and Manuscripts and University Archives, Cornell University.

Elbert, Sarah, Joyce H. Finch, and Gould P. Colman
1976 "The Neirikers. Family No. 3." *How Farm Families Make Decisions*. Rural Sociology Bulletin 79, Agricultural Economics Research 76–11. Ithaca, N.Y.: Departments of Rural Sociology, Agricultural Economics, and Manuscripts and University Archives, Cornell University.

England, Paula
1979 "Women and Occupational Prestige: A Case of Vacuous Sex Equality." *Signs* 5:252–65.
1981 "Assessing Trends in Occupational Sex Segregation, 1900–1976." In *Sociological Perspectives on Labor Markets*, edited by Ivar E. Berg, pp. 273–95. New York: Academic Press.
1982 "Explanations of Occupational Sex Segregation: An Interdisciplinary Review." Manuscript. Department of Sociology and Political Economy, University of Texas at Dallas.

England, Paula, and Steven D. McLaughlin
1979 "Sex Segregation of Jobs and Male-Female Income Differentials." In *Discrimination in Organizations: Using Social Indicators to Manage Social Change*, edited by Rodolfo Alvarez, Kenneth Lutterman and associates, pp. 189–213. San Francisco: Jossey-Bass.

Epstein, Cynthia Fuchs
1981 "Women and Power: The Roles of Women in Politics in the United States." In *Access to Power: Cross-National Studies of Women and Elites*, edited by Cynthia Fuchs Epstein and Rose Laub Coser, pp. 124–46. London: George Allen and Unwin.

Fassinger, Polly A., and Harry K. Schwarzweller
1982 "Work Patterns of Farm Wives in Mid-Michigan." Research Report No. 425, Home and Family Living. East Lansing: Michigan State University Agricultural Experiment Station.

Featherman, David L., and Robert M. Hauser
1976 "Sexual Inequalities and Socioeconomic Achievement in the U.S., 1962–1973." *American Sociological Review* 41:462–83.

Feldberg, Roslyn L., and Evelyn Nakano Glenn
1979 "Male and Female: Job Versus Gender Models in the Sociology of Work." *Social Problems* 26:524–38.

Field, Anne
1982 "The Powers That Be." *Ms* 11 (12):78.

Filiatrault, Pierre, and J. R. Brent Ritchie
1980 "Joint Purchasing Decisions: A Comparison of Influence Structure in Family and Couple Decision-Making Units." *Journal of Consumer Research* 7:131–40.

Flora, Cornelia Butler
1981 "Farm Women, Farming Systems, and Agricultural Structure: Suggestions for Scholarship." *Rural Sociologist* 1:383–86.

Flora, Cornelia Butler, and Sue Johnson
1977 "Discarding the Distaff: New Roles for Rural Women." In *Rural U.S.A.: Persistence and Change*, edited by Thomas R. Ford, pp. 168–81. Ames: Iowa State University Press.

Flora, Cornelia Butler, and John M. Stitz
1984 "Land Tenure, Patriarchy, and the Family Farm: Changes and Continuities in Dryland Agriculture in Western Kansas." Paper presented at the American Farm Women in Historical Perspective Conference, New Mexico State University, Las Cruces, 2–4 February.

Form, William, and David Byron McMillen
1983 "Women, Men, and Machines." *Work and Occupations* 10:147–78.

Frauendorfer, Sigmund V.
1966 "Part-Time Farming: A Review of World Literature." *World Agricultural Economics and Rural Sociology Abstracts* 8(1): v–xxxviii.

Friedl, Ernestine
1975 *Women and Men: An Anthropologist's View*. New York: Holt, Rinehart and Winston.

Friedmann, Harriet
1978 "World Market, State, and Family Farm: Social Bases of Household Production in the Era of Wage Labor." *Comparative Studies in Society and History* 20:545–86.
1982 "The Family Farm in Advanced Capitalism: Outline of a Theory of Simple Commodity Production in Agriculture." Structural Analysis Programme. Working Paper Series no. 33. Toronto, Ontario: Department of Sociology, University of Toronto.

Fuguitt, Glenn V., Anthony Fuller, Heather Fuller, Ruth Gasson, and Gwyn Jones
1977 "Part-Time Farming: Its Nature and Implications. A Workshop Report." Centre for European Agricultural Studies, Seminar Papers no. 2. Ashford, Kent, England: Wyn College, University of London.

Geisler, Charles C., William F. Waters, and Katrina L. Eadie
1985 "The Changing Structure of Female Agricultural Land Ownership, 1946 and 1978." *Rural Sociology* 50:74–87.

Gill, Sandra
1983 "Class and Attitude Toward the Equal Rights Amendment." Paper presented at the annual meeting of the Southern Sociological Society, Atlanta, April.

Gladwin, Christina, and Masuma Downie
1982 "The Complementary Role of Florida Farm Wives: How They Help the Family Farm Survive." Manuscript. Food and Resource Economics Department, Institute of Food and Agricultural Sciences, University of Florida, Gainesville.

Glasgow, Nina
c.1978 "Evaluating the Role of Rural Women in the Polity." Manuscript.

Goss, Kevin F., Richard D. Rodefeld, and Frederick H. Buttel
1980 "The Political Economy of Class Structure in U.S. Agriculture." In *The Rural Sociology of Advanced Societies: Critical Perspectives*, edited by Frederick H. Buttel and Howard Newby, pp. 83–132. Montclair, N.J.: Allanheld, Osmun.

Graff, Linda L.
1982 "Industrialization of Agriculture: Implications for the Position of Farm Women." In "Women in Agriculture and Rural Society," special issue of *Resources for Feminist Research* 11:10–11.

Grantham, Marilyn
1982 "Changes in Rural Women's Roles in Volunteerism: The National Extension Homemaker Council and Its Plans for a Volunteer Recognition/Volunteer Development Program." In *World Development and Women. Vol. 2. Women's Roles in Rural United States. Conference Proceedings*, edited by Mary Hill Rojas. Blacksburg, Va.: The Virginia Tech Title XII Women in International Development Office; Washington, D.C.: South-East Consortium for International Development, Office of Women in Development.

Greene, Wade
1978 "How Durable is the Small Farm?" *Blair and Ketchum's Country Journal* 5 (Dec.):90–98.

Greenwald, Maurine Weiner
1980 *Women, War, and Work: The Impact of World War I on Women Workers in the United States*. Westport, Conn.: Greenwood Press.

Gullickson, Gay L.
1981 "The Sexual Division of Labor in Cottage Industry and Agriculture in Pays de Caux: Auffay, 1750–1850." *French Historical Studies* 12:177–99.

Hagood, Margaret Jarman
1939 *Mothers of the South: Portraiture of the White Tenant Farm Woman*. Chapel Hill: University of North Carolina Press. Reprint. New York: W.W. Norton, 1977.

Haney, Wava Gillespie
1983 "Farm Family and the Role of Women." In *Technology and Social Change in Rural Areas*, edited by Gene F. Summers, pp. 179–93. Boulder, Colo.: Westview Press.

Haney, Wava Gillespie, and Eugene A. Wilkening
1984 "From Kerchiefs, Pails and Cans to Plaid Collars, Record Books and Farm Office: Technology, Policy and Wisconsin Dairy Farm Women in the 20th Century." Paper presented at the American Farm Women in Historical Perspective Conference, New Mexico State University, Las Cruces, 2–4 February.

Hanks, Michael, and Bruce K. Eckland
1978 "Adult Voluntary Associations and Adolescent Socialization." *Sociological Quarterly* 19:481–90.

Hannan, Michael T.
1973 "A Fitness Set Model of the Effects of Income Maintenance on Marital Stability." Manuscript. Stanford University, Stanford, Calif.

Hansen, Susan B., Linda M. Franz, and Margaret Netemeyer-Mays
1976 "Women's Political Participation and Policy Preferences." *Social Science Quarterly* 56:576–90.

Hanson, Ronald Jay
1972 "An Economic Analysis of Off-Farm Income as a Factor in the Improvement of the Low Farm Income Farmers in Illinois." Ph.D. diss. University of Illinois, Urbana.

Hanushek, Eric A., and John E. Jackson
1977 *Statistical Methods for Social Scientists*. New York: Academic Press.

Harrell, Frank
1980 "The LOGIST Procedure." In *SAS Supplemental Library User's Guide: 1980 Edition*, edited by Patti S. Reinhardt, pp. 83–102. Cary, N.C.: SAS Institute, Inc.

Hartmann, Heidi I.
1976 "Capitalism, Patriarchy, and Job Segregation by Sex." *Signs* 1(3, pt. 2):137–69.

Hathaway, Dale E., and Brian B. Perkins
1968 "Farm Labor Mobility, Migration, and Income Distribution." *American Journal of Agricultural Economics* 50:342–53.

Hayghe, Howard, and Beverly L. Johnson
1980 *Perspectives on Working Women: A Databook*. Bulletin 2080. Washington, D.C.: United States Bureau of Labor Statistics, United States Department of Labor.

Hepner, Julie A.
1979 "The Role of the Midwestern Farm Wife." Manuscript. Department of Family and Consumer Economics, University of Illinois, Urbana.

Hill, Frances
1981a "Farm Women: Challenge to Scholarship." *Rural Sociologist* 1:370–82.
1981b "Farmwomen and Vocational Education." In *Brake Shoes, Backhoes, and Balance Sheets: The Changing Vocational Education of Rural Women*, edited by Stuart A. Rosenfeld, pp. 67–92. Washington, D.C.: Rural American Women, Inc.

Hill, Wayne, and John Scanzoni
1982 "An Approach for Assessing Marital Decision-Making Processes." *Journal of Marriage and the Family* 44:927–41.

Hodson, Randy
1978 "Labor in the Monopoly, Competitive, and State Sectors of Production." *Politics and Society* 8:429–80.

Hoffmann, Carl, and John Shelton Reed
1981 "Sex Discrimination?—The XYZ Affair." *Public Interest*, no. 62:21–39.

Hoiberg, Eric, and Wallace Huffman
1978 *Profile of Iowa Farms and Farm Families: 1976*. Iowa Agricultural and Home Economics Experiment Station and Cooperative Extension Service. Bulletin no. P-141. Ames: Iowa State University.

Huber, Joan, Cynthia Rexroat, and Glenna Spitze
1978 "A Crucible of Opinion on Women's Status: ERA in Illinois." *Social Forces* 57:549–65.

Huber, Joan, and Glenna Spitze
1983 *Sex Stratification: Children, Housework and Jobs*. New York: Academic Press.

Huffman, Wallace E.
1977 "Interactions between Farm and Nonfarm Labor Markets." *American Journal of Agricultural Economics* 59:1054–61.
1980 "Farm and Off-Farm Work Decisions: The Role of Human Capital." *Review of Economics and Statistics* 62:14–23.

Huffman, Wallace E., and Mark D. Lange
1982 "Farm Household Production: Demand for Wife's Labor, Capital Ser-

vices, and the Capital-Labor Ratio." Manuscript. Department of Economics, Iowa State University, Ames.

Janiewski, Dolores Elizabeth
1979 "From Field to Factory: Race, Class, Sex, and the Woman Worker in Durham, 1880–1940." Ph.D. diss. Duke University, Durham, N.C.

Jaquette, Jane S.
1976 "Political Science." *Signs* 2:147–64.

Jasso, Guillermina
1980 "A New Theory of Distributive Justice." *American Sociological Review* 45:3–32.

Jensen, Joan
1981 *With These Hands: Women Working on the Land.* Old Westbury, N.Y.: Feminist Press.

Johnson, Nan E., C. Shannon Stokes, and Rex H. Warland
1978 "Farm-Nonfarm Differentials in Fertility: The Effects of Compositional and Sex-Role Factors." *Rural Sociology* 43:671–90.

Jones, Calvin
1980 *Agricultural Information: Uses, Needs, and USDA Services.* Chicago: National Opinion Research Center.

Jones, Calvin, and Rachel A. Rosenfeld
1981 *American Farm Women: Findings from a National Survey.* NORC Report no. 130. Chicago: National Opinion Research Center.

Jones, Calvin, Paul Sheatsley, and Arthur Stinchcombe
1979 *Dakota Farmers and Ranchers Evaluate Crop and Livestock Surveys.* Report no. 128. Chicago: National Opinion Research Center.

Jones, Lu Ann
1982 "'Like the Honeysuckle': Views and Images of Women in *The Progressive Farmer,* 1886–1915." Manuscript. Department of History, University of North Carolina at Chapel Hill.

Jones-Webb, Jeannette
1982 "Through the Eyes of a Young Farmer." Paper presented at the Wingspread Seminar on Women's Roles on North American Farms, Racine, Wisc., 7–9 July.

Joyce, Lynda M., and Samuel M. Leadley
1977 *An Assessment of Research Needs of Women in the Rural United States: Literature Review and Annotated Bibliography.* A.E. & R.S. Paper no. 127. University Park: Department of Agricultural Economics and Rural Sociology, Agricultural Experiment Station, Pennsylvania State University.

Kada, Ryohei
1980 *Part-Time Family Farming: Off-Farm Employment and Farm Adjustments in the United States and Japan.* Tokyo: Center for Academic Publications Japan.

Kain, Edward L., and Diana Johnson Divecha
1983 "Rural Women's Attitudes toward Social Change in Work and Family Roles." Paper presented at the annual meeting of the National Council on Family Relations, St. Paul, Minn., 11–15 October.

Kalbacher, Judith Z.
1982 "Women Farmers in America." Paper no. ERS-679. Washington, D.C.: Economic Research Service, United States Department of Agriculture.
1983 "Women Farm Operators." *Family Economics Review* no. 4:17–21.

Kalbacher, Judith Z., with Kathleen K. Scholl
1983 "Profile of Today's American Farm Women." Paper prepared for the American Farm Women in Historical Perspective Conference, New Mexico State University, Las Cruces, 2–4 February 1984.

Kanter, Rosabeth Moss
1977a *Men and Women of the Corporation.* New York: Basic Books.
1977b *Work and the Family in the United States: A Critical Review and Agenda for Research and Policy.* New York: Russell Sage.

Kau, Susan
1976 "Women's Involvement in Wisconsin Cooperatives." Master's thesis, University of Wisconsin, Madison.

Kaufman, Robert L., Randy Hodson, and Neil D. Fligstein
1981 "Defrocking Dualism: A New Approach to Defining Industrial Sectors." *Social Science Research* 10:1–31.

Klecka, William R.
1980 *Discriminant Analysis.* Beverly Hills, Calif.: Sage.

Knoke, David, and Randall Thomson
1977 "Voluntary Association Membership Trends and the Family Life Cycle." *Social Forces* 56:48–65.

Kohl, Barbara.
1979 "The American Agricultural Movement." Paper presented at the annual meeting of the North Central Sociological Association, Akron, Ohio, April.

Kohl, Seena B.
1976 *Working Together: Women and Family in Southwestern Saskatchewan.* Toronto: Holt, Rinehart and Winston of Canada.

Langway, Lynn, with Diane Weathers, Pamela Abramson, and Tenley Ann Jackson
1984 " 'Worksteaders' Clean Up." *Newsweek* 103 (Jan. 9):86–87.

Larson, Olaf F.
1981 "Agriculture and the Community." In *Nonmetropolitan America In Transition*, edited by Amos H. Hawley and Sara Mills Mazie, pp. 147–93. Chapel Hill: University of North Carolina Press.

Lipman-Blumen, Jean, and Ann R. Tickamyer
1975 "Sex Roles in Transition: A Ten-Year Perspective." In *Annual Review of Sociology*, vol. 1, edited by Alex Inkeles, pp. 297–337. Palo Alto, Calif.: Annual Reviews, Inc.

Lodwick, Dora G., and Polly Fassinger
1979 "Variations in Agricultural Production Activities of Women on Family Farms." Paper presented at the annual meeting of the Rural Sociological Society, Burlington, Vt., 24–26 August.

Lodwick, Dora G., and Denton E. Morrison
1982 "Appropriate Technology." In *Rural Society in the US: Issues for the 1980s*, edited by Don A. Dillman and Daryl J. Hobbs, pp. 44–53. Boulder, Colo.: Westview Press.

Low, A. R. C.
1981 "The Effect of Off-Farm Employment on Farm Incomes and Production: Taiwan Contrasted with Southern Africa." *Economic Development and Cultural Change* 29:741–47.

Lynn, Naomi B.
1979 "American Women and the Political Process." In *Women: A Feminist Perspective*, edited by Jo Freeman, 2d ed., pp. 404–29. Palo Alto, Calif.: Mayfield.

Lyson, Thomas A.
c.1980 "Sex Differences in Recruitment to Agricultural Occupations among Southern College Students." Department of Agricultural Economics and Rural Sociology, Clemson University, Clemson, S.C.

McDonald, Gerald W.
1980 "Family Power: The Assessment of a Decade of Theory and Research, 1970–1979." *Journal of Marriage and the Family* 42:841–54.

McIlwee, Judith S.
1982 "Work Satisfaction among Women in Nontraditional Occupations." *Work and Occupations* 9:299–335.

MacNab–de Vries, Georgina, and Pieter J. de Vries
1982 "Subsistence Agriculture, Wage Labour and the Definition of Women's Roles: A Cape Breton Example." In "Women and Agricultural

Production," special issue of *Resources for Feminist Research* 11:8–10.

McPherson, J. Miller
1981 "A Dynamic Model of Voluntary Affiliation." *Social Forces* 59:705–28.

McPherson, J. Miller, and Lynn Smith-Lovin
1982 "Women and Weak Ties: Differences by Sex in the Size of Voluntary Organizations." *American Journal of Sociology* 87:883–904.

Madden, J. Patrick, and Earl J. Partenheimer
1972 "Evidence of Economies and Diseconomies of Farm Size." In *Size, Structure, and Future of Farms*, edited by A. Gordon Ball and Earl O. Heady, pp. 91–107. Ames: Iowa State University Press.

Mage, Julius A.
1976 "Guelph Report 1. A Typology of Part-Time Farming." In *Part-Time Farming. Problem or Resource in Rural Development*, edited by Anthony M. Fuller and Julius A. Mage, pp. 6–37. Proceedings of the First Rural Geography Symposium, Department of Geography, University of Guelph, 18–20 June 1975. Guelph, Ontario: Department of Geography, University of Guelph.

Mann, Susan A., and James M. Dickinson
1978 "Obstacles to the Development of a Capitalist Agriculture." *Journal of Peasant Studies* 5:466–81.

Manski, Charles F.
1981 "Structural Models for Discrete Data: The Analysis of Discrete Choice." In *Sociological Methodology 1981*, edited by Samuel Leinhardt, pp. 58–109. San Francisco: Jossey-Bass.

Martinson, Oscar B., and Gerald R. Campbell
1980 "Betwixt and Between: Farmers and the Marketing of Agricultural Inputs and Outputs." In *The Rural Sociology of Advanced Societies: Critical Perspectives*, edited by Frederick H. Buttel and Howard Newby, pp. 215–53. Montclair, N.J.: Allanheld, Osmun.

Mason, Karen Oppenheim, and Larry L. Bumpass
1975 "U.S. Women's Sex-Role Ideology, 1970." *American Journal of Sociology* 80:1212–19.

Mason, Karen Oppenheim, John L. Czajka, and Sara Arber
1976 "Change in U.S. Women's Sex-Role Attitudes, 1964–1974." *American Sociological Review* 41:573–96.

Meissner, Martin, Elizabeth W. Humphreys, Scott M. Meis, and William J. Scheu
1975 "No Exit for Wives: Sexual Division of Labour and the Cumulation

of Household Demands." *Canadian Review of Sociology and Anthropology* 12:424–39.

Milkman, Ruth
1976 "Women's Work and Economic Crisis: Some Lessons of the Great Depression." *Review of Radical Political Economics* 8:73–97.

Miller, Joanne, and Howard H. Garrison
1982 "Sex Roles: The Division of Labor at Home and in the Workplace." In *Annual Review of Sociology*, vol. 8, edited by Ralph Turner, pp. 237–62. Palo Alto, Calif.: Annual Reviews, Inc.

Mills, C. Wright
1956 *White Collar: The American Middle Classes*. New York: Oxford University Press.

Mincer, Jacob
1974 *Schooling, Experience and Earnings*. New York: National Bureau of Economic Research.

Moen, Elizabeth, Elise Boulding, Jane Lillydahl, and Risa Palm
1981 *Women and the Social Costs of Economic Development: Two Colorado Case Studies*. Boulder, Colo.: Westview Press.

Moore, Tom
1984 "Walters Enjoys Farm Life." *Chapel Hill* [N.C.] *Newspaper*, 27 Nov., A-6.

Moser, Collette, and Deborah Johnson
1973 "Rural Women Workers in the 20th Century: An Annotated Bibliography." Special Paper—Michigan State University Center for Rural Manpower and Public Affairs no. 15. East Lansing: Center for Rural Manpower and Public Affairs, Michigan State University.

Mueller, Marnie W.
1975 "Economic Determinants of Volunteer Work by Women." *Signs* 1:325–38.

Newby, Howard
1980 "Rural Sociology." *Current Sociology* 28 (1).

Newby, Howard, and Frederick Buttel
1980 "Toward a Critical Rural Sociology." In *The Rural Sociology of Advanced Societies: Critical Perspectives*, edited by Frederick H. Buttel and Howard Newby, pp. 1–35. Montclair, N.J.: Allanheld, Osmun.

Nunnally, Jum C.
1973 *Psychometric Theory*. New York: McGraw Hill.

Oakley, Ann
1974 *The Sociology of Housework*. New York: Pantheon Books.

O'Kelly, Charlotte
1980 *Women and Men in Society*. New York: Van Nostrand.

Okun, Bernard
1958 *Trends in Birth Rates in the United States Since 1870*. Baltimore: Johns Hopkins Press.

Oppenheimer, Valerie Kincade
1970 *The Female Labor Force in the United States: Demographic and Economic Factors Governing Its Growth and Changing Composition*. Population Monograph Series no. 5. Berkeley: Institute of International Studies University of California.
1977 "The Sociology of Women's Economic Role in the Family." *American Sociological Review* 42:387–406.

Orr, Richard
1979 "Farm Wives Taking to the Field with Men." *Chicago Tribune* (Oct. 28) 1:10.

Pearson, Jessica
1979 "Note on Female Farmers." *Rural Sociology* 44:189–200.
1980 "Women Who Farm: A Preliminary Portrait." *Sex Roles* 6:561–74.

Petersen, Trond
1985 "A Comment on Presenting Results from Logit and Probit Models." *American Sociological Review* 50:130–31

Pfeffer, Max John
1983 "Social Origins of Three Systems of Farm Production in the United States." *Rural Sociology* 48:540–62.

Pleck, Joseph H.
1979 "Men's Family Work: Three Perspectives and Some New Data." *The Family Coordinator* 28:481–88.

Polachek, Soloman William
1975 "Discontinuous Labor Force Participation and Its Effect on Women's Market Earnings." In *Sex, Discrimination, and the Division of Labor*, edited by Cynthia B. Lloyd, pp. 90–122. New York: Columbia University Press.
1981 "Occupational Self-Selection: A Human Capital Approach to Sex Differences in Occupational Structure." *Review of Economics and Statistics* 63:60–69.

Quance, Leroy, and Luther G. Tweeten
1972 "Policies, 1930–1970." In *Size, Structure, and the Future of Farms*, edited by A. Gordon Ball and Earl O. Heady, pp. 19–39. Ames: Iowa State University Press.

Ray, Subhash, Richard Berk, and William Bielby
1981 "Correcting Sample Selection Bias for Bivariate Logistic Distribution of Disturbances." Manuscript. University of California, Santa Barbara. Revision of a paper presented at the annual meeting of the American Statistical Association, 1980.

Research, Action and Education Centre [Regina, Saskatchewan]
1982 "Keeping Women Down on the Farm." In "Women in Agriculture and Rural Society," special issue of *Resources for Feminist Research* 11:12–14.

Reynolds, Carl, and Robert W. Walker
1975 "Should We Encourage Women to Enter Ag. Ed.?" *Agricultural Education* 47:272+.

Rodefeld, Richard D.
1978 "Trends in U.S. Farm Organizational Structure and Type." In *Change in Rural America. Causes, Consequences, and Alternatives*, edited by Richard D. Rodefeld, Jan Flora, Donald Voth, Isgo Fujimoto, and Jim Converse, pp. 158–77. St. Louis: C. V. Mosby.

Rogers, Susan Carol
1975 "Female Forms of Power and the Myth of Male Dominance: A Model of Female/Male Interaction in Peasant Society." *American Ethnologist* 2:727–56.
1982 "The Illinois Family Farm Project." Paper presented at the Wingspread Seminar on Women's Roles on North American Farms. Racine, Wisc., 7–9 July.

Rose, Margaret
1984 "The Chicana Farm Worker as Unionist: Ranch Committee Women of the United Farm Workers." Paper presented at the American Farm Women in Historical Perspective Conference, New Mexico State University, Las Cruces, 2–4 February.

Rosenfeld, Rachel Ann
1980 "Race and Sex Differences in Career Dynamics." *American Sociological Review* 45:583–609.
1982a "Off-Farm Employment of Farm Wives and Husbands." Paper presented at the Wingspread Seminar on Women's Roles on North American Farms, Racine, Wisc., 7–9 July.
1982b "U.S. Farm Women: Their Work and Self-Perceptions." Paper presented at the annual meeting of the Southern Sociological Society, Memphis, April.

Ross, John E., and Lloyd R. Bostian
1965 *Functional Orientation of Wisconsin Farm Women towards Mass Media*. Bulletin no. 33. [Madison]: Department of Agricultural Journalism, College of Agriculture, University of Wisconsin.

Ross, Peggy Johnston
1982 "Farmwomen's Participation in United States Agricultural Production: Selected Assessments." Ph.D. diss. Ohio State University.

Sachs, Carolyn E.
1981 "The Displacement of Women from Agricultural Production: The Case of the United States." Ph.D. diss. University of Kentucky.
1983 *The Invisible Farmers: Women in Agricultural Production.* Totowa, N.J.: Rowman and Allanheld.

Salamon, Sonya
1978 "Farm Tenancy and Family Values in an Illinois Community." *Illinois Research* (Illinois Agricultural Experiment Station) 20 (1):6–7.

Salamon, Sonya, and Ann Mackey Keim
1979 "Land Ownership and Women's Power in a Midwestern Farming Community." *Journal of Marriage and the Family* 41:109–19.

Salamon, Sonya, and Kathleen K. Markan
1984 "Incorporation and the Family Farm." *Journal of Marriage and the Family* 46:167–78

Salant, Priscilla
1983 *Farm Women: Contribution to Farm and Family.* Agricultural Economics Research Report no. 140. Mississippi State, Miss.: Economic Development Division, Economic Research Service, United States Department of Agriculture in cooperation with Mississippi Agricultural and Forestry Experiment Station.

Sander, William
1981 "Off-Farm Employment and Income of Farm Operator Families." Agricultural Economics Workshop Paper no. 81:40. Chicago: University of Chicago.
1983 "Off-Farm Employment and the Income of Farmers." *Oxford Agrarian Studies* 12:34–47.

Saupe, William E.
1977 "The Rural Income Maintenance Experiment, Welfare Reform, and Programs for Smaller Farms." Institute for Research on Poverty Discussion Paper no. 459–77. Madison: University of Wisconsin, Madison.

Sawer, Barbara J.
1973 "Predictors of the Farm Wife's Involvement in General Management and Adoption Decisions." *Rural Sociology* 38:412–26.

Scanzoni, John, and Maximilliane Szinovacz
1980 *Family Decision-Making: A Developmental Sex Role Model.* Beverly Hills, Calif.: Sage.

Schertz, Lyle P., et al.
1979 *Another Revolution in U.S. Farming?* Agricultural Economic Report no. 441. Washington, D.C.: Economics and Statistics Service, United States Department of Agriculture.

Scholl, Kathleen K.
1983 "Classification of Women as Farmers: Economic Implications." *Family Economics Review* no. 4:8–17.

Schooler, Carmi, Joanne Miller, Karen A. Miller, and Carol N. Richtand
1984 "Work for the Household: Its Nature and Consequences for Husbands and Wives." *American Journal of Sociology* 90:97–124.

Schram, Vicki R., and Marilyn M. Dunsing
1981 "Influence on Married Women's Volunteer Work Participation." *Journal of Consumer Research* 7:372–79.

Scott, Joan W., and Louise A. Tilly
1975 "Women's Work and the Family in Nineteenth-Century Europe." *Comparative Studies in Society and History* 17:36–64.

Siegel, Paul
1971 "Prestige in the American Occupational Structure." Ph.D. diss., University of Chicago.

Simpson, Ida Harper, and John Wilson
1983 "Full and Part-Time Farming: Family Role Configurations and Farm Consciousness." Proposal submitted to the National Science Foundation. Department of Sociology, Trinity College of Arts and Sciences, Duke University, Durham, N.C.

Slocum, Walter L.
1974 *Occupational Careers. A Sociological Perspective.* 2d ed. Chicago: Aldine.

Smuts, Robert W.
1959 *Women and Work in America.* New York: Columbia University Press.

Sokoloff, Natalie J.
1980 *Between Money and Love: The Dialectics of Women's Home and Market Work.* New York: Praeger.

Stafford, Frank P.
1980 "Women's Use of Time Converging with Men's." *Monthly Labor Review* 103 (12): 57–59.

Straus, Carol
1980 "Women, Work and Political Efficacy." Paper presented at the annual meeting of the Rural Sociological Society, Ithaca, N.Y., August.

Sumner, Daniel Alan
1978 "Labor Supply and Earnings of Farm Families with Emphasis on Off-Farm Work." Ph.D. diss. University of Chicago.

Sweet, James A.
1972 "The Employment of Rural Farm Wives." *Rural Sociology* 37:553–77.
1973 *Women in the Labor Force*. New York: Seminar Press.
1974 "The Employment of Rural Farm Wives: 1970." Center for Demography and Ecology Working Paper no. 74–22. Madison: University of Wisconsin, Madison.

Taylor, Norma
1976 "'All This for Three and a Half a Day': The Farm Wife." In *Women in the Canadian Mosaic*, edited by Gwen Matheson, pp. 151–64. Toronto: Peter Martin Associates.

Thadani, Veena
1981 "Women and Migration." Paper presented at the annual meeting of the Southern Sociological Society, Louisville, April.

Thornton, Arland, Duane F. Alwin, and Donald Camburn
1983 "Causes and Consequences of Sex-Role Attitudes and Attitude Change." *American Sociological Review* 48:211–27.

United States Department of Agriculture
1978 *The Yearbook of Agriculture. 1978. Living on a Few Acres*. Washington, D.C.: United States Department of Agriculture.
1979 *Status of the Family Farm*. Second Annual Report to the Congress. Washington, D.C.: United States Department of Agriculture.

______. Office of Governmental and Public Affairs
1979 *Fact Book of U.S. Agriculture*. Miscellaneous Publication-Department of Agriculture no. 1063. Washington, D.C.: Office of Governmental and Public Affairs, United States Department of Agriculture.
1980 *People on the Farm: Black Families*. Washington, D.C.: Office of Governmental and Public Affairs, United States Department of Agriculture.

United States Department of Commerce, Bureau of the Census
1968 *1964 United States Census of Agriculture*. Vol. 3. *Special Reports*. Part 2. *Farm Labor*. Washington, D.C.: Bureau of the Census, United States Department of Commerce.
1980 *Statistical Abstract of the United States: 1980*. 101st ed. Washington, D.C.: Bureau of the Census, United States Department of Commerce.
1981a *1978 Census of Agriculture*. Vol. 1. *Summary and State Data*. Part 51. *United States*. (AC78-A-51) Washington, D.C.: Bureau of the Census, United States Department of Commerce.

1981b *Statistical Abstract of the United States: 1981*. 102d ed. Washington, D.C.: Bureau of the Census, United States Department of Commerce.

1982a *1978 Census of Agriculture*. Vol. 5. *Special Reports*. Part 6. *1979 Farm Finance Survey*. (AC78-SR-6) Washington, D.C.: Bureau of the Census, United States Department of Commerce.

1982b *Statistical Abstract of the United States: 1982–83*. 103d ed. Washington, D.C.: Bureau of the Census, United States Department of Commerce.

1983 *Statistical Abstract of the United States: 1984*. 104th ed. Washington, D.C.: Bureau of the Census, United States Department of Commerce.

1984 *1982 Census of Agriculture: Preliminary Report: United States*. AC82-A-00-000(P). Washington, D.C.: Bureau of the Census, United States Department of Commerce.

Valadez, Joseph J., and Remi Clignet

1984 "Household Work as an Ordeal: Culture of Standards Versus Standardization of Culture." *American Journal of Sociology* 89:812–35.

Vanek, Joann

1974 "Time Spent in Housework." *Scientific American* 231(5):116–20.

1980 "Work, Leisure, and Family Roles: Farm Households in the United States, 1920–1955." *Journal of Family History* 5:422–31.

Waite, Linda J.

1978 "Projecting Female Labor Force Participation from Sex-Role Attitudes." *Social Science Research* 7:299–318.

1981 "U.S. Women at Work." *Population Bulletin* 36(2).

Wandersee, Winifred D.

1981 *Women's Work and Family Values, 1920–1940*. Cambridge, Mass.: Harvard University Press.

Ward, Kathryn

1984 *Women in the World System: The Impact on Status and Fertility*. New York: Praeger.

Wells, Miriam

1984 "The Resurgence of Sharecropping: Historical Anomaly or Political Strategy?" *American Journal of Sociology* 90:1–29.

Wilder, Laura Ingalls

1941 *Little Town on the Prairie*. New York: Harper.

1943 *These Happy Golden Years*. New York: Harper.

Wilkening, Eugene A.

1958 "Joint Decision-making in Farm Families as a Function of Status and Role." *American Sociological Review* 23:187–92.

1981 "Farm Husbands and Wives in Wisconsin. Work Roles, Decision-Making and Satisfaction, 1962 and 1979." Research Bulletin no. R3147. Madison: Research Division, College of Agricultural and Life Sciences, University of Wisconsin, Madison

Wilkening, Eugene A., and Nancy Ahrens
1979 "Involvement of Wives in Farm Tasks as Related to Characteristics of the Farm, the Family and Work off the Farm." Paper presented at the annual meeting of the Rural Sociological Society, Burlington, Vt., 24–26 August.

Wilkening, Eugene A., and Lakshmi Bharadwaj
1967 "Dimensions of Aspirations, Work Roles, and Decision-Making of Farm Husbands and Wives in Wisconsin," *Journal of Marriage and the Family* 29:703–11
1968 "Aspirations and Task Involvement as Related to Decision-Making among Farm Husbands and Wives." *Rural Sociology* 33:30–45.

Wilkening, Eugene A., and Sylvia Guerrero
1969 "Consensus in Aspirations for Farm Improvement and Adoption of Farm Practices." *Rural Sociology* 34:182–96.

Wilkening, Eugene A., and Denton E. Morrison
1963 "A Comparison of Husband and Wife Responses Concerning Who Makes Farm and Home Decisions." *Marriage and Family Living* 25:349–51.

Williams, Gregory
1979 "The Changing U.S. Labor Force and Occupational Differentiation by Sex." *Demography* 16:73–87.

Wiser, Vivian
1976 "Women in Agriculture." *Farm Index* 15(1):3–6.

Wolf, Wendy C., and Neil D. Fligstein
1979 "Sex and Authority in the Workplace: The Causes of Sexual Inequality." *American Sociological Review* 44:235–52.

Wolf, Wendy C., and Rachel Ann Rosenfeld
1978 "Sex Structure of Occupations and Job Mobility." *Social Forces* 56:823–44.

Wright, Erik Olin
1979 *Class Structure and Income Determination*. New York: Academic Press.

Zochert, Donald
1976 *Laura: The Life of Laura Ingalls Wilder*. Chicago: Contemporary Books.

Index